Barrier-free Design

A manual for building designers and managers

James Holmes-Siedle

Architectural Press

Architectural Press
An imprint of Butterworth-Heinemann
Linacre House, Jordan Hill, Oxford OX2 8DP
225 Wildwood Avenue, Woburn, MA01801-2041
A division of Reed Educational and Professional Publishing Ltd

 A member of the Reed Elsevier plc group

OXFORD   AUCKLAND   BOSTON
JOHANNESBURG   MELBOURNE   NEW DELHI

First published 1996
Reprinted 1997, 2000

© James Holmes-Siedle 1996

British Library Cataloguing in Publication Data
A catalogue record for this book is available from the
British Library

Library of Congress Cataloguing in Publication Data
A catalogue record for this book is available from the
Library of Congress

ISBN 0 7506 1636 9

Typeset by Keyword Typesetting Services Ltd, Wallington, Surrey
Printed in Great Britain by Bookcraft (Bath) Ltd, Somerset

Contents

Prologue

There is a misconception that disabled people are just like everyone else. It is a misconception because it assumes that one group of people is identical to another. The problem with that assumption is that both groups of people are the same. Disabled people can be doctors, lawyers, plumbers, artists and writers.

I'd like you to meet someone who has taken me forty years to get to know well. Allow me to introduce myself. My name is Geoff and I am disabled.

I have cerebral palsy as a result of a premature birth. Over the last four decades, I have found that what many would consider a tragedy has been one of the biggest blessings of my life. If the saying 'life is a classroom' holds any truth at all, then my disability has taught me more valuable lessons than any formal schooling could ever hope to accomplish. I do not think I would either have the patience nor would I have the understanding of people that I now possess had I not had to scrupulously examine my feelings of myself and the world around me because of my disability. As a result of this introspection, I became a writer, first, as a means of expression and second, to prove the axiom that the pen is indeed mightier than the sword. I had planned to write about all that is wrong with the world and, through an increased awareness, set the world right. But I soon found that my idealism, however well meaning, was highly unrealistic.

During the first twenty years of my life, I struggled to get out of a wheelchair. In the twenty-first year I succeeded. That effort, more than anything else, taught me that major accomplishments come as a result of small steps. I decided that the realization of my idealistic dreams could best be accomplished by taking those small steps closer to home.

I am relating all this to you for a very important reason. I believe that the more you know about me, the better I will understand you. That is what life is all about, people understanding people. We live in a world where none of us is untouched by disabilities of one kind or another. There isn't one of us who, whether through family, friends or co-workers, hasn't come into contact with a disabled person. As I said at the outset, disabled people aren't like everyone else. They *are* everyone else.

Anonymous, 1994

Acknowledgements

Many people have contributed to the initiation of this book, whom I would like to thank.

First, the publisher, Butterworth-Heinemann, who responded to an approach to publish in an area that is only slowly growing in recognition, and backed a first-time author.

Practical support has come from those most closely involved in the work: Victoria Waddington, ex-director of All Clear Designs who tolerated the growing pains of the company for three years before she left; Vicki Leo, an Australian architect, for many painstaking hours of development of the specifications; and more recently Jane-Anne Hanna who has patiently helped in the final push to produce the book and the production of most of the illustrations contained within it, and for being a brick during the recent transitions of the company.

Moral support has come in large quantities from my family who have seen my transition from psychologist to designer and finally to a researcher in the design of access for disabled people. Friends who are too numerous to mention have supported this book through all of its stages.

Finally, I would like to thank some of our clients, who have known that the conversion work that we have done on their buildings has been the first step on a long journey. Without their support this book would not exist. I would particularly like to thank: Cliff Taylor of the British Broadcasting Corporation for being one of the first to believe in the need for a company like ours; Sam Turner of the Arts Council of England, for his long-standing support and for allowing us an experimental approach to solving the difficulties in the building, including a three-year project to produce tactile maps; and Dominic Tickell, Director of the Royal Court Young People's Theatre. Many of the examples and photographs are taken from work that we have done together.

I would also like to thank the countless commercial companies that have assisted us in the development of the products that we have used in our design work, and who in some cases altered their products to our specifications.

1 Introduction

This book is intended to assist the building designer (architect and interior designer) and building manager (facilities manager) to improve the service that they offer to disabled people in the buildings that they build, adapt and manage. It is important to highlight that this book is not about disability, it is about building use. Buildings exist to allow protection from the external environment, and facilitate the occupants in their activity of living, working or carrying out leisure activities. The building at its best is an enabling product, and at its worst a handicapping product.

At this point it is important to differentiate between the correct use of the words disability and handicap. Disability is a physical or psychological or mental state of being. Handicap is the interaction of the disability with the physical or attitudinal environment. For instance, visual disabilities, such as long- and short-sightedness are disabilities. They only become a handicap in the absence of facilitating equipment, in the shape of glasses. Angina is a potentially fatal disability, leading to restricted effort cycles. Stairs become an obstacle which is overcome by the use of a lift. This book contains the results of having studied the built environment from this point of view, especially in relation to people who have disabilities that are currently translated into handicaps by the built environment.

Several factors have given momentum to this area of work:

1 An increase in the numbers of disabled people available in the workforce
2 An increase in the realization of the disposable income shifting to the older groups of the population, which also house the majority of 'disability'
3 The introduction of legislation reinforcing the equal rights of disabled people to have access to employment and leisure opportunities (this is law only in the USA, but we are moving towards a legislative possibility in the UK and Europe)
4 An increasing willingness by designers and managers to design for this increasingly visible and vocal group of the community.

The fundamental vision of this book is that everyone should be enabled by the built environment. A building that is accessible, and staffed by people who welcome those from all walks of life, will draw the best out of society.

The philosophies are the same as those that have been behind the equal rights movements for many years. In this instance there are physical as well as attitudinal challenges to overcome. While I will touch on the attitudinal aspects of servicing disabled users, most of this book is designed to reduce the ignorance that has allowed the physical barriers to remain intact.

How often have 'expense' and 'fire hazard' been used to sanction the denial of equality to disabled people? There will naturally be expense involved in implementing change. This book is designed to demonstrate how that expense can be minimized, maximizing return for expenditure, as well as reinforcing the fact that reducing inequality is money well spent. Fire hazards are the result of bad design and management. During a long period practising in this field the fire services have never rejected a proposal that they do not consider a risk to life. Their job is to protect life. The designer's and manager's job is to produce designs and management procedures that comply with their requirements. Neither of these requirements conflict with the provision of full access for disabled people.

This book aims to assist the following groups of people:

- *Architects, interior designers* By providing explanations of why and how it is hoped that architects will be able to assimilate the principles into any design solution that they propose. Worked examples and working drawings, with the relevant legislation, will assist in the preparation of designs and the product references are intended to reduce the time taken to find specialist fittings.
- *Building managers* Reference tables for ongoing work such as the refitting of office areas, carpets, electrical outlets, signage and decoration schedules should enable managers gradually to improve their buildings, often at no extra cost, through the normal 'churn' process.
- *Students* Excitement is all-important, especially when surrounded by the mass of legislation and limitations imposed by building control. This book is aimed to demonstrate that 'designing for disabled people' is exciting, and far from the image of 'hospital and daycentre' design with which it is traditionally associated.
- *Disabled people* Disabled people are asked 'Is the drawing OK?' or 'What do you want?' It is hoped that there is sufficient detail in the relevant chapters to assist groups of disabled people to spot where drawings are deviating from what they would expect in an ideal world. Reference to detailed examples should also assist in putting that message into 'technical' terms that will satisfy the designer.
- *Planners* An accessible building without welcoming staff, managers, publicity and programmes of events that welcome and invite disabled people to actively participate will not be used by disabled people. Sections on publications and attitudinal training will assist managers to implement programmes in this area, improving awareness of a group of people that they currently do not serve.

This book does not intend to be the last word on the issue. It has avoided merely reprinting the guidelines that already exist in the area, some of which are impossible to implement. Likewise, as this book is not meant to be exhaustive, there are many areas that have not been covered as they do not fall within the experience of the author. (For completeness, there may be a few.)

This is not an academic book. There are referenced works, but much of what is discussed may come from anecdotal discussions and research carried out by the author, but practised rather than published. References are given in the 'Recommended reading' section for guides and documents that can usefully answer the reader's questions.

The contents of this book have largely arisen from practical experience. Most of the products recommended have been used in buildings and have performed according to expectations. Products that have not performed have not been mentioned or recommended. If the reader has serious doubts about a product, then a call to the author or to the people that may have installed the product is advised. It is often the case that the company supplying and installing the product is the difficulty, rather than the product itself – a quick ring round will soon reveal the types of comment that are not, unfortunately, printable in a book without risk of reprisal!

This book has therefore a strong 'autobiographical' nature, which it is hoped will be more illuminating than the collection and reiterating of existing work in the area. It is hoped also that the practical use of 'case study' material will go some way to demonstrating the detailed installation of the designs discussed. Many of these installations were a first for the building user and the designers – the designs presented in this book represent the 'finished' versions, where the mistakes have been ironed out!

The author is always grateful for comments where readers feel that the specifications are unrealistic, or they have found other solutions to be more beneficial. Comments of any nature are welcome and should be addressed to the author through the publisher.

Recommended reading

Because this book does not intend to be all-encompassing, readers should refer to any of the texts listed below. They all have their specialities and cover different areas. Other references and recommended texts are mentioned in the relevant sections.

1 Bilo, M., Casciato, M., Dilnnocenzo, A., *et al.*, *La Città Accessible: Itinerari senza barriere per Roma Capitale.*

2 Department of Education and Science Architects and Building Branch; Design Note 25, *Lighting and Acoustic Criteria for the Visually Handicapped and Hearing Impaired in Schools.*

3 Earnscliffe, J. (1992), *In through the Front Door; Disabled People and the Visual Arts: Examples of Good Practice*, The Arts Council for England, London.

4 *European Manual for an Accessible Built Environment*, IG Nederland, Utrecht, PO Box 70, 3500 AB Utrecht, The Netherlands.

5 Lifchez, R. (1987), *Rethinking Architecture: Design Students and Physically Disabled People*, University of California Press.

6 Palfreyman, T. and Thorpe, S. (1993), *Designing for Accessibility – an introductory guide*, Centre for Accessible Environments, London.

7 Pearson, Anne (1985), *Arts for Everyone: Guidance on Provision for Disabled People*, Carnegie UK Trust & CEH, London.

8 Thorpe, S., *Specifiers Handbook 2: Wheelchair Stairlifts and Platform Lifts*, Centre for Accessible Environments, London.

2 Disabled people

It is important to note that this chapter is not intended to stereotype disabled people. The basic premise is that human skills operate within a range of ability. At different ages we all exhibit levels of ability that range from totally dependent to independent, and then usually back towards dependence. Society has learnt to harness the ability of the majority of the population with buildings, housing leisure and work equipment, to strive towards the optimum from life. Until recently it has ignored the tools, mechanisms and attitudes to bring a large percentage of the population into the mainstream. This chapter will describe, both statistically and conceptually, those sectors of the population. The conceptual argument is the most important of the two, with the statistical argument reinforcing the momentum for change, based on equal human rights and untapped human potential.

It should also be borne in mind that this chapter represents the views of a white, able-bodied, middle-class male (the author), and much of the information is therefore second-hand.

Definitions

The World Health Organization (WHO) uses the following definitions:

- *Impairment* 'any loss or abnormality of psychological, physiological or anatomical structure or function'
- *Disability* 'any restriction or lack (resulting from an impairment) of ability to perform an activity in the manner or within the range considered normal for a human being'
- *Handicap* 'a disadvantage for an individual, resulting from an impairment or disability, that limits or prevents the fulfilment of a role

that is normal (depending on age, sex, and social and cultural factors) for that individual'.

The British Council of Organizations of Disabled People (BCODP) has agreed on the following definitions:

- *Impairment* 'lacking part or all of a limb, or having a defective limb, organ or mechanism of the body'
- *Disability* 'the disadvantage or restriction of activity caused by contemporary social organization which takes no or little account of people who have physical impairments and thus excludes them from the mainstream of social activities'.

The difference between these two definitions is quite clear. Disability can be removed by improving the interaction of people with the environment. The BCODP definition is biased towards physical impairments, but the same concepts can be applied to mental and psychological impairments.

The other difference between the two is that the WHO definition is a 'medical model' whereas the BCODP definition is a 'social model'.

Medical versus social models

In an article outlining the argument Micheline Mason and Richard Rieser[1] point out the progression of the different models. They show that the original model was the religious one, where disability was seen as a punishment for evil, or the incarnation of evil itself – 'casting out the demons'.

This has progressed to the medical model. This assumes that disability is caused by a mental or physical impairment, and therefore the impairment becomes the focus of attention. The medical establishment then focuses on being able to 'cure' the impairment and remove the disability. Mason and Rieser then state that '. . . the overall picture is that the human being is flexible and "alterable" whilst society is fixed and unalterable . . .', leaving disabled people to adapt to a hostile environment. The disabled person becomes their medical condition, and society searches for the 'miracle cure'.

However, the disabled person's view is also clearly stated '. . . that whilst we may have medical conditions which hamper us and which may or may not need medical treatment, human knowledge, technology and collective resources are already such that our physical or mental impairments need not prevent us from being able to live perfectly good lives'. It is society's unwillingness to employ these means to alter *itself* rather than *us* which causes our disabilities.

The social model then criticizes architectural barriers, inadequate employment protection, toothless legislation and the lack of protection of the rights of disabled people to access the same social privileges as non-disabled people. Mason and Rieser summarize the case eloquently: 'We cannot give the blind person sight. We can give the sighted person the ability to enable the blind person to do what he/she wants.'

Facts and figures

In 1984 the UK Department of Health and Social Security initiated a series of reports to collect information on disabled people, their income and their needs. The results began to be published in 1988 in a series of six reports[2] which examined the prevalence of disabled adults (residential care and private dwellings), children and their financial circumstances.

The other major source of information relating to disabled people in the UK is the General Household Survey.[3] This is a yearly survey of a sample of the population. Questions are asked of the sample population about any long-standing illness that they may have, for example:

Do you have any long-standing illness, disability or infirmity? By long-standing I mean anything that has troubled you over a period of time, or that is likely to affect you over

a period of time?

Does this illness or disability limit your activities in any way?

The OPCS Surveys of Disability in Great Britain, however, carried out a pre-interview screening procedure, so that only people with a disability were interviewed. These included *only* people whose disability was likely to have a *significant* effect on their ability to carry out *normal* daily activities. However, this study then went into significant detail in an attempt to classify the severity of the disability (scored between 1 and 10) and categorize it as one of the following types (see Figure 2.1):

Locomotion
Reaching and stretching
Dexterity
Seeing
Hearing
Personal care
Continence
Communication
Behaviour
Intellectual functioning

Not surprisingly, the OPCS Surveys give a lower prevalence rate of disability than the OPCS GHS – 135 per 1000 population versus 208 per 1000 (16 years and over) translating into population estimates of approximately 6.1 million and 9.35 million based on 1985 figures. This is accounted for in the survey by the fact that the GHS Survey took into account any limitation in any activity, whereas the OPCS Surveys included only the restricted set of activities discussed earlier.

It should therefore be borne in mind that there are no reliable figures on disability in the UK. It is fair to say that the estimates producing figures in the region of 6 million are conservative, but because there is a continuous variation in the definition of disability and because of the detail contained in the OPCS Surveys I will use these figures to illustrate the statistics. It would be wise, however, only to use the patterns illustrated in these figures, rather than rely on the absolute numbers.

The other feature that is interesting to note in the differences between the studies is the reported rates among older people. The GHS reported a drop in the rate of increase in limiting long-standing illness among the 65+, whereas the

Figure 2.1

*Percentage of
disabled adults by
disability type*

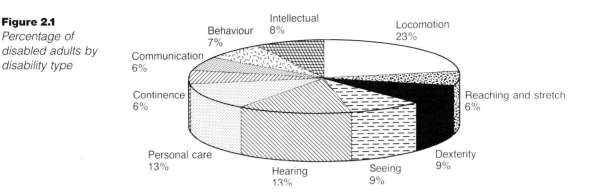

OPCS Surveys report a steady increase. It is suggested that the reason for this is that many elderly people do not think of themselves as having health problems or being disabled; they consider limitations in activities a normal consequence of old age.

Results

It is clear from the results of the research that several characteristics are readily discernible:

1 The majority of disabled people fall into the least severe categories of disability.
2 Disability is primarily found in the older population groups (55+).

3 The majority of disabled people are female (predominantly because of the longer life span of women in the over-75 age groups).
4 The structure of the population is 'ageing', i.e. the proportion of older people (55+) compared to younger people is increasing.

These statistics are illustrated in Figures 2.2 and 2.3 which chart the incidence of disability against age.

The distribution of disability illustrates its nature – i.e. disabled people are not a homogenous group who have one type of disability. It is clear from Figure 2.1 that the majority of disabled people (22.58 per cent) have a locomotion problem. However, most of these people are ambulant. The disabled population who use wheelchairs is vari-

Figure 2.2

*Prevalence of
disability by age and
severity*

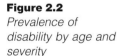

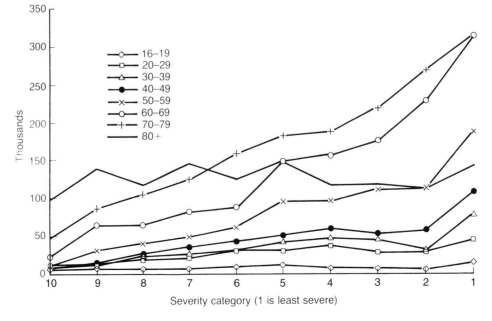

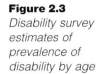

Figure 2.3
Disability survey estimates of prevalence of disability by age

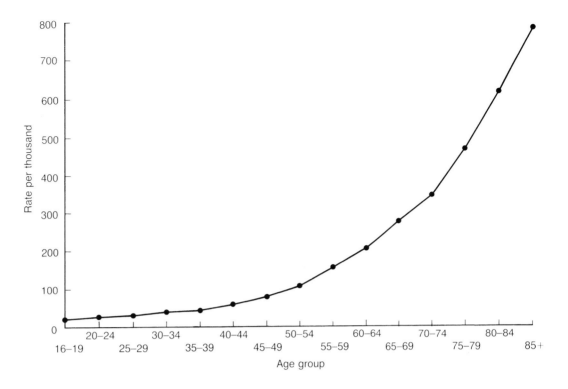

ably estimated as between 4 per cent and 6 per cent of the disabled population.

This figure is at the heart of the common assumption that a disabled person is a wheelchair user, as it can be seen from the statistics that the largest group of disabled people have a mobility disability (largely caused by arthritis), the next largest have a hearing disability (13.55 per cent) and the next largest have difficulty with personal care (12.90 per cent), again caused by arthritis, and followed by dexterity (9.03 per cent) and visual disabilities (8.71 per cent). It is worth noting, therefore, that disabled people in the workplace will tend to have a mobility disability, hearing difficulty, visual disability, and then wheelchair use, in that order, but will more frequently have an element of all the above.

Evidence from research carried out by the Royal National Institute for the Deaf (RNID) in 1989 estimated the prevalence of hearing loss in the population to be approximately 17 per cent – a surprising 7.5 million people. However, they estimated that only 0.08 per cent were profoundly deaf (0.035 million), 0.42 per cent severely deaf (0.185 million), 3.5 per cent moderately deaf (1.58 million), but the majority had a mild hearing disability – 13 per cent of the adult population (5.7 million).

RNIB estimates in 1987 indicated that there were 959 000 people with a severe visual disability – i.e. registered blind. They estimated that there were additionally 740 000 people with a sight disability.

Recent surveys show that only 18 per cent of registered blind people are totally blind, with the remainder having some residual vision. Eighty-six per cent of partially sighted people can at least recognize a friend close-up.

Statistics on Braille reading point to the fact that younger people read Braille – some 14 per cent of 16–59-year-olds, representing 11 000 Braille readers. One per cent of the older population (59+) read Braille, representing approximately 8000 people.

In conclusion, disabled people in the built environment are not a homogenous group. They have disabilities that are, in the main, mild and multiple. This indicates the fact that designers need to consider design for people in areas other than just wheelchair use, and that the increased prevalence of disability among older people, and the increases in the relative numbers of older people, will lead to an increase in the absolute numbers of disabled people in the environment.

References

1 Mason, Micheline and Rieser, Richard, *The Medical Model and the Social Model of Disability.*

2 OPCS Surveys of Disability in Great Britain: *Report 1 – The prevalence of disability among adults*, HMSO, ISBN 0-11-691229-4; OPCS Surveys of Disability in Great Britain: *Report 2 – The financial circumstances of disabled adults living in private households*, HMSO, ISBN 0-11-691235-0; OPCS Surveys of Disability in Great Britain: *Report 3 – The prevalence of disability among children*, HMSO, ISBN 0-11-691250-0; OPCS Surveys of Disability in Great Britain: *Report 4 – Disabled adults: services, transport and employment*, HMSO, ISBN 0-11-691257-X; OPCS Surveys of Disability in Great Britain: *Report 5 – The financial circumstances of families with disabled children living in private households*, HMSO, ISBN 0-11-691264-2; OPCS Surveys of Disability in Great Britain: *Report 6 – Disabled children: services, transport and education*, HMSO, ISBN 0-11-691266-9.

3 OPCS (1988), *General Household Survey*, HMSO, ISBN 0-11-691326-6.

3 Assessing a building for access for disabled people

Assessing a building for access for disabled people has been called an access audit. This is often the first part of the process of improving provision in an existing building, and can, if done correctly, be the start of an ongoing project that will last the lifetime of the building.

This chapter is designed to illustrate the nature of an access audit and the features that should be looked for in such an audit. Sections cover the areas that should be examined and the ways of commissioning an audit on a building.

What is an access audit?

An access audit will examine an existing building against predetermined criteria designed to measure the 'usability' of the building for disabled people. Usability will range from getting in and getting around to getting out. Depending on the measurement criteria, the assessment will examine how much of the facilities can be used *independently* by disabled people. A thorough audit will look at more than just physical mobility and disability. It will also examine use of the services by people with sensory disabilities and mental disabilities. The limit of what is to be assessed will depend on the frame of reference of the project. All-inclusive audits will examine printed material and publicity, staff attitudes and the physical and management issues within the building.

Beginning a project

Before deciding to conduct an audit of a building it is important to have a clear understanding of the following:

- The purpose of the audit

- What the criteria for measurement will be and what will be assessed
- The expected outcomes and their format
- Who is to carry out the audit
- The reporting of the results
- The follow-up procedure and evaluation of progress.

The management of audit information and the construction of the project are key factors in the success of a project.

What are the purposes?

Most access audits are launched with only a vague idea of what they are intended to achieve, high expectations of what they will achieve, and a lack of perception of the management procedures involved in implementing the changes that are required. Audits are conducted for three main reasons:

1 *Comparative surveys*; to gather data on the accessibility of the building or facility to build a comparative table of accessibility of buildings. Projects such as the Audit Commission were designed for this type of collection. This enables a statistical comparison of service provision across a region, and also a longitudinal approach to service provision over time.

2 *Analytical surveys*; to gather data which indicates the accessibility of a building for publication in reference works, directories and guides that disabled people will use to decide where they should go for services. The data is then disseminated through organizations such as Artsline, which provides a telephone enquiry service for disabled people in London

to find details on places of entertainment and, more recently, restaurants.

3   *Adaptive surveys*; to gather information which is designed to generate change. These audits measure areas of inaccessibility and generate recommendations for improvement. Good audits of this nature will also prioritize the improvements and make detailed recommendations. These recommendations may indicate a cost associated with the change and the optimum timescale. This type of audit can be used to generate a 'master plan' for change.

Collection of the same information can be used for all the above objectives, but the intended outcome will determine how the information is collected, the process and by whom it is collected.

Who should do the audit?

Research that we carried out for the Arts Council of England in 1993 indicated that the most successful audits and surveys were undertaken by a mixture of disabled and able-bodied audit teams using questionnaires designed primarily by disabled people. Success is taken to mean that the data collected were accurate and detailed, and represented the difficulties that a disabled person would encounter.

Audits carried out by these groups will often fall into the first two categories of the Comparative and Analytical Survey types. In order to produce the Adaptive Survey the surveying and reporting team should be experienced in the design of buildings for disabled people and the processes required for their implementation. They will also need to assemble their cost recommendations from a knowledge database of products and costs of installation and building work. It is likely therefore that this type of group would include disabled people and architects experienced in adaptive work.

DIY audits

There are guidance documents and books on conducting your own surveys and audits. Packs such as those from RADAR and the Centre on Accessible Environments and All Clear Designs will certainly give a large amount of information to the newcomer to the field, as will questionnaires

designed by The Access Officer's Association for compliance with the Audit Commission surveys of public buildings. However, these guides and questionnaires will result in a mainly mechanistic understanding of access, and are useful only for the most cursory investigation of a building's difficulties or potential.

Kits of questionnaires and measuring devices – for measurement of door-opening forces, lighting levels and ramp gradients – can be purchased from organizations such as All Clear Designs.

The other approach is to attend courses on auditing procedure, such as those run by the Centre on Accessible Environments and longer-term (one-year) courses such as the 'Environmental Access' course run by the Architectural Association.

However, where a thorough assessment of the building is needed it is normally better to employ the services of professional organizations and consultants who are experienced in this area. The Centre on Accessible Environments has an Architectural Advisory Service, based on a register of architect members with experience of access; some of whom will have experience of auditing. The Centre also has experienced auditors who will carry out assessment. A condition of registration is that the organization will give you one hour of their time free to visit the building in question and provide you with advice on how they would proceed. (They may charge travel expenses.) The Arts Council of England has also compiled a directory of consultants in disability and the arts, called *Off the Shelf and Into Action*. The directory breaks down groups by services offered and by geographic region and is available from the Arts Council of England for approximately £15.

Local access groups are extremely useful in having local knowledge as well as a wide range of experienced disabled people. Some local groups are known to the planning departments of the local council, the Social Services Department and may be in the *Yellow Pages*.

Assistance can also be gained in the first instance from Access Officers. These are normally based in the planning department or the Chief Executive's office of the local council. An Access Officer is given the task of implementing equal opportunities where they relate to disabled people, across a council's services. They are an extremely good source of advice on access questions, and should be one of the first people to be consulted.

It is recommended that up to three organizations are contacted to help formulate a strategy. The strategy should be drawn up into a brief, and this can then be issued to gain comparative tenders. Most briefs of this nature will ask for the experience of the organization, measurement methodology and the criteria against which they will be measuring the building, with the output format and the likely outcomes of the survey.

Assessing facilities

Access audits fall into two different categories:

1 Audits that assess the presence of facilities for disabled people
2 Audits that are designed to assess how well the facilities in the building will *work* for disabled people.

The main types of access audits are illustrated in Figure 3.1.

The first type of audit is frequently carried out by questionnaire on a 'ticking' basis – i.e. the question is asked 'Is there an accessible toilet?' The response is entered into a tabular reporting procedure to show the presence or absence of such a facility.

The second type of audit involves a visit to the building where the nature of the facility and how well it will *work* for disabled people are measured. This nature of the assessment is vital to the success of an access audit. Important distinctions can be made, which a simple recording procedure cannot show. For instance, the difference between a *Disabled Toilet* and an *Accessible Toilet* lies in their layout and their ability to be used. Pure recording of the facilities will probably result in a tick for the presence of a disabled toilet if there is a toilet with the wheelchair user symbol on the door. However, due to the poor design and layout of many of these toilet facilities, many would fail the assessment as being an *Accessible Toilet* because they are unusable by disabled people.

The simple recording process is unlikely to point out areas in which the facilities can be improved, other than the complete lack of facilities. The assessment of the *working* of the building can generate sensitive suggestions for improvement, where the improvement can be made by 'fine tuning' of the building.

A description of a facility which does or does not work for disabled people will highlight the difficulties. It should also refer to the solutions required to improve the situation.

Feasibility studies

Feasibility studies take the information from the access audit and use the data to propose detailed architectural changes which will improve the access areas noted in the audit document.

Assessment criteria

Second only to the decision to measure the working of the building is the choice of a commonly accepted criterion for measurement of the building. The reason that acknowledgement of the presence of a toilet marked with a disability symbol is not sufficient is that not all toilets are built to the same standard.

Who are disabled people?

The audit's target group of users must be clarified at the outset. The majority of access audits carried out appear to concentrate on wheelchair use, yet this group represents only 4 per cent of the disabled population. The other 96 per cent are people with mobility difficulties, sensory difficulties (such as visual disability and deafness) and learning disabilities. Most disabled people cannot be placed neatly into categories. The nature of disability is that the majority of disabled people have multiple disabilities, with the largest groups of disabled people being in the population aged over 55 years. At current estimates this group of people are 17 per cent of the population, a figure which will rise to 19 per cent by the year 2025.

The target group to assess therefore ranges from wheelchair users to those who may have reduced vision and who exhibit a degree of mental confusion.

Standards and specifications

With this definition of the disabled population it is important to clarify the areas of a building that will be assessed and the criteria for assessment. It is clear that the current legislative and standards

Figure 3.1
*Types of access
audits available*

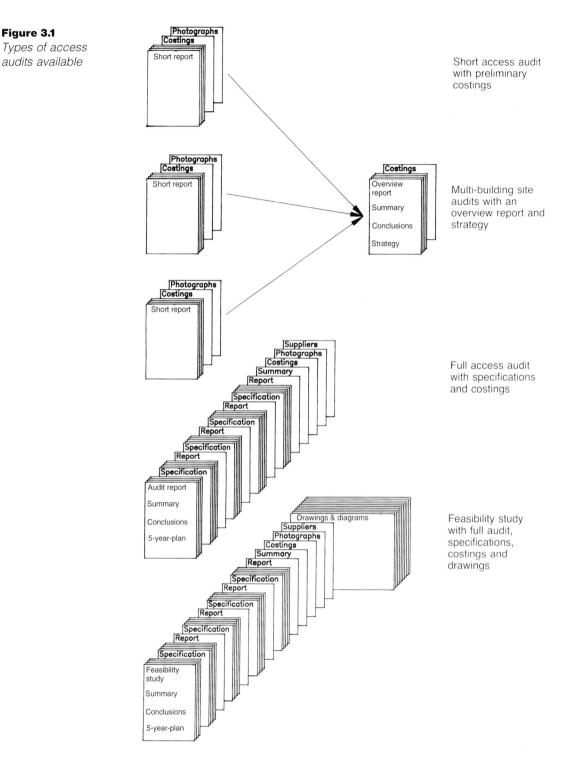

Short access audit
with preliminary
costings

Multi-building site
audits with an
overview report and
strategy

Full access audit
with specifications
and costings

Feasibility study
with full audit,
specifications,
costings and
drawings

documents are not comprehensive enough. Both Part M of the Building Regulations (1991) and BS 5810 are heavily biased towards the needs of wheelchair users, hardly considering sensory disabilities, and paying no reference to people with learning difficulties.

The other difficulty with using documents such as Part M and BS 5810 is that they are descriptions of minimum acceptable specifications which may allow use by disabled people (in wheelchairs). The standards make no reference to the ease of use of the facilities, nor the selection and use of the fixtures and fittings required to use them.

What to assess

Attitudes

Not surprisingly, the attitudes of a building management, front-line staff and management may have more impact on disabled people using a building than the physical aspects of the building. A building that is completely accessible but staffed by people who are not welcoming, helpful and understanding of the issues around disability is likely not to be frequented by disabled people.

Assessing attitudes of the people operating a building is notoriously difficult to do. It is easier and fairly indicative to carry out a *Training Audit* to assess the level of disability equality training, customer care and any other specialist training that the staff may have had.

Publicity/printed material

The design of publicity and marketing information such as leaflets and posters must be sensitive and appropriate to the target market. Use of language, images and media must be accessible, including literature particularly aimed at young people with learning difficulties. It should also be noted that there is a requirement for the production of publicity in formats that include large print, tape and Braille.

Content

Content of publicity material in terms of language, images and portrayals can be assessed for their impact and appropriateness to groups of disabled people.

Layout

The layout and typographic elements contained in the publicity material determine its accessibility to people with visual and cognitive disabilities. Requirements do not necessarily prevent designers from producing exciting and satisfying products.

Physical aspects

The physical aspects of a building form the core of an access audit. Areas which should typically be covered include:

Physical access

- Transport, parking, entrances, entrance matting, ramps (design, platforms, handrails, gradients and lighting)
- Doors – automatic (operation control, safety devices, operation procedure) and manual (closing forces, clear opening widths, vision panel and door furniture)
- Lighting – levels, location, glare and location of control switches
- Short-rise lift platforms – location, size, operation, buttons and alarms
- Wheelchair stair lifts – location, type, controls and size
- Lifts – size, voice enunciation feedback, buttons, lighting and alarm telephones
- Floor finishes (carpet pile, colours, non-slip and visibility)
- Stairs – nosings, handrails, finishes and light levels
- Reception desks/box office desks
- Acoustics and acoustic treatment of spaces

Decoration

- Colours of wall, floor, ceiling and other features
- Contrasts and visual mapping
- Use of colour to distinguish and code areas

Fire escape/evacuation

- Training, escape/evacuation lifts, design of places of refuge (BS 5588 Part 8, to allow access to floors other than the ground floor) and their use, evacuation procedures, evacuation routes, 'Evac' chairs, fire alarms (visual, tactile and auditory), fire extinguishers, automatic building protection
- The design, location and lighting of signs
- Visual fire alarm warning
- Alarm procedures and alarm/emergency response cards

Sanitary facilities

- Toilets – locations, size, alarms (and alarm procedures), fittings (colours, types, location and maintenance), taps/sinks, water temperatures, doors (size, door furniture, signage and automation), sanitary disposal and light levels
- Showers – size, types, fittings, layout, floor surface, temperature, pressure and lighting
- Changing areas – locations, facilities, floor surfaces and light levels

Wayfinding

- Directional signage – size, typefaces, raised lettering, heights, colours, textual and graphic, location, layout, arrows and light levels
- Maps and guides – tactile and taped
- Door/floor signs and other markings (warning)

Communications equipment

- Telephones – minicom systems, inductive couplers, alarm systems and induction loops
- Computers – information technology to assist disabled people, such as text magnification for people with a visual disability
- Tannoy and paging system
- Front of house – induction loops on box office and meeting rooms
- Alarms and alarm procedures

Refreshment/recreational facilities

- Restaurants, bars, tea bars, rest rooms, kitchen and vending areas (machines, etc.)

(these are assessed under similar areas to the physical access section)
- Shops and shopping areas – size, layout, cash desk, price lists and labels

Health and safety

- Signs, first-aid rooms (rest room), first-aid kits and training.

How to report

The report format of an access audit is crucial to the success of the proposed outcome. These were illustrated earlier in Figure 3.1.

It is important to locate the team supervising the audit in a department of the company, council or authority who have an understanding of the issues involved in the audit and, more importantly, of the implementation of change. It will be this group that takes the information that has been collected in the auditing procedure and develops it into an implementation plan.

Conclusion

It is important to have a clear idea of what is being assessed and the purpose of the assessment before any work begins. The purpose of the assessment will determine the areas that are to be assessed, the reporting format and the composition of the report's targets.

There are many consultants who can advise and carry out surveys of this nature or support internal groups undertaking their own surveys. The role of disabled people in the design of assessments and carrying them out cannot be overstressed.

4 Legal aspects of access for disabled people

Access for disabled people to buildings, work and leisure is not currently a right under UK law. Disabled people can legitimately be refused employment or goods and services because they are disabled. The majority of the legislation that exists has not been enacted and relies on the goodwill of those providing employment and services.

This chapter will aim to highlight the major legal aspects for the provision of facilities for disabled people and explore what is happening in other countries. It is not intended to be a comprehensive discussion but will place the legal requirements in perspective.

The chapter has been written from the perspective of a reasonable person, not a frequent campaigner, but who feels that the lack of provision of services for disabled people is a basic denial of human rights. The law insists that there are escape provisions in a building, and non-providers can be sued and shut down. The same rights and controls should exist for disabled people to enter and exit buildings – it is as simple as that.

There have been moves for the past few years to rectify this position by the introduction of a Civil Rights Bill for disabled people, along the lines of the race and gender discrimination legislation. However, successive Conservative governments have blocked the progress of such Bills and have instead proposed their own Disability Discrimination Bill. At the time of writing this is in the form of a White Paper and due to be made law some time in 1995. This Bill is a watered-down version of the Americans with Disabilities Act (discussed later). The prime focus of the Bill is to 'encourage' the provision of employment and goods and services for disabled people. However, the Bill relies on statements such as the 'reasonable adjustment to premises' to define the degree to which employers should adjust to

disabled employees. The government was concerned about the costs of enacting a Civil Rights Bill and estimated the costs to be in the order of £17 billion, which it felt would be borne by industry and thus make it uncompetitive in the world market.

Experience in the USA and Australia has shown that this is not the case, and that a sensible approach to improvement over time is accepted by disabled people and offers a practical proposition. Experience in the building and design of buildings has demonstrated that access improvements are not always accompanied by the 'mythical' large sums of capital expenditure that are cited in the anti-legislation arguments, any more than health and safety or VDU directives have done. Many of the adaptations bring with them benefits to the building operation, which can be added to the equation to reduce the overall costs.

However, one of the most frustrating aspects of the argument is that even a new building need not take full account of the needs of disabled people. The law covering access for disabled people is behind the needs of disabled people, and recently the Building Regulations (Part M, 1991) have only recognized the fact that the majority of disabled people have sensory disabilities. The provision is minimal and is based on BS 5810: 1979, which was published in 1979, and was at the committee stage for many years.

This is compounded by the lack of education for architects and interior designers on how to make buildings accessible. In 1991 Joanne Miller and Dennis Urquhart of The Robert Gordon Institute of Technology in Aberdeen conducted a study into access awareness within architectural education. They sent questionnaires to thirty-eight schools of architecture and received thirty responses. Of these thirty only fourteen provided briefing on access issues, and only then as a precursor to a related project. Only three schools examined the area in the form of a lecture. When asked about the nature of disability, most of these schools defined disabled people as being wheelchair users, with a few recognizing the existence of people with sensory disabilities. Only five widened their definition to include children, people with prams, pregnant women, etc., the remaining twenty-five viewing disabled people as a completely separate category. Fifty-six per cent of the schools felt unable to address the needs of disabled people adequately, largely due to lack of awareness on the part of staff and the feeling that the topic was a specialist area. Where access was considered it was normally the focus of a 'special project' for a school or housing, or the result of a disability in the student carrying out the project.

Legislation would ensure that access issues would be taken seriously in education to comply with the legal rights of disabled people. Lessons from the USA, Canada and Australia point to the fact that the only way to ensure access for disabled people is through legislation, and that the worst fears about greatly increased costs are broadly unfounded.

The brief history of relevant legislation and standards on access and/or rights for disabled people in the UK (partly taken from information provided by The Centre of Accessible Environments) is as follows:

1970 The Chronically Sick and Disabled Persons Act in which section 4 requires that 'Any person undertaking the provision of any building or premises to which the public are admitted, whether on payment or otherwise, shall, in the means of access both to and within the building or premises and in the parking facilities and sanitary conveniences to be available (if any), make provision, in so far as it is in the circumstances both practicable and reasonable, for the needs of members of the public visiting the building or premises who are disabled'. Section 6 requires similar provision at places of accommodation, refreshment or entertainment, and section 8 relates to access and facilities at universities and school buildings.

1976 The Chronically Sick and Disabled Persons (Amendment) Act. This extends the requirements of the 1970 Act to places of employment.

1978 BS 5619: British Standard Code of Practice for the design of Housing for the Convenience of Disabled People. This is a voluntary code of practice which sets down the essential provisions that need to be incorporated into buildings to ensure that they are conveniently used by disabled people.

1979 BS 5810: British Standard Code of Practice for Access for the Disabled to Buildings. This is a voluntary code of practice which sets down the essential provisions that need to be incorporated into buildings to ensure that they are conveniently used by disabled people.

1980 The Disabled Persons Act. This introduced sections to the Town and Country Planning Act 1971. Section 29a places a duty on the local planning authority when granting planning permission for any development covered by section 4 of the CSDP Act of 1970 to draw the attention of developers to the relevant provisions of the 1970 Act and to BS 5810: 1979. Section 29b makes similar provision in relation to educational buildings. Section 6 of the Act provided for the substitution of 'appropriate provision' for the wording 'provision in so far as it is in the circumstances both practicable and reasonable', of the 1970 Act. This section did not come into effect and its purpose is now superseded by Part M of the Building Regulations 1985.

1982 DOE (Department of the Environment) Circular 10/82. This suggests that developers be made aware of their obligations under the CSDP Act 1970 by means of a note accompanying the local planning authority's notice of the grant of planning permission. Local authorities are encouraged to designate one of their staff as an 'access officer' to produce a clearly identified point of contact on questions of access for disabled people. The circular states that 'the arrangements for access to buildings can be a planning matter and the suitability of arrangements for use by the public, which includes disabled people, raises issues of public amenity which can be material to a planning application . . ., where appropriate, conditions may be attached to a grant of planning permission . . .'.

1984 DES (Department of Education and Science) Design Note 18 Access for Disabled People to Educational Buildings. This covers access and facilities for disabled people in educational buildings. The requirements for access stated in Part M of the Building Regulations 1985 are satisfied by the relevant paragraphs of design note 18.

1987 The Building Regulations: Part M: Access for Disabled People. This came into effect on 14 December 1987 superseding Schedule 2 of the 1985 Building Regulations. Part M requires access and facilities for disabled people in offices, shops and the principal storeys of factories, educational establishments and premises to which the public is admitted. It applies to new buildings only: extensions are not covered other than in the maintenance of existing access provision. The approved document gives technical guidance on the design of ramps, stairs, handrails, doors, lobbies, lifts, hotel bedrooms, sanitary accommodation and spectator seating. It is broadly based on BS 5810: 1979.

1988 BS 5588: Part 8: British Standard Code of Practice for Means of Escape for Disabled People. Although not a statutory document this code of practice gives authoritative guidance on the design and management of buildings to enable the safe evacuation of people with disabilities in case of fire. Whereas Part M of the Building Regulations restricts its definition of disabled people to those with mobility difficulties, Part 8 of BS 5588 includes people with hearing or sight loss. The document includes guidance on application of the code of practice to existing buildings.

1991 Part M of the Building Regulations was revised in 1991 and came into force in 1992. The document included people with sensory disabilities for the first time in areas such as the inclusion of induction loops and the placement of obstacles where they may present hazards for people with visual disabilities.

1994 Disability Discrimination Bill. This is a White Paper proposed by the government to ensure the rights of disabled people to 'not be discriminated against when applying for employment or when employed, and provides that this right is infringed where employers do not take reasonable steps to remove physical barriers or adjust their practices to enable a disabled person to be employed'. The Bill also introduces for the first time 'a right of access for disabled people to goods, facilities and services, which will require service providers to adapt their policies, procedures and practices and to remove physical barriers and barriers to communication as long as this is reasonable'. However, the Bill fails to establish a Disability Commission, in favour of a Disability Advisory Body, which is an independent advisory body

with no powers. It is likely to become law in 1995.

The most significant piece of legislation in this list is Part M of the Building Regulations 1991 with that it places a requirement on architects and building designers to include access for disabled people into their original designs for *new buildings* or major adaptations. In practice, building control and planning departments also encourage development in existing buildings to comply with Part M, but often with little success.

The strength of Part M of the Building Regulations has been brought into question with regard to the development of the Tate Gallery in St Ives, Cornwall. In a 1994 article in *Access Action* Sabrina Aaronovitch of ACE discusses the issues concerning the building which was opened in 1993 and covered under the 1985 version of Part M of the Building Regulations. The Gallery is accessed via a flight of steps and a 38-metre ramp with a gradient of 1:12. There are only two platforms and the ramp distances between platforms are 12 and 13 metres. The requirements of Part M at that time required a maximum ramp distance of 10 metres. (This is now 5 metres for 1:12.) Three metres and 2 metres are not an insignificant breach of the Regulations, and most of the ramp is on a semicircle. With this and other breaches of the Regulations the building owners (the county council) were approached, and stated that the building 'meets the functional requirements of Part M'. The Access Committee for England approached a barrister to see whether the Building Regulations Section 36.6 of the Building Act 1984 could be used to force remedial work to the building. The barrister's opinion was that it would be unlikely for an injunction to be granted for a building that had been in use for over a year and felt that in the eyes of the law Part M provided only 'guidance' rather than 'strict rules'. Aaronovitch points out that the judicial review process should really be applied for within three months of the breach. After this period a court would be unlikely to want to disturb the status quo.

If there was a civil rights legislative framework an individual could take an action against the management and designers of a building which, in effect, discriminates against him or her.

European law

Unfortunately, there is not much in European law relating to disabled people. The Treaty of Rome and the Single European Act do not specifically refer to disability. Disability is, however, mentioned in the Charter of the Fundamental Social Rights of Workers (known as the 'Social Charter'). Paragraph 26 states that: 'All disabled persons, whatever the origin and nature of the disablement, must be entitled to additional concrete measures aimed at improving their social and professional integration.' While this section has been used to propose a directive, it is unlikely to affect the UK as the UK did not sign up to the Charter, and will therefore not be tied to directives developed under it.

In a paper written in 1994 Brice Dixon and Carion White point out that one of the most interesting things to note about Europe is that other countries, such as Canada, Australia and the USA, treat the issue of disability differently from Europe. European countries tend to compartmentalize disabled people's lives using non-statutory initiatives to establish the right of disabled people to social and economic integration. Canada, Australia and the USA tend to create legislation which is mindful of the needs of disabled persons in all areas of their lives and enshrines those needs in law.

United States of America

The USA has a history of providing protective legislation for disabled people, culminating in the Americans with Disabilities Act 1990 (ADA). Not all was smooth in the passage of the legislation and President George Bush was finally persuaded to sign the Act following a 'crawl-in' where disabled people left their wheelchairs and climbed the steps outside the White House.

The Act has been in force only since 1992, with remaining features still being phased in. However, the impact has already been considerable, with most states in the USA creating their own local legislation reinforcing and sometimes exceeding those laid down in the ADA.

The Act covers employment, transportation, public accommodation, state and local government and telecommunications. It makes it illegal for an employer to discriminate on the grounds of disability as long as the disability does not significantly reduce the ability of the person to perform essential functions. Therefore the often-quoted situation of a blind person applying for a bus driver's job is protected against.

Employment

The employer must make 'reasonable accommodation' to allow a disabled person to perform their job. This can include making the building physically accessible, altering the work pattern or provision of specialist equipment. Failure to comply with these requirements is interpreted as discrimination, unless 'the accommodation would impose undue hardship on the operation of the business' or would cause a direct threat to employees or the public. 'Undue hardship' is open to interpretation, but it has been found that employers in the USA have often overestimated the cost of provision for a disabled employee, and research by the Honeywell Corporation showed that the average cost of providing accommodation is less than $50. The US Equal Opportunities Commission has suggested that 'undue hardship' would equate to more than 10 per cent of the disabled person's annual salary.

Transport

Transport is viewed as critical under the Act; all railcars ordered after 1990 will have to be accessible, with existing rail systems having at least one accessible carriage by 1995. Key rail and underground stations must be accessible by 1993 and subsidiary stations by 2010. All new intercity buses must be accessible by 1996. Where a severely disabled person cannot use these services, alternative services must be offered.

Public accommodations

This section refers to areas such as hotels, galleries, places of education and places of recreation. These must be accessible by January 1992. An organization can claim 'undue hardship', but if this is found not to be the case then a fine of up to $50 000 is imposed.

State and local government

This section of the Act provided that no qualified disabled person can be excluded from participation in or receiving benefit from a service that receives federal funding. Within a year of being signed all these entities must have evaluated their policies, services and practices with a view to what modifications they should make. Structural changes should have been undertaken by 1995. However, 'historic properties' were excepted.

Telecommunications

Companies offering services via the telephone should offer a relay service or TDD (telecommunications devices for the deaf) for people with hearing or speech difficulties.

Summary

While the measures in the ADA are not perfect, they have had a significant effect on the provision of opportunities for disabled people. Test cases are currently establishing what the exact impact will be, but conversations with disabled people in the USA emphasize that transport, buildings and services are already much more accessible to disabled people.

The important feature of the Act is that it lays down standards that can be measured and assessed. In some cases, such as in the use of raised signage for people with visual disabilities, this is unnecessarily rigid in that signs must use upper-case lettering, whereas upper- and lower-case lettering is more integrationist (but against the 'law' according to the ADA).

Canada and Australia

Canada and Australia have a different legislative make-up, with more reliance on provincial legislation having first set up a 'principle' of 'civil rights'. However, the legislation has proved effective in protecting the rights of disabled people to have access to goods, services and employment in these countries.

Conclusion

The purpose of this chapter has been to provide an answer to the question 'So what are we required to do by law?' and concludes, sadly, that UK legal requirements are currently minimal. The new legislation proposed by the government will not make a great deal of difference unless the Civil Rights Bills are successful at making their way through the parliamentary process.

As an employer, there is a duty of care under the health and safety legislation (dealt with in more detail in the section on fire) to ensure that employees with a disability are protected in the workplace. Most of the improvements to buildings that have taken into account the needs of disabled people result from the equal opportunities policies of the companies concerned as they update their employment practice to accommodate the needs of disabled people.

It is important, therefore, as a purchaser of buildings or building design services from an architect or interior designer, that clients clearly state their requirements in terms of access for disabled people, specifically mention publications that state such requirements and emphasize that these are basic performance criteria that must be reached. Relying on the law or the education of designers, unfortunately, at present is not sufficient.

Recommended reading

1 Aaronovitch, Sabrina (Autumn 1994), *How reasonable is Part M?* Access Action, Access Committee for England.
2 HMSO (1995), Disability Discrimination Bill, White Paper.
3 Lifchez, R. (1987), *Rethinking Architecture: Design Students and Physically Disabled People*, University of California Press.
4 Standing Advisory Commission on Human Rights 1994, *Disability: An assessment of the implications of physical and sensory disability in a Northern Ireland context together with supporting research papers*, HMSO.

5 Training

This chapter is designed to introduce the reader briefly to the types of training that are available to improve an awareness and understanding of the issues of disability. One feature central to all the courses mentioned here and a central tenet to Disability Equality Training is the 'non-experiential' method of learning.

Many groups offer training by subjecting the participants to temporary experiences – use of a wheelchair, blindfold and ear-defenders. These courses are not approved by organizations of disabled people, and can be seen to contribute little to the understanding of disability in the built environment. The experiences gained during these exercises are not transferable. Disabled people are not a homogenous group. How can sitting in a wheelchair help to understand the requirements of someone who has been a wheelchair user all their life?

It is important to emphasize that the disabled people in courses such as those listed below are used because of their professional ability. It will also be the first time for many participants that they have worked alongside a disabled professional. This will have more long-term impact than a short period of wheelchair use. The training is designed to change 'attitude' and 'mindset' to begin to include disabled people in the vocabulary of people attending the courses. Once the trainee has the 'tools' to talk to disabled people he or she will be able to debrief clients. They will be able to talk to them, and ask them questions, rather than asking them if they can borrow their wheelchair!

Disability Equality Training

Disability Equality Training was first formalized by the Disability Resource Team. This type of training employs only qualified disabled trainers and explores the issues of disability from society's attitudes to the historical models of disability. Participants are encouraged to examine issues related to disability so that they are better equipped to talk to disabled people about their experiences. This form of training leaves the participant with tools to gain understanding from a wide range of disabled people rather than the narrow experiences of awareness training.

Where do we get a trainer?

The Arts Council of England publishes a directory *Off the Shelf and Into Action* which lists a large number of training agencies. It is important, when seeking a training group to use, to ask about the degree of tailoring to your organization, and how much the course will concentrate on practical 'work'-related issues. It is wise to set a brief with the expectations for the trainers and ask how the organization will achieve the expected outcome. There are groups who merely apply a formula type of training, and these should be avoided.

Who to train?

There are several groups of people to train when looking at access for disabled people: architects and designers; building control departments; building management; management executives and front-line staff.

Architects and designers

The training of architects and designers was briefly discussed in Chapter 4. It is worth repeating here that this area of training is not taken seriously in UK architectural schools, and that there are some novel approaches that should be adopted and integrated into architectural training. This area of work should pervade all aspects of a design project rather than being treated as a specialist area.

So often discussion of access for disabled people is covered in association with housing for older people, hospices and day centres. Projects should emphasize that disabled people become involved in all aspects of daily life. Architects and interior designers have responded extremely well to projects that revolve around a subterranean night club, ship or cinema complex.

Training and information resources should be used throughout the education process and disabled people included in the continuum of people for whom architects are designing. Training exercises should include practical exercises and break away from the examination of wheelchair access as a 'single' issue.

Building control and planning departments

As the people responsible for implementation of access provision in new buildings it is critical that this group of people have a clear understanding of 'barrier-free' design. Their background and experience is extremely diverse. Time is normally short and their understanding of political issues well developed.

As this book emphasizes, access for disabled people is about use and attention to detail. Many planning and building control departments will encourage accessible development by giving a certain level of guidance and, where necessary, do a certain amount of problem solving with applicants, and in the case of building control, on-site. Training in this area should therefore concentrate on how people use buildings and the critical features of designs and detailing requirements. Because this group of people is used to reading plans they can be used extensively. However, the training should be kept light and fast-moving. In the past, tests such as 'spot the difference' have been useful short exercises to emphasize important features of a design.

Building managers

To ensure that all the access improvements to the building are used to their greatest extent it is important that disabled people feel welcomed by the centre's staff, tutors, resident groups and other users. In many instances accessible buildings are not used by disabled people because of staff attitudes which may include the feeling that 'disabled people can't do that'.

Training related to disability falls roughly into three groups:

1 Attitudes; where people's attitudes and perceptions of disabled people are examined and addressed. Disability is a misunderstood concept, with the misunderstanding often determining the limits of expectations of activity.
2 Practical; where specific skills relating to disability can be learned. Courses on sign language will give the user an ability to communicate with people who use it on a regular basis.
3 Service provision; where staff train to discover how their services, planning and provision can be altered, improved or maintained to meet the needs of the disabled population.

Obviously this separation is slightly artificial, as all three groups overlap to a degree and will contain similar exercises and skills. However, divided as above the courses fall into groups that are more appropriate to aim at different sectors of the staff structure within an organization.

Course structures will vary to relate to the staff function and composition as follows:

1 *Front-line staff* These are often the 'shop window' of an organization. They can either welcome disabled people into the building or exclude them before they arrive. Front-line staff service people face to face, by telephone and letter. Being aware of the facilities that the centre offers and communicating them is an everyday part of their job, and this relates equally to the facilities that are offered for disabled people.

There is often a high turnover of front-line staff, with many working on a temporary or seasonal basis. It is recommended that they attend an initial one-day course, with specialist topics such as sign language being offered on an ongoing basis. This type of training is best carried out on the actual site with guest trainers. It is also useful to include awareness training in the induction courses that new staff attend.

Many staff now attend some form of 'customer care' courses. These consist of 'modules' or training packets. This is an ideal opportunity to introduce equality training as a package that spans the other modules.

2 *Middle-level managers*   These are critical to the implementation of an organization's equal opportunities policies, and are often involved in policy formulation as well. There is also a degree of face-to-face work with clients entering the building.

A two-day course is recommended for middle management, which is specifically tailored to the needs of an arts-based manager. The first day will be used to examine the basics of disability equality training, with the second used to focus on job-specific issues. Further training, which is more profession-specific (e.g. portrayal of disabled people in the media for television production teams) is also recommended. This type of training is best carried out at the place of work using outside trainers.

3 *Executives*   People responsible for policy formulation at the executive level should examine disability issues in a broader context to explore the issues surrounding the integration of anti-discriminatory and positive policies throughout the organization. This group will also be responsible for setting targets and establishing a system to monitor and evaluate the success of these policies. Executives should attend the courses run on-site, but should also have access to courses which unite executives from other organizations who are making policy decisions on a project-wide basis and across other art forms.

The types of course and their availability are normally based on cost and time. In a small organization it is recommended that all groups are trained together, especially as staff in these situations tend to be more multi-functional in their roles. In larger organizations the front-line training should be more face to face with a mixture of attitudinal and practical skills training, with middle and upper management being a mixture of attitudinal and policy-based exercises.

Specialist courses will need to be arranged for staff looking at educational programmes or responsible for areas of outreach/publicity and employment practice in the organization.

Recommended reading

1 Arts and Disability Unit, *Off the Shelf and Into Action*, Arts Council of England.

6 Access to advertising and publicity material

Printed material is one of the primary means of outreach of an organization. It is commonly the initial means of informing the user of the organization's activities and calendar, and may be a useful reminder for diary events.

Because the material is normally a purely visual medium, it is important to consider its impact on those with a visual disability. However, there are many other issues related to the written and illustrated message, such as the language that is used and the degree to which pictograms are used instead of words. (People with learning difficulties or low literacy skills may find pictograms useful when combined with words.)

General rules related to printed material should be taken as guidelines, rather than a 'straitjacket' and are as follows. (See Figure 6.1 for an illustration of the fonts mentioned below.)

Type

As a general rule sans serif typefaces are most acceptable, such as Avant Garde, Gothic Book and Helvetica. The headings in this book are in a sans serif typeface. Other typefaces have reduced serifs, such as Palatino, but the sans serif typefaces are preferred.

Serif fonts such as Times Roman and New Century Schoolbook present the reader with more difficulty as they fill the page with more black, and the serifs confuse the complete word shape. (Words are read as shapes rather than by decoding each letter in turn, so the overall shape of the word is important.)

Italicized text is more difficult to read than non-italic even with sans serif typefaces, and it makes the reading of the serif typefaces even more difficult – such as Times Roman Italic or ITC Zapf Chancery Medium Italic, where the word shape is less legible.

Case

Because word shape and the envelope surrounding the risers and fallers in the word are so important in its interpretation, lower-case lettering is more easily and quickly read and interpreted. Therefore this lettering is recommended on all

Figure 6.1
Selected font types

Avant Garde Gothic Book
Helvetica
Platino
Times Roman
New Century Schoolbook
Times Roman Italic
ITC Zapf Chancery Medium Italic

signs, including where emphasis is intended. The difference is quite profound; for example, UPPER and Upper have very different outlines.

Weight

The weight or boldness of the type is an important feature in the legibility of the text. The stem width of letters should be in proportion to the letter's height, so that the features of the letter are readily distinguishable, at the same time presenting a dark enough image against the background. A typeface such as Helvetica presents an ideal weight ratio, with the bolder version being less easy to read.

The same typeface in the heavier font is less easy to read because of the increase in the amount of black on the page and the thickness of the stem in comparison to the letter's features/height. However, weight can be used to emphasize headings and differentiate features of text – but it should be avoided in large blocks.

Size

Choosing a size of text to suit every reader is impossible. Different visual disabilities require text in different font sizes which range from 14 point to 24 point. It is not proposed that all publications be issued in the largest font required, as it is assumed that people requiring the largest of fonts will have equipment at home to magnify text for detailed perusal. However, it is recommended that vital pieces of information should be legible without great magnification. To this end, important information, such as the diary section, telephone/contact details, prices and course names should be large enough for most people with a visual disability to read.

The minimum body text size recommended for print is 14 point, which generates a capital letter height of approximately 4 mm. (*Note*: fallers will drop approximately 1.5 mm below the line, therefore requiring a reasonable line-to-line separation – something like a 14/16 point combination.)

Titles should begin at approximately 18 point and increase to whatever is practical on the page. However, it should be remembered that the title is easier to read if it can be readily scanned. See Figure 6.2 for examples of font sizes.

Background

A significant feature of the legibility of the text is the contrast between the text colour and the background that it is printed on. The higher the contrast between the two, the greater the legibility. It is important to note that it is not the differences in the colours but in their reflectance – i.e. how much light bounces off them. Therefore blue on blue is a possible combination as long as the difference in the reflectance is maintained. Using different colours improves the contrast, but reflectance is the important feature – imagine black on purple. Similarly, text printed on any type of background shading will have a reduced legibility because of the reduced contrast between text and background. As the shading increases, the legibility reduces. See Figure 6.3 for examples of

Figure 6.2
Selected font sizes

14 pt text is this size
16 pt text is this size
18 pt text is this size
24 pt text is this size

Figure 6.3
Degrees of shading obscuring background text

background shading and its effect on figure legibility.

Density

The density of the text itself is also important and type styles which reduce the darkness of the text, either by using Outline or Texture, will have an effect on the legibility of the text. This type of effect should therefore be used sparingly, with non-vital information. See Figure 6.4 for examples of outline and textured text.

Figure 6.4
Outline and textured fonts

Reversed

Light text on a dark background (see Figure 6.5) presents an image which appears to be larger and whiter than non-reversed text (see Figure 6.6) of identical size (through a psychological effect called the 'halo' effect). However, this technique should be used sparingly, as the massive increase in the amount of black on the page reduces its legibility, and we are more used to decoding the white space around lettering rather than the black space.

Layout

The justification of the text is an important feature to guide the eye and interpret sentences. The sentence structure is read as a whole, detecting a body of text. Opinion is varied on the use of justified margins or whether a ragged right-hand side should be used.

The argument for using a ragged right-hand edge is less clear-cut. It is proposed that this avoids the uneven and somewhat arbitrary spacing created by the use of proportionally spaced text. However, a counter-argument proposes that a standard sentence length helps to detect the extent of blocks of body text, especially in multi-column documents.

We therefore tend to prefer a fully justified body of text, though this is more a matter of individual preference. Left justification, however, does appear to play a significant role in informing the eye's search pattern to place the text in sequence.

Where there is an alteration in the use of the left-hand justification then the most appropriate form is to use a regular stagger, as opposed to radical and unpredictable alterations to margins, which

give the reader no
indication where the next
piece of text will
appear, making it
difficult to follow the
sequence of the sentences.

Orientation

The orientation of wording has a great effect on its legibility. It is difficult for many users to read a

Figure 6.5
Reversed text showing the halo effect, looking larger than it is

Figure 6.6
Non-reversed text which does not have the same effect as that shown in Figure 6.5

Figure 6.7
Text in this orientation is difficult to read

Figure 6.8
Text in this orientation is extremely difficult to read

word that is on its side. (See Figures 6.7 and 6.8.) Sometimes this orientation is necessary for graphic effect, or because it is the only way to fit in a title with a large enough typeface. However, when the lettering is orientated differently from the reading direction, the difficulty in reading and interpreting is magnified as there are no clues given by the word shape. Each letter must be processed separately and built into the word, which is then interpreted.

Advertising

Advertising for disabled people should take place on a regular basis to invite applications from disabled people. Most of the networks for disabled people operate on a national basis. It is also worth bearing in mind that the boundaries for disabled people are more significant. There are few organizations that are accessible for disabled people. It may be worth considering, therefore, that the catchment area for disabled people should be significantly wider than for their able-bodied counterparts. It is therefore recommended that the national publications and organizations below are contacted, and used for advertising courses and exhibitions:

Publications

Dail **(0171) 916 6351** 34 Osnaburgh Street, London NW1 (Disability Arts in London)
Disability Now **(0171) 383 4575** 16 Fitzroy Square, London W1P 6LP
Mail Out **(0422) 310161** 9 Chapel Street, Hollywell Green, Halifax HX4 9AY

Organizations

Action for Disability **(0171) 702 7173** Dame Collett House, Ben Johnson Road, London E1
Artsline Ltd **(0171) 388 2227** 54 Chalton Street, London NW1
BCODP **(01332) 295551** British Council of Organisations of Disabled People, Litchurch Plaza, Litchurch Lane, Derby DE24 8AA
SKILL **(0171) 274 0565** National Bureau for Students with Disabilities, 336 Brixton Road, London SW9 7AA
Disability Alliance **(0171) 247 8776** Universal House, Wentworth Street, London E1

Disability Resource Team **(0171) 482 5062** Bedford House, 125–133 Camden High Street, London N1 7JR

London Disability Arts Forum **(0171) 916 5484** 34 Osnaburgh Street, London NW1

National Disability Arts Forum **(0171) 813 1431** 34 Osnaburgh Street, London NW1

Shape London **(0171) 700 0100** London Volunteers Bureau, Resource Centre, 365 Holloway Road, London N7 6PA

Artists with Disabilities 22 Seymour House, Church Way, Somerstown, London NW1 1LR

Disability Arts in Bromley **(0181) 290 5546** 14 Rodway Road, Bromley, Kent BR1 3JL

Society for Disabled Artists **(0895) 32675** 13 Harvil Road, Ickenham, Middlesex

GLAD **(0171) 274 0107** 336 Brixton Road, London SW9 7AA

Production formats and techniques

This section briefly examines the methods of making printed material available to people with a disability. It is intended only as a guide and is the result of research in 1994. It is important to monitor the changes in technology, and advisable therefore to contact organizations such as the Royal National Institute for the Blind, AIRS and especially other libraries and institutions that have implemented some of these systems.

Documents come in many formats and types. They range from those that are being produced internally on word processors as memos, to a back catalogue of printed material in a library. Each type of document is discussed, and the options laid out for the production of versions which will satisfy people with visual disabilities and improve access to printed information.

The recommendations follow an inclusive approach and point towards the adoption of 14 point text (5 mm high capital height and 75% × to capital height ratio) as a minimum standard large print for published documents, with other sizes available for those who request them.

Facts and figures – the need

Analysing the need for the production of print formats for people with visual disabilities is dependent on where figures are drawn from. (Refer to the section on disability for a more detailed dis-

cussion of the figures.) OPCS figures from 1988 show that there are currently 15 000 registered blind people, with a further 1 700 000 people with a severe or appreciable sight impairment. In 1989 a survey conducted by Bill Kirby and Marcus Weisen (of the RNIB) reported that 312 museums received visits from groups of people with partial vision, despite the fact that, in a survey of 1400 Museums Association members, only 2.5 per cent provide a Braille guide, 4.5 per cent a taped guide and 3.9 per cent a large-print guide. The figures in this small survey demonstrate the hidden market of people with visual disabilities who are currently being denied ready access to the majority of printed information.

In a recent piece of research, carried out for The Arts Council of England into students who have successfully trained in the arts, out of approximately 400 students who successfully completed their academic courses in 1994, approximately 20 per cent had visual disabilities. When the field of music is examined, approximately 90 per cent of disabled students successfully graduating have a visual disability. It is also clear that demand rises in response to facilities being available and widely advertised. A lack of previous demand does not generally indicate a lack of need.

Types of business information

Printed information considered in a business context generally falls into three categories.

Internal information

Internal information is either generated directly within the workplace or received from outside the workplace, but then used and/or circulated internally:

- Faxes produced for sending outside the building or faxes received into the building and then circulated
- Memos produced and circulated either within the building or for outside consumption, or received into the building; letters produced for distribution outside the building, or letters received and circulated
- Reports/papers produced within the building for circulation or reports received into the building and then circulated.

External information

External information is produced within the organization but intended for external consumption by the general public or other organizations. Examples include:

- Leaflets which advertise or inform the reader as to the service of the organization or department
- Reports (printed) from the departments on a regular basis
- Newsletters published periodically and circulated to readers
- Surveys/questionnaires circulated to gather information and data from other bodies and the general public
- Annual reports, produced in large numbers
- Books commissioned, written and published by or on behalf of the organization.

Back catalogue/library

Most organizations have a library facility of some sort, which is either used by staff or open for use by members of the public. The back catalogue of information stored in a traditional print form is not available to members of the public who have visual disabilities.

Output types

People with a visual disability are not a homogenous group. The visual ability of people within these groups will vary widely and will range from the need of a larger print size to Braille and taped messages. The formats which people will require fall largely into the following groups:

- *Large print* This is anything which is larger than the standard IBM typewriter Courier type, which is 10 CPI. At its minimum, large print means 14 point (5 mm capital height) text, but the actual size needed will vary with the user, with some requiring as large as 24 point text (8 mm capital height). 'Large print' normally also refers to the font type and is conventionally accepted to be sans serif. Conventional wisdom dictates that serif text is more readable as body text, and this is generally accepted. However, discussions with all disability groups that deal with large

print have categorically stated that sans serif is much easier to read for people with visual disabilities. Large print means different things in different uses. On items such as letters and short reports, large print should be taken to mean whatever size the user needs. Twenty-four point sans serif text has become accepted as a standard if the requirement is not known, with 14 point sans serif as acceptable where longer documents are required (unless a larger point size is requested). Sizes up to 72 point may be requested, though any larger than this produces a document that is completely unwieldy, and this is seen as the largest sensible size (though if the user is operating at this size, it is likely that he or she should be using tape).

- *Braille* This is produced with a Brailling printer on specialist heavyweight paper, and is used by Braille readers, even for long documents. The Braille referred to here is type 2 condensed version, which is for experienced Braille users.
- *Tape* This will contain a narrated version of the documents that replaces the printed output. The tapes are professionally narrated to maintain the listenability of the document under question, especially for long documents.
- *CCTV* This is a closed-circuit television camera, mounted to look at and magnify written text onto a screen. It allows people with reduced vision to read printed documents in 'real time' in a magnified form, but does not capture the text in any form. It is mainly used in libraries for browsing.
- *Synthesized speech* Speech output can effectively 'read' a document to the user in real time, or read an existing computer file. The document is scanned a line at a time and a synthesized voice will read the words.
- *Multimedia* These presentations are altering the way that information is stored, retrieved and available to disabled people. Organizations such as the Open University are revolutionizing access to course materials. Complex searches of the compact disc can be made and synthesized speech can be used to translate text on the screen. Real 'sound bites' of the original event can also be accessed. With a speech, the transcript can either be translated by

synthesized voice in the computer or the digitally recorded speech can be played. This allows the user to access information randomly as sighted people do, rather than use the sequential access system that tapes dictate. This system is not yet available to most organizations, and will not be discussed in more detail.

Conversion methods

Converting printed information into one of the above formats depends on the origin of the information. This will be either computer generated or printed on paper. (There is feasibly a third category of documents received on tape, which will be either transcribed into a computer or typed onto paper.)

Computers

Computer-generated text either exists as a formatted document in a word processing (WP) or Desk Top Publishing (DTP) package or as ASCII text files. (ASCII is the lowest common textual language that the computer will work with. It has no formatting codes, such as margins or typeface, and is purely text.) Most word processors/DTP systems have a facility to save their formatted text as ASCII files for conversion into other packages.

- *Large print* The production of large print from computer-generated text can be achieved from within the software (WP or DTP) that is being used to control the text. At its simplest the printer is merely told to print in the selected font size and reformat the page layout accordingly. This process can simply be achieved using macros, which are miniature programs called up by the user from within the software. A 'postscript' laser printer, or a printer with a selectable font cartridge, or a printer with a windows-compatible driver and windows program are required for the production of large print.
- *Braille* The starting point for producing Braille is an ASCII file in a computer. This is produced by the word processing software. The file is then entered into a Braille conversion program, which reads the text

and produces a Braille version, which is then output to a Braille printer. Braille printers are specialist printers which can be linked to any PC with a print output, and the conversion software. They require special paper which they emboss with Braille. Once again, a 'macro' can be produced within most programs which means that the user can remain in his or her word processing/ DTP package, and it will automatically send the text into ASCII and to the Brailling converter for printing. The Braille printer can be attached to a large network, and therefore accessed by any computer on the network in a large organization. (Although someone will have to be able to read Braille to identify whose the Brailled document is!)
- *Tape* Taped output can be produced in one of two ways, for different purposes:
  - Internally produced short documents required for limited circulation can be produced on relatively inexpensive recording equipment, and narrated by members of staff – this is suitable for memos and short letters
  - Longer reports and widely circulated documents are produced professionally by specialist agencies, where narrators with good reading and listening quality voices are used for the transcription.
  For either method, the narrator will work from a printed script to produce a master tape, which can be copied, personalized and labelled, and distributed along with the original script.
- *CCTV* This would not be used where text was already contained within the computer. A screen-enhancement piece of software such as 'Zoomtext' or 'Lunar' would be used to increase the size of the text on the computer screen to a size that the partially sighted user could access directly.
- *Speech synthesis* Speech can be produced simply from a computer file, as long as the computer has a sound card and speech synthesis software/recognition. This was seldom used due to the poor quality of the synthesized voice, but the technology has improved and is heavily used by people with little remaining vision who are intensive computer users. The other method is using speech-to-text converters to enter the text. Systems produced by Dragon Software and IBM have reached speeds of up to 100

words per minute, which is faster than typing!

Printed information

Converting printed information into Braille, large print or synthesized speech requires the use of a scanner and optical character recognition software (OCR). This software can take an image from a scanned page and 'recognize' the text, which is then converted either into ASCII text or into your favourite word processor. The printed text is placed on the scanner, which is connected to a computer (286, 386, 486 or Pentium). The text is scanned and saved as a file. The file is then interpreted by the OCR software and converted. However, a scanned and analysed sheet of text will always contain a percentage of errors, and will have to be edited and cleaned up by the user. The computer files then produced can be converted into any of the above formats.

Implementing a print accessibility policy

This is designed to show the steps, example products and 'ballpark' figures to implement the formats described above. It is important to note that the costing exercise was carried out in 1994, so the costs are guideline only.

Internal information

Large print

Faxes, letters, memos and reports can all easily be produced in large print when they are targeted at people with a visual disability. A record of the preferences of the recipient should be maintained and their preferred font type and size produced.

To make the production of these formats as simple as possible a technical department should be able to produce a 'macro' for the particular computer program in use to allow conversion into large print. Several word processors have the facility of a 'style library' which can be invoked when the 'merge' command is enacted. If one of the fields in the merge file is a font-size command, then the font size for the specific letter/memo/fax of that person will be merged, for their letter only, and returned to the standard setting in the next

letter requiring standard fonts. It should be noted that the address section of a letter is not required to change if it makes use of the windowed envelope facility.

The success of this approach relies on good data tracking and maintenance. A successful procedure in the past has been the inclusion of a questionnaire in all mail-outs for a three-month period. The questionnaire specifically asks people about their print requirements. The responses should be analysed and the data entered into the merge records. (The questionnaire should be available in large print, tape and Braille!)

Action requirements are as follows:

1 Produce standardized merge files/address lists.
2 Add facility for large print into the address list merge files.
3 Design macro command for the conversion of faxes and memos into large print size required.
4 Examine and anticipate the conversion problems into windows-based software.
5 Provide publicity within the organization and training on the production of large-print material.

The cost implications of this system will be minimal. In fact, there will be a slight saving in time and effort, due to the automatic nature of the merge and the simplicity of employing a manual. There will be an initial resourcing implication from a computer maintenance team.

Scanning

The simplest solution to this problem is to employ a scanner and OCR software (as discussed above).

- *Recognita Plus* is widely acknowledged as one of the best OCR software packages for people with visual disabilities as it offers a special menu system called 'Auge'.
- Scanners vary in quality and price. The OCR software will work with most scanners, but the Hewlett-Packard 'IIP' (300dpi) is recommended because of its wide compatibility with other systems and the excellent hardware support. The HP scanners are also TWAIN-compliant, which means that they comply with an international standard and are likely to work with software.

Flatbed scanners are preferable, as they do not rely on the operator having a steady hand, and can be used by people with a visual disability.

As a combined package the scanner and software can be purchased for approximately £1400 from Concept Systems.

Braille

There is a need in the day-to-day activities of large organizations to produce Braille documents that will range in size from one to twenty-five sheets of A4 (one sheet of A4 translates into roughly three sheets of Brailled type). The production of Braille requires the document to be on computer, a Braille conversion program and a Braille printer. According to the manufacturers, the printer can act as any other printer on the network, and can therefore be located anywhere in the building. The printing process is quite noisy, and the printer should therefore be equipped with an acoustic hood.

As stated above, a user could move from a letter on the screen in, say, WordPerfect '5.1' to a Brailled document with the use of a macro, without having to understand the Brailling system. According to Dolphin Systems a macro could be written from Windows software, using a full DOS window – though this would be more complex.

There appear to be three options open for the production of Braille:

1 The use of a Brailling service from an outside organization, such as the RNIB, AIRS or the DRT. Transcription from printed A4 is approximately £1.65 per page of Braille, with £0.12 per copy of Braille sheet. Turnaround time is approximately 24 to 48 hours. AIRS offer the additional service of distributing the Brailled items to the target addresses as long as these are supplied.
2 The provision of a separate Brailling facility, which includes computer and operator of the Brailling system.
3 A medium-grade Brailling printer, connected to the network and used by all departments via macros.

An example of option 3 is the Dolphin software (CIPHER) and 'Index Everest' printer, which is a medium-weight Braille printer which is also able to print sideways for spreadsheets, etc. available from Sensory Visionaid and an acoustic hood, also from Sensory Visionaid.

The printer should be sited centrally, and logically should be located in the library/post/resource area, and supervised by their staff, who should also receive training on its use. Cost implications are as follows:

		£
1	Translation program	130.00
2	Braille printer	3500.00
3	Acoustic hood	300.00
4	One-day training/installation	250.00
5	Braille paper (per 1000)	28.00
	Total cost	4208.00

Tape production

Taped versions of printed literature fall into two categories:

1 Small documents, such as memos and letters, which are required in small numbers of tapes
2 Small documents required in large numbers and large documents required in any number.

There are three methods of achieving transcription onto tape, which should use a standard domestic cassette rather than small dictaphone-type cassettes:

1 A medium-quality recording system such as a 'ghetto blaster' maintained within the building and a method of producing and personalizing copies of the tapes and a supply of tapes
2 A high-quality recording facility within the building with access to studio quality recording equipment and a roster of people with good voice/reading ability
3 Using transcription services provided by the RNIB, AIRS and the DRT. These organizations have professional studios and tape-copying facilities. AIRS has the facilities for sound effects and distribution of the taped material. AIRS will handle from one to 100 000 copies of a tape.

For the production of small documents it is recommended that internal resources be used. A compact system such as the Sony 'Studioman' produces high-quality recordings and is extremely portable. A low-cost copying twin-tape system, such as those produced by Panasonic, has the facility to copy tapes at high speed. They can also record, and can act as a standby for the Studioman, but should largely be kept free of duplication.

Large numbers of small documents and larger documents should be handled by professional recording services. Of the services contacted, AIRS offered the most professional, with a minimum charge of £5 for a memo, and £0.75 per tape copy. They offer single-voice recording from £30 per hour (it takes approximately 3 minutes to read an A4 sheet) and two voices (for variety) from £70 per hour. Turnaround can be achieved the same day if short documents are faxed to them.

The following cost implications have been put together for a medium-size organization of approximately 200 staff, for approximately one year of operation:

		£
1	Studioman or equivalent	130.00
2	Panasonic tape to tape	69.00
3	Tapes C30 × 200	100.00
4	Professional studio (AIRS), one voice, at approximately 200 sheets of A4 per year at £5 minimum	1000.00
	Total cost	1299.00

External information

Production of external information such as leaflets and annual reports will involve a year-on-year cost, which will have to be attached to the individual publication's budget. It is important to note that this process is more difficult if there is not a house style or method for purchasing print. If each designer is briefed with a different briefing document then it is unlikely that the following measures will succeed.

While not in favour of briefings and manuals that restrict a designer's creativity there is a need for a common approach to implement these recommendations via the production of common briefing documents which contain a mixture of hard-and-fast rules/requirements and guidance.

In printed material which is intended for general consumption, large print takes on a different meaning from that for letters, memos and paper-based reports. With each increase in print size, publication and distribution costs rise. On a large published document an increase of 2 points in the text size can result in a 100 per cent increase in the production cost and a 75 per cent increase in the distribution cost. However, on small publications like leaflets, the increase in production cost can be as little as 3 per cent, with no increase in the cost of distribution.

Leaflets

Large print

Most leaflets take the form of A4 folded twice or a variation of this. Point sizes used vary between 10 and 12, all of which fall below the 14 point minimum recommended. Increasing the type size of a leaflet like this will considerably facilitate its use by people with a visual disability, and those using magnification equipment will also benefit. Increasing the type size to approximately 14 point typically adds an extra flap to a leaflet that is currently A4.

At 1994 prices this increased the cost of production on Hi-Speed Blade Paper, two colours, from £220.00 for 1000 A4 sheets (three-flap leaflet of A4 folded into three) to £228.87 for 1000 four-flap (A4 plus a flap).

Braille

As most leaflets are generated from text documents they can easily be saved to disk in ASCII text format. When any leaflet is produced a disk with the labelled files on it should be placed with the organization's library. When requests for Brailled versions arrive they can then be printed on demand. (**Note**: There should be a Braille catalogue listing all the publications available.)

There is the minimal cost of Braille paper at £26 per 1000 sheets, the printer set-up and the extra storage space.

Tape

All leaflets can be recorded onto tape at the time of production to create a library of master tapes which can be used for duplication. (**Note:** there should be a tape catalogue listing all the publications available.) Based on the likely production of four leaflets per year the cost will be approximately £150 per year for the recording costs plus storage of the tapes and the copying facilities.

Newsletters

Large print

Newsletters and periodicals with a circulation of 1000 copies tend to use 11 point serif text and often adopt an A3 folded into A4 format. Increasing the body text to 14 point would make this publication accessible to people with visual disabilities. Increasing the font size would increase the publication to at least two A3 folded sheets, which is typical of publications which are accessible to people with visual disabilities. There is a larger percentage price rise involved in this alteration of approximately 62 per cent (from £326.87 to £533.56 = £206.69) which will total approximately £2500 per year. However, this cost should be compared with the alternative approach advocated by some organizations, which involves the production of large-print run-offs, which take time and effort to produce and do not communicate the 'design' nature of the business. The stories would have to be placed on disk in order, the photograph captions extracted and photocopied and the headlines added to the text. A person would have to be detailed to collect and respond to requests for the format and produce the requested copies. It is suggested that this would involve a larger ongoing expense than £2500 per year, and would provide a 'back-door' type of access for people with visual disabilities. Cost implications are approximately £2500 per year.

Braille

Newsletters tend to be generated from text documents, from which they can easily be saved to disk in ASCII text format. When a newsletter is produced a disk with the labelled files on it should be placed in the library. When requests for Brailled versions are received they can then be printed on demand. (**Note:** there should be a Braille catalogue listing all the publications available.) Cost implications are a minimal cost of £26 per 1000 sheets of Braille paper.

Tape

Newsletters can be recorded onto tape at the time of production. The cost for the master tape will be approximately £30. (**Note:** there should be a tape catalogue listing all the publications available.) Based on the likely production of twelve annual reports per year the cost will be approximately £360.

Annual reports

Annual reports are produced in a print run of approximately 10 000 and are widely circulated. The documents tend to be approximately 120 pages long.

Large print

Were this format merely translated into large print it would significantly increase the document to approximately twice the size. However, existing formats make great use of white space and a layout which employs wide margins. Through careful layout and editing of report lengths it is predicted that there need be only approximately a 30 per cent increase in the size of reports and consequently a corresponding 30 per cent increase in the cost of production. Cost implications are approximately 30 per cent increase in current production.

Braille

The text contents of an annual report normally originate in text format on the computer, and should be saved to disk in ASCII text format, ready for use in the Brailler. Accounting information should be laid out according to instructions in the Brailling software – spreadsheets can be produced in Braille. One hundred and fifteen pages would produce approximately a 370-page Braille document. Cost implications are the cost of Braille sheets (£26/1000).

Tape

A master tape should be produced from the finished annual report as soon as it is available. As a rough estimate one page of A4 takes 3 minutes to read, which gives a studio time of 6 hours and therefore a four-tape set. Cost implications are approximately £500 for the master set.

Multimedia compact disc

More and more annual reports are being produced in a multimedia format on compact disc. A key advantage of this format is the many ways that the same information and data can be displayed and relayed to the reader. The use of screen readers and the need to search and scan information should be taken into account when deciding on the capabilities of the format. Briefing documents for the designers should include people with visual disabilities as a target audience.

Books

Many organizations now produce publications in 'book' format. These formats present the largest difficulty for those planning to make their information accessible to disabled people, due to the commercial pressures of publishing.

Large print

The implications of producing a book in large print are such that the publisher may consider that it is not economical to publish the book because of the production costs. There are several options available to be considered:

1 Produce the complete book in large print, increasing the size of the book by approximately 65 per cent from the standard 10/11 point type.
2 Produce elements of the book in large print – e.g. the foreword, contents, index, glossary, address lists, etc. – with the body text increased to 12 point and headings at 14 point or larger. Associated with the book would be a larger-print manuscript which is ordered separately (at no charge).
3 Print the book as normal. Associated with the book would be a larger-print manuscript which is ordered separately (at no charge).

It is felt that the best compromise is to produce elements of the book in a larger print. These facilitate use and navigation of the book, allowing people with a visual disability to find more easily the section that they want. They can then use magnification systems to interpret the print, if they are unable to do so.

The increase in print size to 12 point has been shown to be acceptable to publishers and the introduction of large-print indexes and tables will only increase the numbers of pages by a few, so the cost increase will not be great.

Back catalogue

The back catalogue of items contained in a library can be made accessible to disabled people by use of the scanner and for browsing by use of a CCTV reading system. CCTVs come in many shapes and sizes, in either colour or black and white. While the colour CCTVs are not much more expensive than the black and white versions, they have fewer features – such as single-line viewing and screen clarity. The black and white systems are more versatile for everyday reading, and functions such as the single-line reading (using a masking system) make them easier to use by people with a visual disability. The 'Vantage' CCD black and white system offers many advanced features in this area and is obtainable from Sensory Visionaid. The 'Vantage' CCD 14-inch black and white system costs £2000, plus training and installation.

Conclusion

The proposals in this section have shown some of the ways in which printed information can be made available to people with visual disabilities. Access to print ranges from the way that designers are briefed to the facilities that are contained within the library for staff and public.

This chapter has been researched by consulting specialist organizations, and other libraries that have successfully implemented systems of this nature. It is important to take the steps mentioned as a starting point for research. Different people prefer different products and features and prices change rapidly. It is recommended that the specialist organizations are contacted for an up-to-date view of what is on the market.

Recommended reading

1 McLean, Ruari (1980), *The Thames and Hudson Manual of Typography*, Thames and Hudson, London.

7 Communication equipment

Communication issues primarily affect users who have a hearing disability but also include the location and height of telephones. In a large space such as a meeting room or theatre there are basically two choices for electronic communication with people with hearing disabilities – either induction loops or infra-red transmission systems. There is also the use of sign-language interpreters and of hearing-aware staff. (**Note**: The correct symbol should be used to indicate the induction loop, infra-red or hearing-aware symbols (see Figure 7.1).)

Hearing-aware schemes

Hearing aware means that the staff behind the box office counter have been on a course to understand the issues related to people with hearing difficulties. They will know not to shout – which makes things worse as the hearing becomes less clear with volume. They will understand the value of using simple gestures and clear lip movements. It is unlikely that the staff will have any understanding of sign language.

Figure 7.1

Symbols indicating the types of assistance for users with hearing difficulties

Induction loop

Hearing aware

Infra-red system

Sign language

Sign language is the use of the hands to communicate. It is more than this simple interpretation as sign language has a grammatical structure that is different from that of English. British Sign Language (BSL) uses both hands (unlike the American Sign Language) for most gestures and has a condensed grammatical structure and different word order from spoken English. In Sign Supported English (SSE) the signing follows the grammar and word order of the simultaneously spoken English.

While sign language is complicated and rich – requiring up to five years to learn – basic sign language can be learned at evening classes at adult education institutes, and is well worth the effort. A ten-week course will equip you with the capability to ask a deaf sign language user basic questions and understand requests.

Electronic systems

It is worth immediately clarifying the two systems for the transmission of sound to people with hearing disabilities. These are discussed in more detail later in this chapter. Both systems take sound inputs and communicate them to people with hearing equipment. Their basic layout is summarized in Figure 7.2.

Inductive devices make use of the facility in most hearing aids to take input from an induction coil in the hearing device which picks up radio waves instead of sound, which is detected by the microphones. Sound is taken from a microphone, passed through an amplifier into a radio loop aerial – the induction loop. The sound picked up from the microphone is converted into radio signals that are detected by the receiver. Most hearing aids have the capability of switching to a 'T' position, which switches off the microphone and switches on the loop input. Loops to interact with this receiver are found in telephone handsets, box office counters, in meeting rooms and theatres and in the headsets of devices which are designed for use by people with hearing aids. If the user who is hard of hearing does not have a hearing aid or has an aid without the 'T' switch, then they will not be able to make use of induction loop installations.

Infra-red devices use the same technology as found in a television remote control. The microphone passes the sound into an amplifier and a

Figure 7.2
Basic layout for amplification, loop and infra-red systems

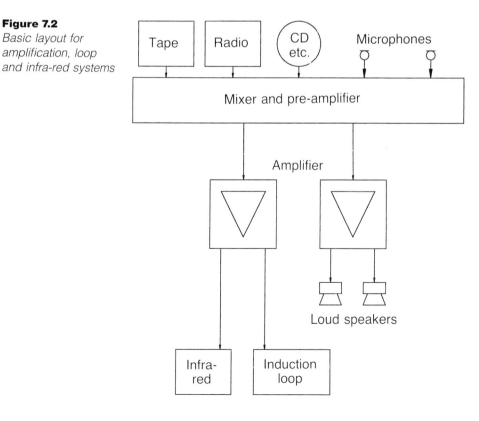

coding device that converts the sound signals into bursts of infra-red light that are emitted by the transmitter. The light, in the infra-red wavelength, is not visible to the naked eye (although, strangely, it appears as a white light if viewed through a camcorder). This light shines around the space where it is picked up by specialized infra-red receivers which decode the signal and convert it into sound. This system requires the user to wear a specialist headset to receive the signal. There are also headsets that can receive the infra-red signal and convert this into a radio signal that can be used by people with hearing aid loop settings so that someone with a hearing aid can make use of the infra-red system.

The reason for either of these systems instead of purely using amplification on a hearing aid is to relay the sound directly to the user. If a microphone on the user is amplified to the extent that it will pick up the performance on stage, then all the sound around the user will also be amplified – coughs, opening of crisp packets and any other noise will be amplified and mask out the stage sound. The microphone placed on the stage will pick up the sound and transmit it direct to the user without picking up the audience noise. Obviously, positioning of the microphone is therefore extremely important.

Telephones

Public telephones should be clearly signposted to indicate accessibility as per signage specification, and located with the telephone, operating parts (including coin slot and display) no higher than 1200 mm AFFL where the approach is from the front, and 1400 mm AFFL where it is possible to approach from the side. The telephone should incorporate an inductive coupler in the handset, e.g. British Telecom 'Payphone' 190MP, 200 Mk II, 500, 600 and Phonecard, and Mercury handset M204. Most public telephones can be fitted with inductive coils on the handset, either at the time of ordering or retrospectively. The cord from the telephone to the handset should be no less than 750 mm long, and dialling should be by means of large pushbutton controls.

Public telephones should be provided with unobstructed access to within 300 mm in front of the telephone with such access at least 800 mm wide. Where acoustic hoods are used they should be contained within an area where they would not constitute a hazard to people with visual disabilities and should be a contrasting colour to the background. A small shelf should be provided beside the telephone for change, etc.

A folding seat (e.g. Hewi 33.4020 or Neaco DF 5805) should be provided beside the telephone for people who may need to sit while making their call. Permanent seats should not be used as they will obstruct access for wheelchair users.

Office/internal telephones

Telephones should incorporate an inductive coupler in the handset, e.g. British Telecom 'Vanguard', 'Tribune' with the 'Tribune E1' having an amplified handset, lamp signalling and inductive coupler; and Mercury M204. The cord from the telephone to the handset should be no less than 750 mm long, and dialling should be by means of large pushbutton controls. (In certain instances, it may be necessary to provide a telephone with an amplified handset or an amplified voice output, e.g. for people who are hard of hearing, speak quietly or work in a noisy environment.)

Deaf people require additional equipment to signal visually the presence of an incoming call. There are strobe lights and systems that can dim the lights in a room when there is an incoming call. These are specialist systems and British Telecom should be contacted directly.

Minicom

A Minicom, also referred to as a text phone or TDD, is a piece of equipment used by deaf people to communicate over the telephone. The Minicom unit allows two-way textual information transfer across a telephone line. These units should be located within the main switchboard/reception, with further units located throughout departments. In use a Minicom user will dial into another Minicom. Once connected, both users can type messages on their keyboards and see the message typed by the other on a small liquid crystal screen on the unit. This either scrolls into memory or can be printed for a permanent record. The Minicom Textphone 7 also has the capability of acting as answer-phone for Minicom messages, which means that text messages can be left and retrieved. This version is strongly recommended for this feature and costs approximately £290. The availability of Minicom (from Teletec

International or Sound Advantage PLC) should be clearly indicated on all literature.

Where an organization has capacity on its telephone lines then this should be dedicated to the Minicom and training in the use of the Minicom given. Where the organization is small, or all the lines are taken, then the Minicom can share a line using a device called a 'Micro network manager' from Sound Advantage PLC. This device will take input from a normal telephone point and detect the type of call – Minicom, voice, fax and modem – and automatically route the call to the appropriate device. At approximately £120 the Micro network manager costs the same as installing a new line, but saves the running costs of the extra line, and therefore pays for itself within approximately one year.

Induction loops

As outlined above, the induction loop consists of three components – the loop, the amplifier and the microphone. (See Figure 7.3 for a basic room layout.) These are available as permanent installations or as portable devices that can be used for temporary spaces, or where a single user makes use of a large number of meeting rooms. It is preferable for a permanent installation to be made, or at least for the loop aerial to be permanently installed so that only the amplifier and microphone are carried around.

A single turn of loop is required for a room and the loop can be installed at a low level around the skirting board, behind the skirting or under the floor. Less optimum performance is provided by an installation at high picture level as the field strength is not so close to the user. It is recommended that a specialist installer/supplier is asked for advice on the strength of the amplifier required to achieve reliable and satisfactory results.

In a large stage area several microphones should be used, focused towards the area of action. On conference tables there are specialist microphones which are optimized to pick up voices around the table.

Advice and equipment can be obtained from Sound Advantage PLC, who are the commercial arm of the RNIB, though advice and better value for money can be obtained from Connevans Ltd who also offer a wider range of equipment.

Counter communication

An area often overlooked for induction loops is provision at box offices or booking counters. It is often also assumed that the user of the loop will be a member of the public, though he or she may well be a member of staff. Care should therefore be taken in the location of the microphone or use of a loop that can have two microphones, such as the ILD20 from Connevans or the Across the Counter Communication Aid from Connevans.

Infra-red systems

The most popular infra-red system is manufactured by Sennheiser but distributed in the UK by several companies such as Infratech. The system has a microphone input, amplifier, sender and receiving headsets. The headset has an adjustable volume control and rechargeable battery. The advantage of an infra-red system is that it can be supplied with several channels. Different information – such as translation and audio description – can be transmitted down the different channels and selected by users on their headsets. Newer headsets have also been produced which will interface with users of hearing aids that use the 'T' setting, thus providing a solution for all the users.

The main advantage of the infra-red system is that it is usable by people who do not have hearing aids. It is well known that older people tolerate a high degree of hearing loss before considering any type of hearing aid. The newer within-the-ear aids do not have the facility for the 'T' setting but are popular for their low profile. The infra-red headsets thus allow this group to experience clearer hearing in places such as theatres, where they might otherwise hear little. In the experience of the Royal National Theatre the headsets that they have are most in demand during matinée performances where the older people form a higher percentage of users, and they are heavily used by people who are not 'deaf'.

As the proportion of the population in the older age ranges is increasing, the provision of facilities such as infra-red headsets may offer the theatre a commercial advantage.

In general, it is probably best for a small operation to install an induction loop, which can be obtained for approximately £800. The installation of an infra-red system is considerably more

Figure 7.3

Basic layout for an induction loop in a small room

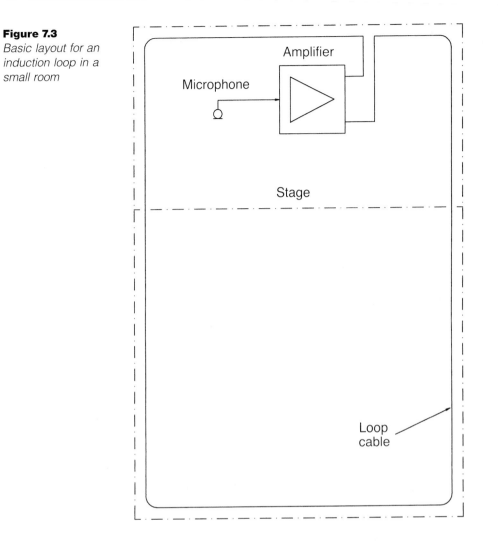

expensive and will involve the management and distribution of the headsets, recharging of batteries and maintenance of the headsets. Each headset costs approximately £90 and the theatre should aim to have at least 5 per cent of audience capacity supplied with headsets.

8 External areas, parking and paths

The external areas of the built environment cover a wide range of topics which deserve more detailed treatment than they will be given here. However, this does not indicate their lack of importance – the route that a disabled person takes in getting to a building is extremely important – but these areas are dealt with well in the documents recommended at the end of the chapter, and do not form a great part of the author's experience.

The treatment of the site of a building and the relative locations of the entrances, service entrances and points of arrival contribute to the ease of use of the building by disabled people. Examples of good practice in the shaping of a complicated external environment can be found in the Docklands Development at Canary Wharf, where textured and coloured pavements and well-landscaped entrances and exits have considered pedestrians as well as car drivers.

Figure 8.1
Reserved symbol

Figure 8.2
Good sign prominently showing a reserved bay

Accessible car parking

Accessible parking bays should be clearly signposted, located as close as possible to accessible entrances and, if possible, under cover. Parking bays need to be wide enough to allow wheelchair transfer to and from the car. The parking bays should be designated for use by disabled people and clearly signed at the entrance to a car park. The International Access Symbol of a wheelchair user should be yellow or white on tarmac and at least 1400 mm high. (See Figures 8.1 and 8.2.)

Signs indicating that the space is reserved should be located on a wall or post next to the accessible parking bay and should utilize white, 50 mm high, upper- and lower-case lettering on a blue background and the International Access Symbols which should be at least 200 mm high, white on a blue background. Wording on the sign should indicate that the space is reserved for the use of disabled drivers. The signs should not be obscured by a vehicle parked in the space and should be located with the top of the sign beginning at 1600 mm AFFL.

Directional signs leading to accessible parking bays should display the International Access Symbol and utilize at least 75 mm high, upper- and lower-case lettering:

Bays and transfer zones should be clearly marked in yellow so that the bays are easily identifiable from standard bays. Each bay should display the International Access Symbol on both the road surface and on a signpost or wall. The sign should also state that regular checks will be made to see that only disabled people use these parking spaces (Hounslow Planning Department, August 1989).

The recommended allocation of spaces in the Hounslow Department, in employment-generating developments not normally visited by the public, are as follows:

Up to 25 parking spaces: one wider space
Up to 50 parking spaces: two wider spaces

Up to 75 parking spaces: three wider spaces
Up to 100 parking spaces: four wider spaces
Thereafter one per 100 or part thereof.

The recommended allocation of spaces in the Hounslow Document in shops and buildings to which the public has access is as follows:

Up to 25 parking spaces: one wider space
Up to 50 parking spaces: three wider spaces
Up to 100 parking spaces: five wider spaces
Thereafter three per 100 or part thereof.

Bank of parking bays

The *minimum* dimensions of a standard parking bay are 2400 mm wide × 4800 mm deep. Parking bays for wheelchair users should be at least 3600 mm wide. Parking bays for ambulant disabled users should be at least 3000 mm wide. (See Figure 8.3 for the recommended layout of parking bays.)

Accessible parking spaces should have a 1200 mm wide transfer zone marked at the rear of the

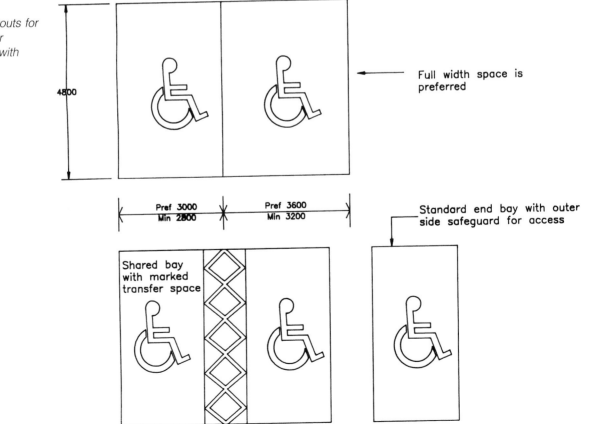

Figure 8.3
Alternative layouts for accessible car parking bays with dimensions

4800

Full width space is preferred

Pref 3000
Min 2500

Pref 3600
Min 3200

Standard end bay with outer side safeguard for access

Shared bay with marked transfer space

space. Accessible parking bays may be grouped in pairs of standard-sized bays with a shared 1200 mm wide transfer between them. Transfer zones should have yellow cross-hatch road markings.

Kerbside parking

In-line parking bays should allow access to the rear of the vehicle where wheelchairs are often stored, and be at least 6600 mm long × 2400 mm (3300 mm preferred) wide. Where a disabled person can transfer directly onto the pavement, a 2400 mm wide bay is sufficient. However, a 3300 mm wide bay should be provided wherever possible as a disabled driver or passenger may be forced to disembark on the roadside of the vehicle.

Pathways

The ideal pathway is well illuminated, even, firm and well drained, presenting a non-slip surface in both wet and dry conditions. Sudden or irregular changes in gradient and gaps more than 10 mm wide in the surface of the path should be avoided.

Corners and edges

Angles at intersections of paths should be splayed or rounded to make turning the corner easier for wheelchair users. Paths should be clearly marked using a contrast between surface colour, brightness and texture, with path edges defined with a kerb or tapping rail (no higher than 300 mm above the ground). Examples of a less subtle use of marking of a pathway can be found on the pavement leading to Morley Eye Hospital at Old Street Roundabout, London. A green stripe leads from the Underground station at Old Street and follows the path to the eye hospital. All the obstacles that used to be a hazard on this path – used by many thousands of people visiting the eye hospital – have been relocated so that there is a clear path to the hospital. This was the result of a study carried out in 1989 on behalf of the Islington Safer Cities Campaign where the author performed a survey of the area on behalf of CILT (The Centre for Inner London Transport Research). During the survey it was noted that there was an abundance of street furniture, which was grey or black, against a grey or

black background, presenting a low target value to people with a visual disability.

Less subtle use of tactile paving has been used, for instance, at the Town Hall in Hammersmith, where a tactile strip leads from the pavement to the front door of the Town Hall, which is located some distance from the pavement and benefits from the clearly marked path. In fact, anecdotal reports have indicated that people without visual disabilities tend to follow the lines and routes indicated by this paving.

A word of caution is required when installing paving, as there are incorrect uses of the red and yellow blister paving appearing in the environment. The type of paving used is designed to have a very specific meaning to people with visual disabilities who rely on the information that they impart. The wrong use of a paving type will reduce their usefulness considerably and the ability for disabled people tc use them.

The Guidelines from the Department of Transport should be followed strictly and people with a visual disability should be asked to comment on the proposals before they are implemented.

Signage

As well as using indicators in the pavement to facilitate movement through the built environment, signs have as significant a role to play outside a building as they do inside one. Viewing distances have increased and lettering heights will have to be increased accordingly, with a 25 mm letter height translating into a viewing distance of 15 metres for people with perfect vision and 25 mm letter height into 7.5 metres for people with a visual disability. It is also important that external signage be well illuminated to approximately 50 lux above the background illumination level.

In an external area there are less likely to be people who know the layout of the space or are available to be asked. Signs can therefore play a role in a 'question-and-answer' format. A central signboard is used to display the most commonly asked questions and provide the answers. Questions such as 'Which way is the main entrance?' can be answered by a sign giving the directions to that entrance.

In conjunction with the question-and-answer signs clear and regular use of maps and colours can considerably improve the ability of people to navigate through a building. Tactile maps and tactile signage can be used to good effect, but it should be remembered that this type of sign should be located in 'obvious' locations. There is a rumour that a Braille and tactile signage system has been installed in a European city under a handrail system that is located in the central square. The difficulty is that people who read Braille do not know that it is there and no dog has yet been trained to find the system! (Refer to the signage section for more detail on signage.)

Width, gradient and crossfall

The width required for two wheelchair users to pass on a path is approximately 1800 mm. Where there are unavoidable obstacles on the path the *minimum* width of clear path should be no less than 900 mm (1350 mm preferred).

The longitudinal gradient of any newly constructed path should be limited to no more than 1:20 (or 5 per cent). However, where this cannot be achieved because of site limitations, the longitudinal gradient of a path should not exceed 1:15 (or 7 per cent maximum). Where the gradient of a path is greater than 1:15 (or 7 per cent), there should be an alternative route via a ramp complying with the ramp specification. The crossfall (i.e. the gradient across a path) can make steering extremely difficult and should not exceed 1:40 (or 2.5 per cent).

Channel gratings and manhole covers

Channel gratings and manhole covers should have a non-slip surface, flush with the pavement. Openings in gratings should be no larger than 13 mm in one direction. Gratings with elongated openings should be positioned so that the long dimension is perpendicular to the predominant direction of traffic.

Pedestrian crossings

Pedestrian crossings should be well-illuminated with well-defined and maintained road markings.

Tactile surfaces

To assist visually disabled people to find pedestrian crossings, tactile surfaces (with flat-topped domes) should be used on all crossings, and should be detectable underfoot, even to people wearing thick-soled shoes. Refer to the Department of Transport Disability Unit Circular 1/91 for full details on the types and layout of tactile surfaces at pedestrian crossings.

Dropped kerbs

Dropped kerbs should be provided wherever possible at all pedestrian crossing points and where level access is required between the pavement and carriageway (e.g. in a car park). There should be double yellow line road markings across dropped kerbs to prevent parked cars becoming an obstruction. (See Figure 8.4 for details on kerb layouts.)

Where they are provided, dropped kerbs should: finish completely flush with the carriageway as a lip can cause difficulties for wheelchair users; be complemented by a dropped kerb on the other side of the road; and provide indication of its presence to partially sighted people.

Dropped kerbs may be indicated to visually disabled people by a contrast in colour to the adjacent ground surfaces, and a tactile warning texture on the dropped kerb surface (see below). Red, textured dropped kerbs should be used at controlled crossings (e.g. pelican, zebra, traffic lights) and buff-coloured, textured dropped kerbs at uncontrolled crossings (i.e. side streets).

The least possible gradient should be used for any dropped kerb, and the maximum gradient of ramps and flares should be no more than 1:15 (or 6 per cent). Dropped kerb ramps should be at least 1200 mm wide (2000 mm preferred).

Traffic islands or median strips should have textured dropped kerbs on both sides, or be cut through level with the carriageway and have textured paving.

In use, a dropped kerb can present a significant hazard to a wheelchair user. The waiting user is anxious to cross the road as soon as it is safe to do so, which necessitates being as close to the edge of the pavement as possible. However, this section of the kerb has the maximum gradient of the dropped kerb and requires the wheelchair user to 'hold' on this gradient while waiting for

Figure 8.4
Dropped kerb types. The upper one is more difficult for wheelchair users than the lower one

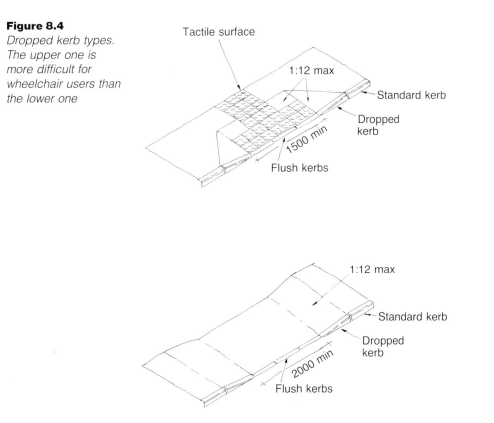

Tactile surface

1:12 max

Standard kerb

Dropped kerb

1500 min

Flush kerbs

1:12 max

Standard kerb

Dropped kerb

2000 min

Flush kerbs

the traffic to clear. For this reason the type of dropped kerb which uses a fall on either side of the crossing, with a platform spanning the full width of the crossing, is preferred. The user can wait on a level platform without any danger or need for difficult manoeuvres.

Street furniture

Street furniture should be located so that wheelchair users do not find difficulty in manoeuvring around obstructions, and blind or partially sighted people can walk in safety without colliding with unexpected obstacles. Care should especially be taken in avoiding the location of items such as bollards in the centre of dropped kerbs. This is more common than would be expected, as illustrated in Figure 8.5.

There should be a *minimum* distance between obstacles of 900 mm and a vertical clearance of 2500 mm between the ground and overhead obstacles (e.g. signs and canopies). A contrasting colour and texture immediately around obstacles on the ground can assist visually disabled people to locate obstacles in their path.

Bollards

Bollards are used to protect pedestrians from vehicular traffic and to prevent vehicles parking on the pavement. However, they present a tripping hazard to people with a visual disability. To reduce this hazard, bollards should be no less than 1000 mm high (putting the obstruction at waist rather than knee level), and be of a contrast-

Figure 8.5
Bollard in the centre of a dropped kerb preventing use of the kerb

ing colour to the surrounding area. There should be no horizontal projections on the bollards. Bollards should be located at regular intervals with no less than 900 mm between them.

Tapering obstructions

Tapering obstructions include spaces below ramps and staircases and stabilizing wires on telegraph poles – these can present considerable hazards to blind and partially sighted people. Such obstructions are difficult to detect with a cane and are not always avoided by guide dogs.

To reduce this hazard, the spaces below ramps and staircases should be either totally enclosed and handrails, tapping rails or a kerb installed around the obstruction. The obstruction may also be indicated by a change in ground surface around or below the obstruction.

Dispensers

Coin slots, card slots, cash dispensers and displays of stamp machines, cash points, etc. should all be located within reach of wheelchair users (i.e. displays no higher than 900 mm above the ground, and card/coin slots no higher than 1200 mm above the ground) and not recessed too far within the wall. The display should incorporate clearly defined and well-spaced buttons with raised numerals to assist partially sighted people.

Recent research by the Centre on Accessible Environments found that the majority of cash dispensers had not been installed with wheelchair users in mind. They have produced information and guidelines, which are available directly from the Centre.

Lighting

Lighting should comply with the standards set in the British Standard 5489. *Minimum* light level required for partially sighted people in external areas, especially staircases and ramps, is 50–75 lux. However, higher light levels are desirable, especially where there are obstacles such as steps to negotiate.

In areas where continuous lighting would be obtrusive, it is useful to install automatic PIR (photo infra-red) detecting light units. These should be installed at a high level to avoid vandalism.

Low-pressure sodium light sources are an economic light source, but the light produced has a restricted spectrum that tends to reduce the colour definition which assists partially sighted people. Thus, 'whiter' light sources (e.g. high-pressure sodium, low-consumption fluorescent and, for occasional use, halogen) are preferable.

The route from the building to car parks and transport routes for disabled people should be clearly lit to improve the ability to navigate and the safety of users of the area.

Recommended reading

1 Department of Transport Disability Unit Circular 1/91.
2 *Reducing Mobility Handicaps Towards a Barrier-Free Environment* (1991), The Institution of Highways and Transportation.
3 Stephen Thorpe, *External Surfaces: Access Design Sheet: 3, Design for Special Needs*, Centre on Accessible Environments.
4 *Think Access* (1989), Hounslow Planning Guide, London Borough of Hounslow Planning Department.

9 Stairs

Stairs represent one of the primary methods that we use for vertical circulation in a building, and are the heaviest used as means of escape. As stated earlier, the majority of disabled people will also be users of stairs, as they do not have a major mobility difficulty. In some buildings there is no alternative but to use stairs, as they are the only method for changing level. Because there will be a high percentage of disabled people using this medium, it is important to examine some of the features discussed below.

Treads

The detailed design of stairs is covered in Part M of the Building Regulations. The designs are aimed at providing a large enough going for safe footing and a riser that is not too high for people with mobility difficulties as well as children (see Figure 9.1).

For external steps, on the approach to a building, tread/going should be uniform and at least 280 mm, which for tapered treads should be measured at a point 270 mm from the inside of the stair. For internal steps, within a building, tread/going should be uniform and at least 250 mm, which for tapered treads should be measured at a point 270 mm from the inside of the stair.

Tread nosings

Ideally, stair nosings should be splayed or rounded to at least a 6 mm radius, and there should be no overhang on the nosing to avoid tripping.

Nosing strips

To people with a visual disability a set of stairs with a uniform carpet or colouring provides a disorientating experience (see Figure 9.2). Nosing

Figure 9.2
Lack of nosings on the stairs is dangerous

Figure 9.1
Section through a stair showing dimensional requirements

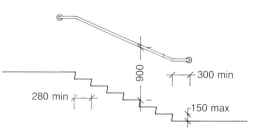

280 min   900   300 min   150 max

Figure 9.3
High-contrast nosings give a good visual indication

strips are used to highlight the edges of individual treads, which makes them easier to detect by people with a visual disability (as seen in Figure 9.3). The nosing strips do not have to be made from plain stripes – an example of a more adventurous use of stair decoration is shown in Figure 9.4, which is located in the Institute of Contemporary Arts, London. The nosing colour/hue should be chosen to provide a contrast with the floor surface (i.e. carpet or linoleum). The nosing strip also has the purpose of preventing carpet from slipping and from suffering excessive wear. (White strips often provide a good contrast with a darker background, but colour combinations may be used, as long as there is an acceptable level of contrast between the hue of the two materials – so the same colour can be used as long as one is light and one is dark.)

There are several ways of marking tread nosings. Metal stair nosings which can carry a solid PVC strip, such as those manufactured by Gradus and Altro housed in an aluminium, brass or plastic extrusion which is screwed to the stair nosing are primarily used on carpeted stairs and steps in level. The PVC strips come in a wide range of colours allowing the best colour contrast to be chosen; e.g. white, yellow or light grey against a dark carpet, black, blue or dark green against a light carpet.

Single-piece plastic stair nosing, again from Gradus, can either be solid PVC or contain a solid PVC strip and is used either where there is no stair finish or where there is one such as linoleum. The colour of the nosing should be chosen to provide the greatest contrast with the stair finish; e.g. white, yellow or light grey against a dark carpet, black or dark green against a light carpet.

With light stair nosings it is essential to regularly maintain the stair nosing using a non-abrasive cleaner. If an abrasive cleaner is used there is a danger of creating a surface which will attract dirt and therefore become ineffective as a warning.

In buildings where existing treads are not of a high enough contrast, it is sufficient, as a short-term plan until sufficient funding is found, to alter the treads that would clearly indicate the landings and change in level, i.e. initially changing only the treads that are first and last on the landing.

Non-slip nosings

The majority of stairs in public buildings appear to be cast concrete and have low-frequency use. These tend to be too expensive for the contrasting nosings as above. A lower-cost but equally effective treatment is to paint a contrasting nosing onto the stair tread. The painted strip should be at least 40 mm wide, and be no more than 10 mm from the front edge of the tread.

Figure 9.4
Good nosings can be used to decorative effect

Better than just the white paint are self-adhesive non-slip nosing strips which provide a low-cost temporary alternative to the permanent nosings above or can be used on stairs with low traffic. This type of nosing is available in a variety of forms, shapes and colours from safety catalogues in strips, such as Signs and Labels and Stocksigns.

Signs and Labels also produce a product which is better still, in that it is hard-wearing and provides superior non-slip qualities. This comes in the form of a kit where a resin is painted onto the stair nosing, using masking tape as a mask, and a non-slip aggregate is sprinkled onto the wet resin. Once the resin has cured and the tape been removed an extremely durable non-slip strip is left.

Risers

Open risers present a tripping hazard to people climbing stairs, especially those wearing callipers or who have stiffness in hip or knee joints. To minimize the risk of people catching their feet beneath the nosings or treads when climbing stairs, risers should not be open and nosings should be detailed as above.

Riser heights

For external steps, on the approach to a building, risers should be uniform and no more than 150 mm. For internal steps, within a building, risers should be uniform and no more than 170 mm.

Riser markings

The top and bottom riser in a flight of steps should be marked in a colour contrasting with the stair finish (conventionally white). This indicates the location of the top and bottom of a flight of stairs and the position of intermediate landings. This can be effected using paint or a high-visibility riser material.

Handrails

Handrails are essential for people with mobility difficulty or who are unsteady on their feet. Also, people with visual disabilities often rely heavily on handrails to orient themselves on staircases, that

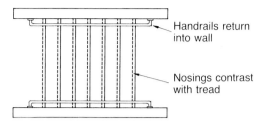

Figure 9.5
Plan of a stair showing handrail and tread layout

is, when they reach the top, bottom or a landing, or where there is a change in direction (see Figure 9.5). Flights should have handrails on both sides if they are more than 1.0 m wide, and at least one handrail if they are less than 1.0 m wide.

Height

The handrail should be located at 900 mm above tread level (the line traced by joining all the fronts of the tread together) and at 1000 mm above the landings. On balustrades, the bottom rails should prevent a 100 mm spherical object from passing between the treads and the guarding.

Detailing

Handrails should be easily gripped, well supported and not rotate within their fittings. People with limited manual dexterity or arthritic hands encounter difficulty in gripping. Circular section handrails (e.g. solid timber, nylon or powder-coated steel tube), 40–50 mm outer diameter, have been found to be most comfortable to grip. Handrails should be in a contrasting colour or hue to their immediate surroundings. The nylon and timber handrails are best for people who might be affected by the temperature of a handrail as these are pleasant to the touch, whereas the mild steel handrails will tend to be cold to the touch.

There should be a minimum clearance of 45 mm between the wall and the handrail, and 50 mm vertical distance between the bottom of the handrail and the handrail support (see Figure 9.5). This is to allow the hand to grip the handrail firmly for support.

As handrails are used extensively for following, they should continue around corners, across landings and extend horizontally at least 300 mm beyond the last treads of the stairs. This will allow some steadying action at the base and beginning of the stair, and sufficient warning that the stair is about to begin or end. Handrails should finish with a positive stop at each end without encroaching upon the unobstructed width of the stair (i.e. either rounded or returned smoothly into the wall, floor or post). This informs visually disabled people of changes in direction or that the stair has ended.

Light level

The majority of stairs are extremely poorly lit. The *minimum* light levels on stair treads should be in the order of 75–100 lux, rising to 200 lux for people with visual disabilities.

Emergency lighting

> All parts of the premises to which the public have access and all external exit ways should be provided with emergency lighting capable of providing sufficient illumination for the public to leave the premises safely . . . any corridor, not included in parts of the premises . . . which may be used by staff . . . in the case of an emergency, should be provided with normal lighting and an escape lighting system (*Guide to Fire Precautions in Existing Places of Entertainment and Like Premises*, HMSO, 1990).

While BS 5266 stipulates that escape routes have a *minimum* illumination of 0.2 lux, it is recommended that a *minimum* illumination of 10 lux is provided at floor level along the centre of the route.

Wall-side and open stair markings

PVC or rubber products such as those from Jaymart exist which are used to define the wall-side and the open edge of a stairway. The colour of the edging strips should be chosen to provide the greatest contrast with the wall finish. These side markings help to locate the stairs for people with a visual disability.

Tactile warning strips

Part M of the Building Regulations stipulates the use of tactile warning strips before the beginning of a flight of stairs. In practical terms, one has to be extremely careful not to design in a trip hazard, so care should be taken in the laying and placement of the paving. The first thing that someone with a visual disability will do on detecting the paving and the stair is to reach for the handrail, which is then extremely important.

Signage

Signage is often ignored in stairwells, leading to long and wasted journeys. The requirements for stairwells is the same as that in lift areas, with the need for the floor number to be clearly indicated with a 100 mm high letter on a contrasting signface, which also contrasts with the background wall colour.

The sign should be located consistently within the stairwell, and preferably be a tactile sign type, or, failing that, a vinyl or screen-printed version. In areas where there is likely to be a high degree of vandalism then a reverse-printed polycarbonate sign is preferred to vinyl or surface-printed signs. Further information on tactile signs can be found in the section on signage or obtained from All Clear Designs.

Areas of refuge

When designing staircases from scratch it is important to examine the opportunity to use the stairwell as an area of refuge to BS 5588, Part 8. Stairwells offer the perfect opportunity to create areas of refuge and thus allow people with a mobility disability safer access into the building. There is more discussion about this area of design in Chapter 13.

Recommended reading

1 *Guide to Fire Precautions in Existing Places of Entertainment and Like Premises*, HMSO, 1990.
2 Part M of the Building Regulations (1991).

10 Ramps

Introduction

Ramps are an essential method for assisting wheeled traffic to cope with changes in level that are traditionally overcome by using steps. Wheeled traffic can include wheelchairs, parents with prams, trolleys and other vehicles. Ramps are not a replacement for stairs and steps, but are needed as an additional method for dealing with a change in level.

The principal document governing the design of ramps is Part M of the Building Regulations 1991. However, it is worth noting that ramps designed to comply with building regulations and guidelines may not be independently accessible to all wheelchair users. Again, it is important to refer to the section dealing with disabled people – few wheelchair users have the strong upper body that we conventionally envisage. The majority of wheelchair users will have limited upper body mobility, and will not be able to self-propel up a gradient of 1:12, nor be able to control their rapid descent down a ramp of 1:12. However, a ramp of 1:15 or 1:20 will not present a great difficulty to these users.

Likewise, the Regulations allow for ramps of extreme length where a mechanical device would clearly allow more disabled people to access the facility. Mechanical devices are not generally preferred to ramps, as there is always the possibility of a mechanical device developing a fault. But a faultless ramp that is unusable by disabled people is not preferable to a mechanical device that will have occasional breakdowns. For more information on mechanical devices refer to Chapter 11 dealing with lifts.

Part M provides design guidelines which comply with the Building Regulations 1991. However, it should be stressed that Part M lays down a *minimum* legal obligation. This chapter presents the minimum of accepted *good practice*.

Design considerations

All entrances to a building should provide wheelchair access. Part M of the Building Regulations states (Objective 1.5) '. . . Disabled people should be able to use the principal entrance provided for visitors or customers and an entrance which is intended, exclusively, for members of staff . . .'. Thus, ramps are required to overcome changes in level not only at the 'front door' of a building but also at rear entrances.

Not all wheelchair users possess the strength and dexterity to propel themselves up steep ramps (and in this case 1:12 is considered steep), to control their speed or direction, or to stop themselves when descending ramps. Some disabled people (or their assistants) need to stop frequently along ramps, in order to rest or catch their breath. Wheelchair users require sufficient space to stop on landings, and to open and pass through doors without having to reverse into circulation routes or roll back down the ramp. There should be adequate space for people heading in opposite directions to pass each other, especially on long ramps. Some disabled people are weaker down one side of their body and require support rails on both sides of the ramp.

Wheelchair users with limited manual dexterity and control are at risk of their feet catching beneath bottom rails or in gaps in the balustrade. This risk should be minimized in the choice and design of ramp balustrades.

In wet-weather conditions, external ramps may become slippery, especially for people who are already unsteady on their feet. Moreover, in cold conditions, any moisture on the ramp surface may freeze, making the surface even more hazardous. External ramps should employ non-slip surfaces to overcome this hazard. Many people have difficulty traversing slopes, and find steps easier to use. Visually impaired people generally require higher light levels to enable them to perceive changes in their environment, such as direction, level and gradient.

The surface of the ramp and the design should ensure a non-slip surface in all weathers and avoid ponding of water, with effective drainage. The ramp structure should be stable and well secured to the surrounding structures.

Layout

There are many ways to ramp the entrance of a building. What is important at the entrance of a building is to ensure that the wheelchair user enters from the 'front'. The layouts in Figures 10.1 to 10.5 show alternative entrances to the building. Figure 10.1 shows the existing entrance to the building. Figure 10.2 illustrates a straight ramp entrance to the building that separates the entrance for wheelchair users from that of ambulant people. This design, while entering at the front of the building, is not preferred. Figure 10.3 shows an alternative entrance which brings the entrance to the ramp to the front of the building. Figure 10.4 also brings the entrance to the front, but makes worse use of the space, as it requires an extra platform and therefore more space. Figure 10.5 shows a preferred layout where the user enters from the 'front' of the building through the shortest route. It is always worth testing these alternatives for their 'architectural' as well as 'integrational' significance. Figures 10.6 and 10.7 show the entrance to a school which has efficiently used a ramp to gain entrance to both front doors, at the same time as using a stepped entrance. The stepped entrance shown in Figure 10.8 uses a corduroyed paving stone to provide tactile warning of the presence of the steps.

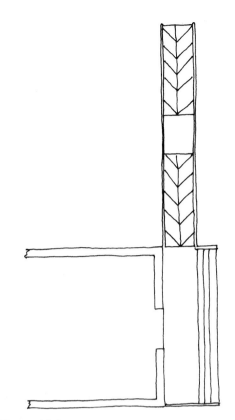

Figure 10.2
The simplest ramped approach has the user entering a long way from the building

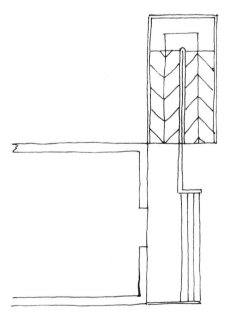

Figure 10.3
Folded ramp allowing the user to enter at the same point as ambulant users

Figure 10.1
Building requiring a ramped approach to a stepped entrance

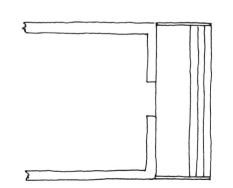

Figure 10.4
Double folded ramp allowing users to enter in the same orientation as the ambulant user

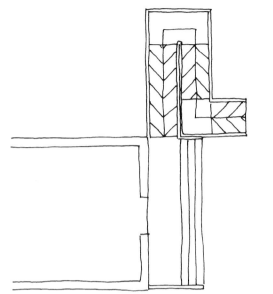

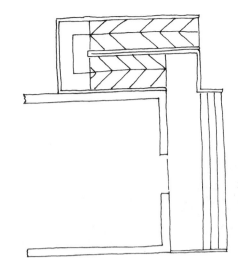

Figure 10.5
Simple folded ramp allowing users to enter in the same orientation as the ambulant user

Figure 10.6
Good entrance ramp to the school front door

Figure 10.7
*Ramp providing
stepped as well as
ramped entrance*

Figure 10.8
*Steps using corduroy
paving strips to warn
of their presence*

Design guidelines

Part M (Building Regulations 1992): Section 1: Means of Access to and into the Building – Ramped Approach: Provisions states:

A ramped approach will satisfy Requirement M2 if it:

(a) Has a surface which reduces the risk of slipping

(b) Has flights whose surface widths are at least 1.2 m and whose unobstructed widths are at least 1.0 m

(c) Is not steeper than 1 in 15, if individual flights are not longer than 10.0 m, or not steeper than 1:12, if individual flights are not longer than 5.0 m

(d) Has top and bottom landings, each of whose lengths is not less than 1.2 m and, if necessary, intermediate landings, each of whose lengths is not less than 1.5 m, in all cases clear of any door swing

(e) Has a raised kerb at least 100 mm high on any open side of a flight or a landing

(f) Has a continuous suitable handrail on each side of flights and landings, if the length of the ramp exceeds 2.0 m.

Gradient

While the Building Regulations (Part M) recommend 1:12 as a maximum gradient (for slopes less than 5.0 m long), it is worth pointing out that this gradient can be impossible or may present serious difficulties to the wheelchair user over even a short distance. A gradient of 1:12 may deny access to many wheelchair users in the upward direction, and is highly likely to make a safe descent, even in an emergency, dangerous and difficult to achieve.

It is better to aim for a gradient of 1:20, with a maximum preferred gradient of 1:15. These gradients should allow use by most disabled people who self-propel their wheelchairs.

Figure 10.9 shows the comparative gradients of ramps of 1:12, 1:15 and 1:20, but Figure 10.10 shows that the regulation to insert a platform at every 5 metres on a 1:12 ramp and every 10 metres on a 1:15 and 1:20 ramp actually increases the ramp distance needed to comply with the regulations.

Width

Building Regulations (Part M) recommend a minimum unobstructed width of 1000 mm (surface width of 1200 mm). However, this does not allow users – both wheelchair users and other users of the ramp – heading in opposite directions to pass on the ramp.

For short, infrequently used ramps (i.e. less than 5.0 m long), or where there is limited space available to install a ramp in an existing building, it is acceptable to waive the need for people to be

Figure 10.9

If simple gradients are taken into account there is a 1:1 relationship between gradient and distance

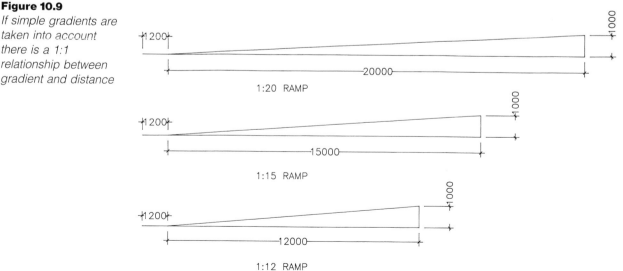

1:20 RAMP

1:15 RAMP

1:12 RAMP

Figure 10.10
If the requirement for platforms is included the difference between 1:12 and 1:15 is reduced

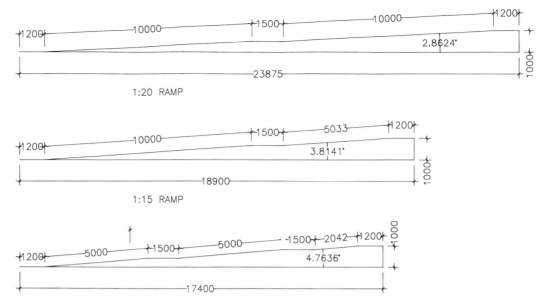

1:20 RAMP

1:15 RAMP

1:12 RAMP

able to pass on the ramp. However, for longer ramps and ramps in busy public areas there should be provision for people to pass on the ramp. An unobstructed width of 1800 mm (surface width of 2000 mm) will allow a wheelchair user to pass other users on the ramp, including other wheelchair users (see Figures 10.11 and 10.12).

Landings

Level landings are required at the bottom and top of each ramp, where there is a change in direction of the ramp, after every 10.0 m length of a 1:15 ramp (after every 5.0 m length of a 1:12 ramp) and where there are doors or gates located along the ramp. These landings are used as resting points for people using a ramp, or to rest and allow other people to pass. Landings should be at least as wide as the full width of the ramp leading to them and approximately 1200 mm long.

Top and bottom landings

Additional landing length should be provided on top or bottom landings to account for doors or gates opening onto the landings. Where a door opens out onto a landing, the total length of the landing should be the required minimum of 1500 mm plus the length of the door swing. However, if

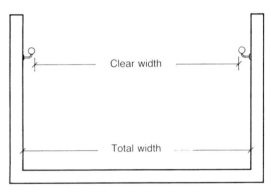

Figure 10.11
The width of a ramp is the clear, usable width between any obstructions

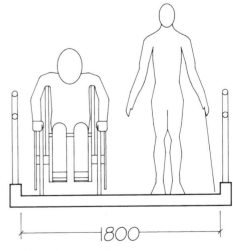

Figure 10.12
A ramp which is 1800 mm wide allows two users to pass each other on the ramp

Figure 10.13
Doors opening onto the platform need a longer platform. Ideally they should open off the platform

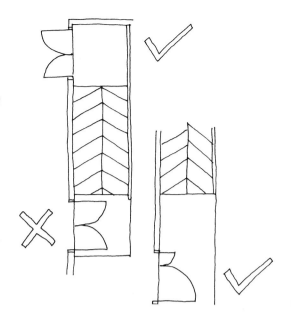

the door swings inwards, away from the landing, the length of the landing need only be the required minimum (see Figure 10.13). While the Building Regulations (Part M) recommend a minimum landing length of 1200 mm, at the top and bottom of a ramp (clear of door swing obstructions), a length of between 1500 mm and 1800 mm is preferred.

Intermediate landings

An intermediate landing is required wherever there is a change in direction of the ramp and/or every 10.0 metres of a straight run at a gradient of 1:15 (and/or every 5.0 metres of a straight run at a gradient of a 1:12 ramp). While the Building Regulations (Part M) recommend a minimum intermediate landing length of 1500 mm, a length of 1800 mm is preferred.

Flush door thresholds

To allow wheelchair access, entrance thresholds need to be flush. To provide weatherproofing to the thresholds, doors may require threshold seals to be fitted. Weatherproof, flush thresholds can be achieved on hinged doors using a variety of threshold seals, e.g. Sealmaster or Athmer and Wellington. Further details on the designs of these thresholds can be found in Chapter 14.

Handrails

Handrails serve as balustrades (Building Regulations, Part K) and to assist wheelchair users and pedestrians (Building Regulations, Part M). They are useful for people to steady themselves when they negotiate the stairs, changes in level and slope. Building Regulations (Part M) recommend that only ramps exceeding 2.0 m in length require handrails, but some people may become unsteady on any slope regardless of the length and so handrails are recommended for ramps of any length (not kerb ramps) and especially on ramps where the gradient is 1:12. Where handrails are not employed, some kind of visual warning is needed to indicate the presence of the ramp (e.g. a change in surface colour or texture, or warning strips placed where there is a change in gradient).

Part M of the Building Regulations (1991), Section 1, Handrail Provisions, states:

(a) The top of a handrail is 900 mm above the surface of a ramp
(b) The handrail extends at least 300 mm beyond the top and bottom of a ramp . . . and terminates in a closed end which does not project into a route of travel
(c) The profile of the handrail and its projection from a wall is suitable.

Handrails to assist wheelchair users and pedestrians should be located at 900 mm above the ramp surface. Handrails functioning as a balustrade should be located at approximately 1100 mm above the ramp surface (Building Regulations, Part K).

Where a balustrade is required along a ramp, i.e. if it is above a hazardous area or at a great height where there is a danger of falling off, it is recommended that handrails are located at both 1100 mm and 900 mm above the ramp surface. However, on a normal ramp the upper handrail will not be needed on the ramp.

Handrails should be easily gripped, well supported and not rotate within their fittings. People with arthritic hands or limited manual dexterity may experience difficulty in gripping handrails. Circular-section handrails (e.g. solid timber, nylon or powder-coated steel tube), 40–50 mm outer diameter (see Figure 10.14) may be easiest to grip (e.g. the Hewi balustrade system which is made from nylon). However, the majority of hand-

Figure 10.14
Handrails should be secured 900/1000 mm off the floor and use 45 mm diameter handrails

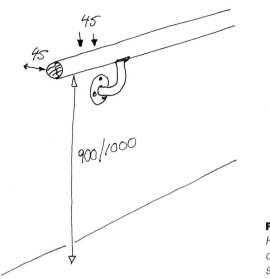

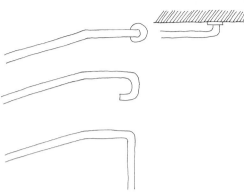

Figure 10.16
Handrails should end in a manner which communicates the end of the flight to a partially sighted user

rails are lower cost if they are fabricated from scratch from mild steel and powder coated by companies such as Sapphire. See the case study below for more details. Structurally, handrails have been found to be strongest where a lower flange is welded to the base of the rail and bolted into the ramp, rather than grouted into the ramp as a pole (see Figure 10.15). To be either a long section of unsupported handrail or a short section of single rail it is advisable to provide a 'kink' to the rail to give the rail more stability. There should be a minimum clearance of 45 mm between any wall holding the handrail and 50 mm vertical distance between the bottom of the handrail and the handrail support.

Handrails should be continuous across landings and extend horizontally at least 300 mm beyond the inclined sections of the ramp. Handrails should finish with a positive stop at each end without encroaching upon the unob-

structed width of the ramp (i.e. either rounded or returned smoothly into the wall, floor or post). (See details in Figure 10.16.)

Guardings

Guardings and balustrades should be designed to minimize the risk of wheelchair users catching their feet between balusters (e.g. solid balustrades) (see Figure 10.17). Any glazing in the guarding/balustrades should be of glass blocks, toughened glass or laminated safety glass, e.g. the Hewi balustrade system. Wired glass should not be used (Building Regulations, Part K).

Figure 10.15
Handrails should be securely fastened using sufficient bolts and a plate

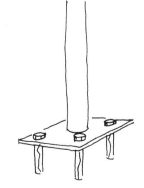

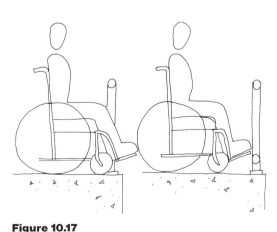

Figure 10.17
Handrails can be used to protect against rolling off the edge of a ramp with a rail at 100 mm AFFL

Figure 10.18

Upstands can be formed from concrete, brick or rails providing they are 100 mm AFFL

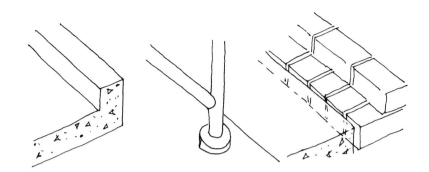

Kerbs and bottom rails

In the absence of walls along the sides of a ramp, kerbs should be provided to prevent wheelchair users from rolling off the edge, and guide people with partial vision who use canes. Kerbs should be of solid construction and at least 100 mm high. They can be constructed in the laying of a concrete ramp and should be added to the shuttering during pouring, so that the upstand is integral with the lower part of the ramp, or has reinforced rods poured into it. Alternatively, bricks to match the building or engineering bricks such as the 'Yorkshire Blue' can be used, though these are expensive. A brick placed sideways on its long side will provide an upstand of approximately 125 mm high (see Figure 10.18).

Case study: Ramp detail

Client: St Anne's Church Hall

This 27-year-old church hall had a 100 mm step at the entrance to the hall. The use of the hall was being adapted to improve access for disabled people. There was a fair amount of space in front of the hall, but there was a need to allow large traffic such as refuse lorries for the rubbish collection. The ramp was therefore taken down the side of the building with a dampproof expansion joint between the building and the ramp. (See Figure 10.19 for the building plan and ramp locations.) The design of the kink in the ramp was used to strengthen the handrail design so that it would not be destroyed by the children playing on it (see Figures 10.20 and 10.21). The balustrade was attached to the concrete ramp using welded flanges which were bolted into the concrete. The upstand was created using engineering bricks to complement the building and reduce the 'new' nature of the ramp (see Figure 10.22 of the ramp details).

Note should be taken that the handrails were broken opposite the exit doors to allow safe exit from the hall and the kitchen.

The cost of the concrete element of the ramp was approximately £1700 (excluding VAT). The balustrade was costed in two ways. The first, using the Hewi balustrade system, was costed at £3847 (excluding VAT). However, this was considered too expensive so a purpose-made mild-steel powder-coated handrail was fabricated by Sapphire for £1388 (excluding VAT) plus contractor's cost of £592 (excluding VAT).

Alternatively, in lieu of a kerb and for ease of construction, a bottom rail may be added to a guarding. To prevent the front wheels of a wheelchair rolling under the rail, centre bottom rails about 100 mm above the ramp surface.

External surfaces

While the surface should be as smooth as possible to allow ease of travel for the small wheelchair front wheels, it must be a non-slip surface in all weather conditions, especially external ramps. Non-slip surfaces include laid concrete, roughened concrete paving slabs, herringbone-pattern paving bricks, and concrete coated with a non-slip material.

For superior non-slip treatment several systems can be used: (1) grit applied to an epoxy carrier – common applications include surfacing of external ramps; (2) paint types like Carbo-Grip and Flowcoat, which are suitable for low-traffic situations where they will be renewed on a regular

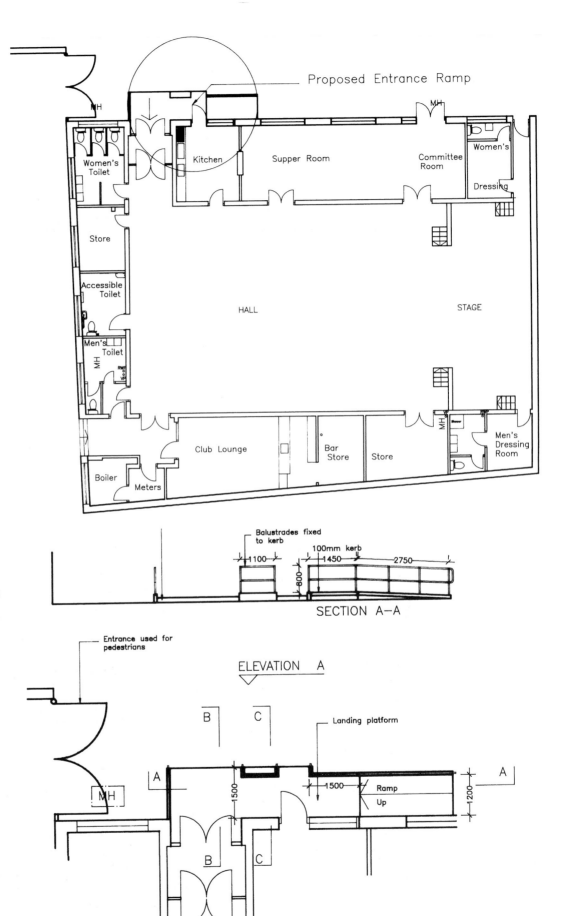

Figure 10.19

Location for a ramp on an existing 1968 building plan

Proposed Entrance Ramp

MH

Women's Toilet

Store

Accessible Toilet

Men's Toilet

MH

RWP VP

Boiler

Meters

Kitchen

Supper Room

HALL

Club Lounge

Bar Store

Store

MH

Committee Room

STAGE

Women's Dressing

Men's Dressing Room

MH

Figure 10.20

Plan and section A–A of the entrance ramp showing handrail and upstand

Balustrades fixed to kerb

100mm kerb

1100

800

1450

2750

SECTION A–A

Entrance used for pedestrians

ELEVATION   A

MH

B

C

Landing platform

A

1500

1500

Ramp

Up

A

1200

B

C

Figure 10.21
*Elevations of the
entrance ramp
showing upstand and
handrail detail*

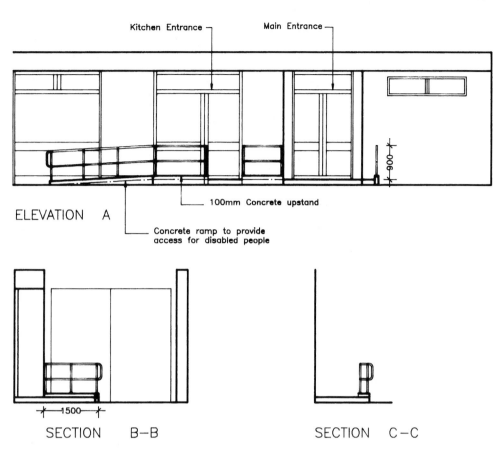

Kitchen Entrance

Main Entrance

900

ELEVATION A

100mm Concrete upstand

Concrete ramp to provide
access for disabled people

SECTION B—B

1500

SECTION C—C

Figure 10.22
*Brick upstand and
handrail on a new
ramp*

Figure 10.23
*Non-slip surfacing on
an external ramp*

basis (yearly in some cases); and (3) harder-wearing and thicker polyurethane substrate with a grit, such as Scotch-Clad, or a faster-curing Acrydur which has an acrylic base and grit. These systems offer a more durable solution which has the ability to flex slightly and therefore reduce cracking.

Where possible, some form of patterning should be used to provide a visual warning for people with visual disabilities of the existence of the ramp. Patterns such as yellow chevrons which can be painted onto the non-slip surface can be used, but care should be taken to avoid reducing the non-slip nature of the coating. (See Figure 10.23, which illustrates a non-slip coating used to create a chevron pattern as well as improving grip.)

Internal surfaces

Internal ramps can make use of the wide range of non-slip vinyl and rubber flooring systems which now offer a wide range of attractive colours. The two primary flooring systems include:

- Welded abrasive vinyl sheets, which offer a hard-wearing flooring with a range of applications (especially internal wet areas) and colourways. They conform to use requirements in areas where hygiene is necessary (e.g. kitchens) and offer the opportunity to incorporate coloured patterns into the floor surface. They are adhered to the floor surface and hot-welded to form a seamless flooring. Such types of flooring are

manufactured by companies like Altro Ltd and can use an inlaid panel 100 mm wide and contrasting with the main floor surface. Landings should also use a different colour from the ramp surface.

- Rubberized flooring, which is a slightly lower-cost floor and wall covering and offers a larger colour range than the above flooring systems (except external UV-safe versions), and a large variety in the surface textures is available. The rubber systems, such as those produced by Jaymart, can be used on areas such as stairs, in a complete tread, riser and nosing piece, which is adhered directly to the prepared floor surface.

Cross-slope

Ramps should be constructed to avoid pooling of water on the landing surfaces. It may be necessary, for surface-drainage purposes on external ramps, to provide a cross-slope across the width of the landings. In such cases, the cross-slope should be no more than 1:50. On landings with edge kerbs or a side wall, there should be a drainage hole to prevent water collecting along the edges.

Where the ramp is going to be subjected to large amounts of water, or where it is leading to a floor level that is lower than the outside floor level (this being the logical route for the water to take), more substantial drainage precautions should be taken.

Drainage gulleys should have small grilles that traverse the ramp surface rather than being parallel with the direction of the ramp. The drainage should be fitted with rodding eyes to ensure that it can be adequately cleaned, and in areas where there is a large flow of water and high wash of silt then a silt trap should be installed. This is an area in the pipe run that allows the silt to fall out of the water and into a bucket that can be removed and emptied on a regular basis. This is especially important if the rainwater is going into a soakaway, which would be expensive to clean if it silts up.

Case study: Ramp drainage

Client: St Anne's Church Hall, London E2

This building had been constructed on the outside of a church hall building to provide a covered entrance from the churchyard to a newly installed lift. The finished floor level inside the building was below the level of the tarmac path in the churchyard, which itself was the lowest level of the churchyard. Water was a problem in the building, and flowed in torrents even when the rain was light, swiftly overpowering the capacity of the drains which were soon blocked with silt.

The churchyard entrance ramp was a secondary entrance ramp used by people who would largely have a facilitator, and could therefore cope with a short section of ramp. The design of the ramp was optimized for access use as well as to act as a barrier against the floods which would naturally flow down into the building. The top platform was given a slight gradient to reduce the tendency of the water to flow in this direction. The main slope of only 1.5 metres had a gradient of 1:12 finishing on a level platform in front of the entrance door (see Figures 10.24, 10.25 and 10.32). The drainage channel was designed for a high flow of silt-laden water and designed with two rodding eyes and a silt trap for maintenance. Despite the water and the fact that the door has no weather protection at the sill level, and a completely flush threshold, there is limited water penetration into the building. Users of the ramp have been extremely impressed by the ease with which they can now enter the building and are pleased with the automatic lighting that comes on when they are present and illuminates the ramp to approximately 300 lux.

The cost of excavation of this ramp and the laying of a reinforced concrete ramp with drainage was approximately £3100 (1995), including the door joinery work.

Lighting

It is important to have good illumination on ramps, both qualitative and quantitative, especially for people with partial vision. Good illumination may be achieved by employing a combination of low-level directional light sources (e.g. bollard lights or recessed light fittings) and high-level general or diffuse sources.

Generally, minimum illumination levels for external and circulation routes do not account for the higher lighting levels required by people with visual disabilities. A *minimum* of 100 lux illumination (at ramp level) is recommended.

Maintenance

The accessibility of a ramp is dependent not only on a well-designed ramp but also on regular maintenance. Ramp surface coatings may require periodic renewal and regular clearing of drains and snow in winter.

Stepped ramps

Stepped and ramped approaches to buildings are preferred, as ambulant people with mobility disabilities have difficulties using a ramp only. Steps should also have handrails and are discussed in Chapter 9.

However, there are examples where the steps are formed by different runs of a ramp to-ing and fro-ing back to front, where the surface of the ramp is also the stair tread. In such cases, not only are the risers of the steps not uniform but the tread surfaces are not flat. It is also likely that there would be no physical barrier to prevent a person in a wheelchair from rolling down the steps if they lose control on the ramp.

Thus, combining steps and ramps in this manner is not recommended. However, if such a ramp is included as a design 'feature', it is recom-

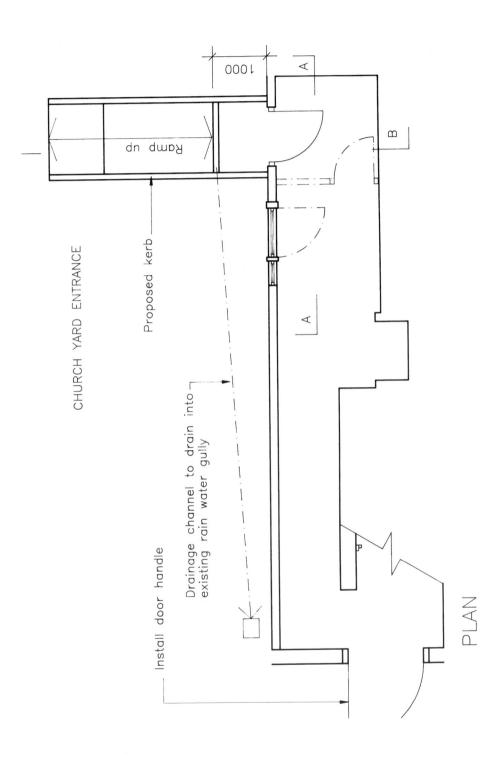

CHURCH YARD ENTRANCE

Install door handle

Proposed kerb

Drainage channel to drain into
existing rain water gully

Ramp up

1000

A

B

A

PLAN

Figure 10.24
Ramp with considerable water protection measures, but no door threshold

Figure 10.25
Section B–B through the ramp showing the fall and drainage location

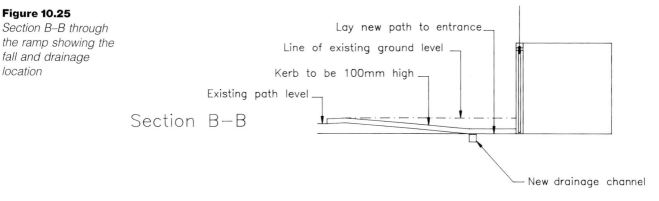

Section B-B

Lay new path to entrance
Line of existing ground level
Kerb to be 100mm high
Existing path level
New drainage channel

mended that alternative means of adjacent separate stepped and ramped approaches be provided. A good example of a ramp which combines steps and ramps is the entrance to the Royal Institute of British Architects (RIBA) at 66 Portland Place, London.

Pavement vaulting

Pavement vaulting is the process of adapting the pavement to provide a ramped entrance to a building. This process is useful where there is no way to provide a ramp within the boundary of the building itself or of supplying a reliable mechanical device. This can be a small change in level such as that discussed in the case study below, or a large change in level (up to 150–180 mm AFFL) as shown in Figures 10.26 to 10.28, which show proposals for the adaptation of the entrance of the Council for National Vocational Qualifications, London.

Where there is enough room on the pavement, and a gradient of not more than 1:15, or, in exceptional circumstances, 1:12 can be achieved, the pavement can be relaid to provide a level platform outside the entrance of the building. The local authority is likely to object to the use of this technique, so it should be explored with them at the earliest opportunity and with the assistance of the Access Officer. However, it has been done successfully in the London Borough of Islington (County Court), Hammersmith and Fulham (Post Office) and The Royal Borough of Kensington and Chelsea (The Royal Court Young People's Theatre) (see case study below).

Care must be taken not to provide a hazard as all the pedestrians will have to use the slope, and it is recommended that a balustrade be installed at kerb level to prevent wheelchair users leaving the building and overshooting onto the road.

Case study: Pavement vaulting

Client: The Royal Court Young People's Theatre, London W10

The entrance to the building was located on a sloping pavement with an entrance step that varied between 80 mm and 40 mm. There was not enough room within the step area to produce a satisfactory ramp or to install a reliable mechanical device to overcome the short step.

It was proposed to create a level platform outside the building using the pavement (see Figures 10.29–10.32), and sloping the pavement either side of the platform to rejoin the pavement. The maximum gradient required on the slope was 1:20, which is barely noticeable in use.

The local authority's Borough Engineers were not immediately enamoured of the idea, but eventually gave their permission. The pavement was relaid in the traditional sand and slab, over a period of three days and at a cost of approximately £800 (excluding VAT) (see Figures 10.33–35).

Conclusion

There is more to making an effective ramp than laying a slope to a required gradient. There are many aspects that make ramps usable, some of which are summarized in Figure 10.36.

Figure 10.26
*Plan of an entrance
ramp using a vaulted
pavement*

ENTRANCE PLAN

Figure 10.27
Section A–A showing the difference in pavement and entrance level

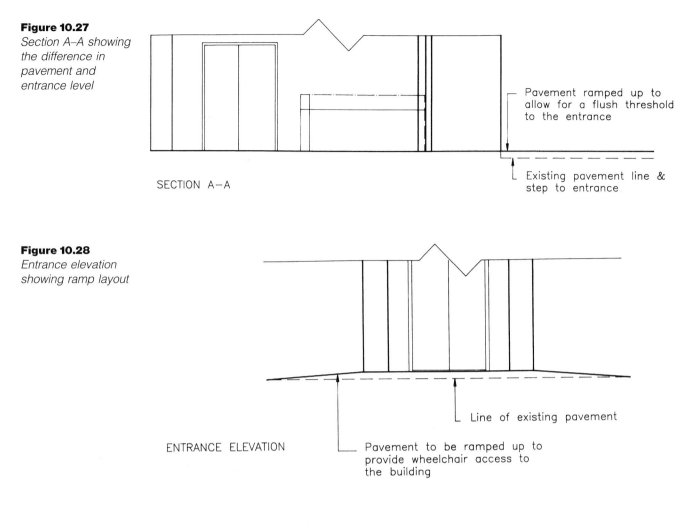

SECTION A—A

Pavement ramped up to allow for a flush threshold to the entrance

Existing pavement line & step to entrance

Figure 10.28
Entrance elevation showing ramp layout

ENTRANCE ELEVATION

Line of existing pavement

Pavement to be ramped up to provide wheelchair access to the building

Figure 10.29
Entrance plan showing layout of a vaulted pavement entrance ramp

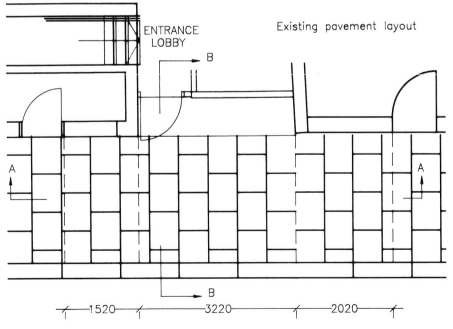

ENTRANCE LOBBY

Existing pavement layout

B

A   A

B

|←—1520—→|←———3220———→|←——2020——→|

Figure 10.30
Section A–A showing the 1 in 20 layout of the ramp fall that was constructed

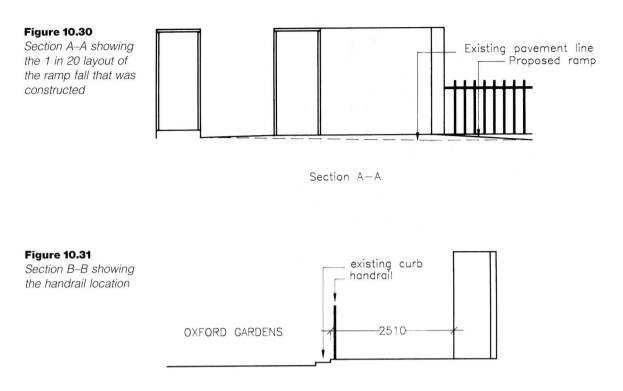

Existing pavement line
Proposed ramp

Section A—A

Figure 10.31
Section B–B showing the handrail location

existing curb
handrail

OXFORD GARDENS

2510

Section B—B

Figure 10.32
Ramp designed to stop water – short slope at the front, the entrance slope and drainage

Figure 10.33
Entrance to building before work was done to the pavement showing the drop

Figure 10.34
Close-up after the work showing flush entrance from the pavement

Figure 10.35
Longer shot showing vaulted pavement with a barely perceptible ramp

Figure 10.36
Summary of ramp requirements

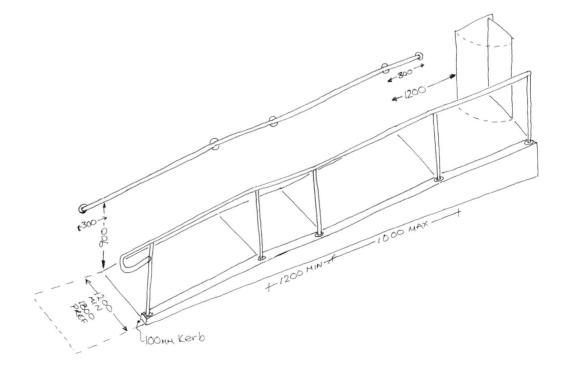

Recommended reading

1 *Barrier-Free Design: Access to and use of buildings by physically disabled people*, 1985, Public Works, Canada.
2 Building Regulations, Part K, *Stairways, ramps and guards*, 1985, HMSO, London.
3 Building Regulations, Part M, *Access and facilities for disabled people*, 1991, HMSO, London.
4 Federal Register, Vol. 56, No. 144, Part III, Friday, 26 July 1991, Rules and Regulations, Appendix A.
5 Voutsadakis, Stelios (1989), *Housing for people with disabilities – A design guide* (second edition), Islington Council Press, London.

11 Lifts

Associated information

Information on the use and requirements of evacuation lifts can be found in Chapter 13. Details are found in BS 5588: 1988, Part 8.

Introduction

Lifts are a critical element in most people's use of a building. They convey much more than just disabled people, often overcoming travel distances that would defeat all but the fittest members of the population. If it is possible to avoid the installation of a mechanical lifting device (for instance, by installing a ramp) then do so – mechanical devices need regular servicing and will inevitably have periods out of service and be subject to vandalism. If it is possible to install a lift inside rather than outside then, again, do so – water and dirt will penetrate the best insulated of mechanisms, and outdoor products will require more frequent maintenance and are at a higher risk of vandalism.

When selecting a lift it is equally important to select the company installing and servicing it. Installation and back-up are critical to the completion of site work, and the difference between a good company and a bad one is enormous. Several manufacturers have been omitted from this chapter because of problems that they exhibited during installation. It is sound practice to ring round other architects to ask about the performance of a company, and ask the lift company for satisfied customers to ring (we have warned off a few people contemplating a particular supplier!)

Servicing is equally important. A client will probably spend more on the servicing and maintenance of a lift in its lifetime than the original purchase price. It is recommended that clients shop around for a call-out and maintenance contract, as our feedback has shown there to be large differences between the charges of large and small operators, with no difference in service.

When ordering a lift always specify a kit of spare parts – if they are available – and place an instruction sign in the lift area stating what parts are in stock and where they are. This will reduce repair and servicing times.

The recommendations in this chapter are concerned with widening the usability of lifts that already exist and increasing the specification of lifts that are in the process of being designed.

Once the car dimensions have been assessed there are many areas of the basic functioning of the lift that will determine the degree of usability for disabled people. All lifts have pushbuttons for operation – making these easy to see and locating them at a height available to wheelchair users is not a great problem. Preventing the doors from closing onto delicate limbs seems a sensible course of action.

This chapter will deal broadly with three types of lift:

1 Passenger lifts, which represent the great majority of installed lifting mechanisms, usually carrying six or more passengers over two or more floors
2 Platform lifts, which are usually designed to overcome a stepped entrance or change in level for a single wheelchair user and his or her facilitator. These types of lift are increasingly becoming used for more adventurous applications, travelling up to 4000 mm and through floors
3 Wheelchair stair lifts, which are used to traverse flights of stairs, either in a straight line or travelling round corners and bends. The range

of these lifts has increased over the years and a single lift can now connect several floors.

The key function of all these products is to provide 'independence' to their user. The degree of independence will depend on the 'operation' of the lift. Extreme care must be taken in the specification of the lift operation, as a case history later in this chapter will show.

We would advocate the use of a 'performance specification' where the profile of the user has been assessed and the operating nature of the lift is recorded. An example is located in the performance specification for a short-rise lifting platform.

Passenger lifts

Passenger lifts represent the most frequently used method of vertical circulation in the majority of buildings over two or more floors. The lifting mechanism and the interior finish may vary between manufacturers, but the basic principles in their design will be similar.

There is a difference between the smaller lift with a hinged door and manual gate and the larger automated telescopic doors – these will be discussed in their specific sections. The basic requirements of a passenger lift are shown in Figure 11.1.

Control buttons

Call buttons located inside and outside the lift need to be within reach and visible to the users. Pushing the button should give a positive indication (feedback) that the call has been acknowledged with, preferably, an indication of the likely time of arrival of the lift.

Landing station

Control buttons should be in a panel which contrasts with the background (wall) and with the buttons. The pushbuttons should be between 20 and

Figure 11.1
Summary of passenger lift requirements

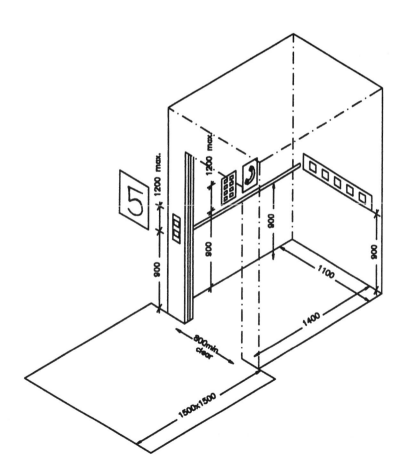

30 mm in width and either light up when depressed or be continually lit (half-light rising to full light on pressing). Light guides/surrounds/halos do not offer as good a feedback as an illuminated numeral or button. Wherever possible, larger buttons approximately 50 mm in width should be used with large, black, filled, etched numerals (e.g. the Dewhurst US85 Pushbutton).

Button legends should be raised at least 1 mm from the face of the button, to give a tactile representation of the numeral, with a *minimum* numeral height of 15 mm and a numeral line width of approximately 3 mm (e.g. the Dewhurst US89, which has an illuminated, raised numeral). The alarm button should be marked with a raised bell symbol.

Legends should be located in the centre of buttons – if not immediately to the left of the buttons. (Refer to the signage specification for choice of typefaces.)

Braille

Braille markings can be useful where there is likely to be a high percentage of blind or partially sighted people. However, it should be remembered that only a small number (2 per cent) of the 400 000 registered blind people in the UK read Braille, with a further 2 per cent of sighted people capable of reading Braille. It should also be noted that the angle that Braille would be presented at in a lift panel would be difficult for Braille readers to read. (Braille is normally read on a horizontal surface.)

Where Braille is to be specified, a combination of Braille and raised lettering on the button is recommended (e.g. the Dewhurst US81 Braille Pushbutton). It should be borne in mind that Braille is most successful in a mild steel panel as brass is too soft to retain the characters.

Tactile legends

More successful than Braille is the use of buttons with a raised and illuminated legend (e.g. Dewhurst US89). With this button the legend contrast is heightened by passing light through it from behind, so that it performs well both visually and in a tactile mode. Discussion with people with a visual disability and the RNIB indicate that the purely tactile button is preferred, and that Braille buttons are regarded as an able-bodied

approach to demonstrate 'awareness' but are not actually much use. (This is not to argue against Braille signage in general – see the signage section for more details.)

Location/height

Ideally, the location of external call buttons should not be more than 1070 mm AFFL to the centre of the top button or to the centre of a single button. Internal buttons should be located with the uppermost button no more than 1400 mm AFFL. The exception to this is where a repeater 'strip' panel of floor selection buttons is also arranged in a horizontal position, placed along the rear of the car at approximately 1070 mm AFFL (to the centre of the buttons). This panel enables wheelchair users, who cannot turn in the lift, to activate the lift. On an illuminated button, such as the Dewhurst US89, the light level can be made to change from medium to high illuminance when the button is depressed.

Lighting

Light levels in the car, on the controls, and on the threshold should be a *minimum* of between 75 and 100 lux, preferably from a diffuse light source rather than a point source.

Feedback

Feedback is an essential element for reducing the stress of using a lift and allowing an assessment of the waiting period to be made by the user. Even indicating that the lift has acknowledged the call will reduce the user's stress.

1 *Button* Depressing the button should cause one or more positive responses: illuminate the button; fully illuminate a part-illuminated button; activate a short sounder (frequency between 500 Hz and 2000 Hz) or both.

2 *Auditory feedback* This is important for people with limited vision or out of the line of sight of the information. It is extremely useful where a bank of lifts is used to indicate which lift is available. Care should be taken not to contribute heavily to the environmental noise level and to set sound levels so that they are heard only on the relevant floor. Lift manufacturers tend to mount the speaker unit on the car,

leading to overspill between floors if the volume is set too high. Therefore gongs are preferred on each floor, with verbal announcement in the lift car.

- *Position* An audible announcement (talking lift) of the floor reached and the direction of travel assists people with visual disabilities (as well as users in general). The announcers should clearly state the floor and direction *twice* on arrival. These announcers can also indicate that the doors are about to open or close (e.g. Dewhurst CF11).
- *Arrival* The lift should announce its arrival audibly. Many types of announcement are acceptable, but those that generate a range of frequencies are preferred (such as the 'gong' type) to a single high-frequency 'ping'). (The high-frequency hearing ranges are the first to decline as a result of ear damage and ageing.) The ideal frequency range is between 500 Hz and 2000 Hz (or a two-tone announcer, alternating between 500 Hz and 4000 Hz). To differentiate the direction of travel of the lift the announcer should sound *once* for up and *twice* for down (e.g. Dewhurst CJ20).

3 *Visual feedback* This can be used to indicate the location of the lift and is used by passengers to ready themselves to mount or depart from the lift.

- *Position* A car position indicator should be provided, both inside and out, to indicate the location of the car in the lift-shaft. The indicator should be approximately 60 mm × 50 mm (e.g. a high-efficiency segmented LED or Dewhurst Digital Display Unit – CE50). It should be located to provide a clear view (i.e. at 1830 mm AFFL above the heads of other passengers).
- *Arrival* The arrival of the lift should activate a visual indication to passengers of its direction of travel. The indicator should be located at least 1830 mm AFFL and should be at least 60 mm in width/height.

Doors

The doors to the lift often present the greatest hazard or barrier to the disabled user. Short cycle times and insensitive leading-edge pressure sensors lead to 'mechanical Rotweilers'

chewing users who are too slow to cross the threshold.

- *Timing sensors* Leading-edge door sensors should prevent the doors from closing when there is someone in their path. The mechanical type of sensor exerts a considerable force before reopening the doors. A LED array/'magic eye' is recommended so that the door automatically reopens without having to make physical contact. Where discreet proximity detectors are used they should be positioned 125 mm and 735 mm AFFL. Where this is not possible a timed interval of approximately 15 seconds is required for safe negotiation. (Many systems allow this to be overridden by a double press on the floor button by the user – reducing the closing time.)
- *Audible warning* There should be an audible announcement to warn that the doors are about to close.
- *Opening width* The minimum allowed under Part M of the Building Regulations is a clear open width of 800 mm. This is considered too small by most users and a minimum of 820 mm is preferred.
- *Hinged doors* On smaller lifts the use of hinged doors and a manual gate is common. Where possible, the use of a gate should be avoided and the hinged door powered with an automatic opening device.

Lift car

The lift car has features that make it more usable by disabled people.

- *Internal dimensions* Lifts are now being categorized in Europe into four types: (1) inaccessible; (2) straight in and reversing out; (3) a three-point turn required to get out; and (4) a lift with sufficient space for a wheelchair turning circle to get out. The minimum internal area of the lift car required by Part M has dimensions 1100 mm × 1400 mm. However, this is now considered to be in category 3, with a 1275 kg lift being considered fully accessible.
- *Handrail* A handrail should be attached to the side and back walls at 1000 mm high

AFFL. The handrail should have at least 45 mm clearance from the wall.

Telephone

The emergency telephone is essential to the safety and comfort of mind of lift passengers.

- *Operation* An emergency telephone should alert the building's security system once it is lifted from its cradle. It should indicate automatically which lift is the source of the call, or carry a sign which clearly identifies the lift. It should then allow two-way conversation. Telephone systems which require dialling on the handset should be avoided. Where the building is not covered by a central control room the telephone should be equipped with a dial facility. In some instances it is possible to alert the security system when the door to the telephone cabinet is opened, although notices to this effect are needed.
- *Location* The emergency telephone should be located so that the base of the handset is no more than 1100 mm AFFL. The telephone should be located either on the wall surface or in a recessed cabinet which is clearly marked (see below).
- *Cabinet door* The door to the cabinet should open so that it does not obstruct access to the telephone (i.e. away from the

user). The door handle should facilitate opening by a user with reduced manual dexterity. It should not be proud of the surface of the door more than 30 mm and should avoid sharp edges. The initial force required to open the door should be minimized by avoiding the use of magnetic holders (e.g. by use of friction hinges) (see Figure 11.2).
- *Telephone signs* To indicate that the emergency telephone is inside the cabinet there should be a sign on the door in words and symbols. The words 'Emergency Telephone' and the telephone symbol should use lettering 20 mm high, red upper and lower case on a white background in bold type. The symbol should be a *minimum* of 100 mm high and red on a white background. Instruction signs should utilize red lettering of 10 mm (*minimum*) upper and lower case, on a white background. This should be positioned either on the telephone itself or on the inside of the door to the telephone cabinet (not more than 1200 mm AFFL).

Signage

Signage in and around lifts should be kept to a minimum to allow the few that are needed to be prominent.

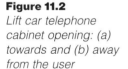

Figure 11.2
Lift car telephone cabinet opening: (a) towards and (b) away from the user

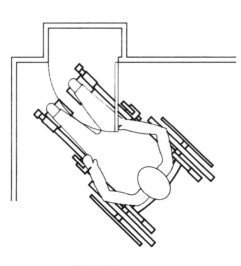

Bad design opens towards the user

(a)

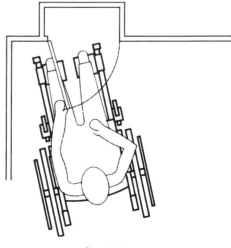

Good design opens away from the user

(b)

- *Warning signs* Lift landing signs (e.g. 'Do not use this lift in the event of fire') should utilize upper- and lower-case lettering, at least 20 mm high. In the case of warning signs, white lettering on a red background should be used. (See the signage specification for a discussion of fonts and contrasts.)
- *Floor identification* The lift door frame should carry an indication of the floor number. The letter/numeral should be a *minimum* of 100 mm high raised (*minimum* of 1 mm) from the signface. The colour of the letter/numeral should contrast with the colour of the signface, which should also contrast with the surface that it is mounted on (e.g. white/black/white, black/white/black, yellow/blue/yellow, blue/yellow/blue, etc.). The sign should be located at approximately 1525 mm AFFL so that it is visible from within the lift car.

Wheelchair stair lifts

Wheelchair stair lifts are horizontal lifting platforms that can lift a wheelchair user along a track beside the risers of a stair. They are extremely useful where there is not a means of installing a ramp or a platform lift.

Wheelchair stair lifts come in a variety of shapes and sizes, with prices that reflect the company policy and the capabilities of the product. It is always worth getting a range of quotations from up to three companies, and ensure that they are all quoting for the same product particulars. Lift companies appear to have extremely complicated methods of quoting, and what might be standard on a particular model may well be an optional extra on others!

Stairs

Not all stairs will be capable of carrying wheelchair stair lifts and acting as escape stairs. It is important to consult the fire authorities to consider the use and location of the stair lift.

Platform

The platform on a wheelchair stair lift is a crucial element in the design. In most of the products the platform is hinged against the body of the lift and folds away when not in use. The width of the lift when stowed away is important where the stair or entrance is not generous.

Most makes of stair lift have automatic platforms as an option. More and more lifts now have the automatic platforms as a standard option. This is an important feature for independent use of a stair lift. Folding down a platform which is not automatic requires extremely good upper-body mobility and some dexterity when balancing at the top of a flight of stairs. Adding an automatic platform to a product can vary between £700 and £3000 depending on the manufacturer. However, there are some lifts that cost under £6000 in total which include an automatic platform as a standard specification.

Straight or spiral?

Most manufacturers now offer lifts that can perform a straight run of stairs or can follow the curve of a stair and even traverse several flights before stopping at a landing. Products by Gimson can now deliver the user to one of several landings on a stair, traversing several floors. The two types are illustrated in Figures 11.3 and 11.4.

Operating switches

The most frequent complaint about wheelchair stair lifts is that they are not working or that they require key activation. Independent use means that a visitor can activate a lift without the need to call for assistance. It is important to specify large well-mounted buttons on the landing posts, with the optional use of a large joystick or pressure button on the lift car. If key switches or on/off switches have been used then it is important to wire them in so that the lift can be energized from either the top or bottom landing.

If earth circuit return breakers have been installed then they also should be wired so that they can be reset from either the top or bottom. These devices are frequently tripped by passers-by, isolating the lift from the supply. A user arriving at the opposite platform cannot reset the device and is prevented from using the lift.

Figure 11.3
*Straight-run
wheelchair stair lift
with elevation showing
the unfolded position*

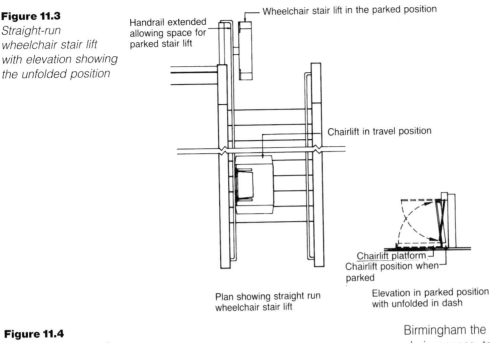

Wheelchair stair lift in the parked position

Handrail extended
allowing space for
parked stair lift

Chairlift in travel position

Chairlift platform
Chairlift position when
parked

Plan showing straight run
wheelchair stair lift

Elevation in parked position
with unfolded in dash

Figure 11.4
*Ninety degree bend
wheelchair stair lift
showing lower parking
position*

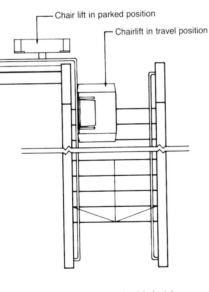

Chair lift in parked position

Chairlift in travel position

Plan showing wheelchair stair
lift with 90 degree turn

Case study: Stair lifts

Client: Central Television PLC
Location: Abingdon, Oxford
Date of installation: 1994

Central Television has a commitment to improving access for disabled people to all its premises. Following a survey of its Central studios in Birmingham the station wanted to provide wheelchair access to its news-gathering service in Abingdon.

The building is leased and has two staircases (one at either end of the building), one of which is communal. The newsroom and news-gathering areas for journalists were located on the upper floor, and it was therefore necessary to look for a low-cost method of overcoming the stairs.

Two options were proposed (see Figure 11.5):

1   Using a Gimson Spiralift mounted in the well of the stair – this would allow the lift to park away from the escape stair when not in use (see Figure 11.6).
2   Using a Wessex VC63 which was wall-mounted and would rest at the bottom of the stair when not in use. As can be seen from the drawings, the well version makes better use of the stair width than the Wessex version, which was significantly less expensive (see Figure 11.7).

The Spiralift was chosen because it would allow an easier mounting arrangement for wheelchair users on the ground floor, and this was the preference of the fire officer.

Additional changes made to the building included adaptation of a male toilet into an accessible cubicle – if a female user wanted to use the toilet, then there would have to be a guard placed on the door. Normally this is not desirable, but

Figure 11.5
Existing layout of building requiring wheelchair access to upper floors

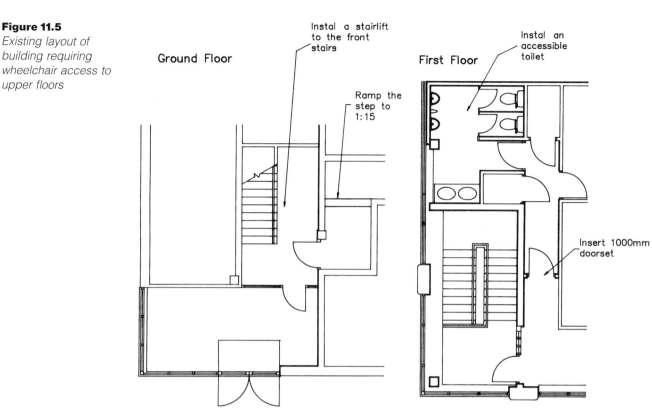

Ground Floor

Instal a stairlift to the front stairs

Ramp the step to 1:15

First Floor

Instal an accessible toilet

Insert 1000mm doorset

Figure 11.6
Ground floor showing two types of wheelchair stair lift: well (Gimson) and wall-mounted (Wessex)

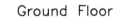

Ground Floor

Option 1

Option 2

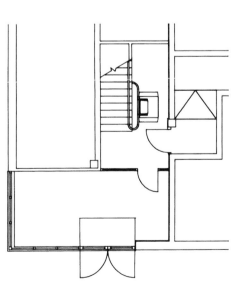

Gimson Spiralift

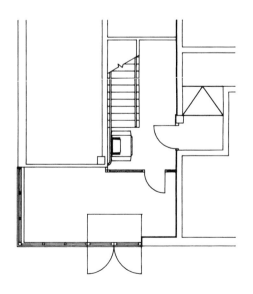

Wessex VC63

Figure 11.7
First floor showing two types of wheelchair stair lift (Gimson and Wessex). The wall-mounted version was chosen

First Floor

Option 1

Option 2

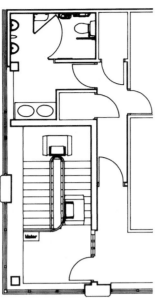

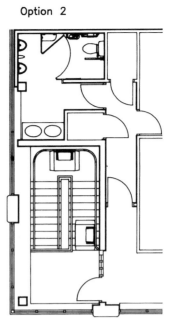

Gimson Spiralift

Wessex VC63

these were the only adaptable toilets in a building heavily staffed by men.

Platform lifts

Platform lifts are probably the most commonly known methods for enabling wheelchair users to overcome a set of steps or change in level. There are broadly three types of platform lifts (see Figure 11.8):

1 *Step lifts*   These are mainly manufactured by Terrys and consist of an air bag and a platform. Inflating the bag raises the platform and allowing the air to escape causes the platform to lower. These devices are really intended for domestic use, and are extremely noisy in use, but cost from £3500.

2 *Scissor lifts*   These platforms are developments of dock levellers and lifting platforms. They use a scissor mechanism and a hydraulic ram. These products require a pit for installation, which adds considerably to the installa-

tion cost. The lifts are very heavy, which means that they are a permanent solution. These lifts can lift up to the BS 6440 1983 height of 1.98 metres.

3 *Lifting platforms*   These are non-scissor mechanisms that use either a screw drive or a hydraulic ram to lift a platform up a column – similar to a forklift truck. These platforms are capable of lifting up to the European Standard (ISO 4000) as well as the 1.98 metres allowed in the British Standard. It is important to note that the screw mechanism lifts, largely imported from the USA, are extremely noisy in operation, and are not recommended in areas where noise would be an issue.

Placement

Platform lifts are normally used in conjunction with steps, where they can be located in a variety of places depending on the design of the building. Some of the likely locations are illustrated in Figure 11.9.

Figure 11.8
*Lift types: (a)
wheelchair stair lift;
(b) wheelchair step
lift; (c) wheelchair
platform lift*

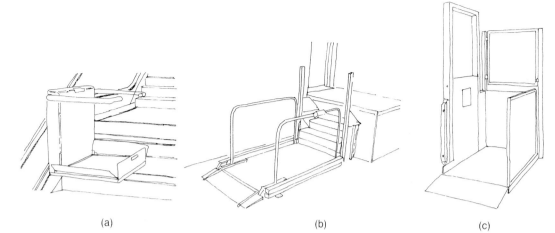

(a)   (b)   (c)

Figure 11.9
*Possible locations for
platform lifts with
stepped entrances: a
step lift with bridge
and two platform lifts*

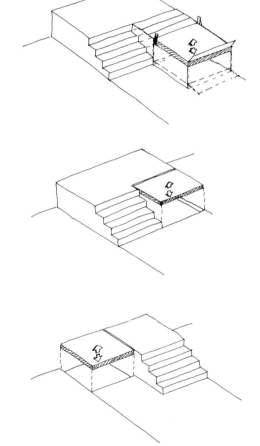

Travel height

At present, the height of travel of a powered plat-form lift is restricted by BS 6440: 1983 to no more than 1.98 metres. Until comparatively recently this was considered to be the limit of travel that was acceptable. However, a European standard (ISO 4000) has recently described standards for a lift-ing platform with travel distances up to 4000 mm.

The British Standards Institution is carefully considering the upgrading of BS 6440, which is currently a code of practice, and rewriting it to allow for travel distances up to 4000 mm. The greater travel distance means that, according to the Factories Act, the lift should be fully enclosed. Where there appears to be the use for a lift travel-ling up to 4000 mm the local building control offi-cer and the client's insurers must be consulted for approval.

It has been noted over the last few years that there is an increasing demand for lifts of this type. They represent a low-cost option to a passenger lift (normally the lift is in the £10 000 range, as opposed to £25 000 for a passenger lift). The use and specification of this type of lift will be dealt with later, and described in detail in the case study.

Gates

Except in the rarest of instances it is important to provide automatic gates. The purpose of a short-rise lift is to provide *independent* access for a disabled person. Many disabled people who use power wheelchairs will not be able to open and close a gate to enter a lift. Figure 11.10 illustrates the difficulty that a wheelchair user will have clos-ing a non-automated gate. Failure to specify pow-ered gates at the beginning of the project can be an expensive exercise, as shown in the case study later.

When automatic gates are installed there should be some form of visual warning to indicate

Figure 11.10
Wheelchair user stretching round with difficulty for a non-automated short-rise lift gate (single automated)

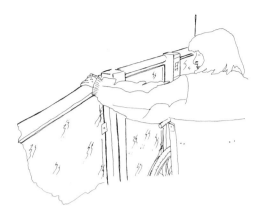

the swing of the gate. Figures 11.11 and 11.12 show the installation of a warning strip in the matting that is in front of the lift. This reinforces the fact that coir mats (illustrated in Figure 11.11) are not good for wheelchair use, and this one prevented manoeuvring in front of the lift platform. The replacement with Construction Specialities 'Pedimat' allowed for the installation of a contrasting arc of colour to mimic the opening swing of the door and thus give a warning as to its action, as well as a matting which is good at dirt removal and has a good surface for wheeled traffic.

Figure 11.11
Entrance to the short-rise lift on the left has coir matting which stops wheelchair users

Figure 11.12
Coir matting replaced by a grid system which has the door opening swing inset

Buttons

These have requirements similar to those of a passenger lift. As there are normally fewer buttons to deal with, the larger Dewhurst US85 pushbuttons are preferred where possible.

Operation

All these lifts will have automatic sensing edges to detect obstacles in their path. It is therefore recommended, where possible, that a continuous control mechanism is installed on the lift. In operation the call or send button is pressed only once to activate the lift and the lift will then complete its travel without pressure on the button. This requirement is important as many wheelchair users do not have the strength or dexterity to keep the constant pressure required on a pushbutton for periods of up to 60 seconds.

Specifications for alteration to existing short-rise lift

(1) Automate existing lift gates, top and bottom of rise using the FAAC 402 compact swing gate operator. Provide electrical control so that the unit operates in the following way:
  (a) If the lift is at the level required then a press of the call button will automatically open the gate, which will remain open until either:
    (i) the send button is pressed inside the lift car, in which case the gate will close, and the lift will move to the required level; or
    (ii) a period of time has elapsed (120 seconds), after which the user can be assumed to have left the lift car, the gate will close automatically; or
    (iii) the call button at the destination platform of the lift (this option being for facilitated use of the lift).
  (b) When the lift arrives at the desired platform the gate will open automatically as soon as the lift is safely stationary.
(2) Install continuous control mechanism to allow a single press on the button to call the lift. The controller should respond to a 'call' button on the top and bottom landing stations, a single press calling the lift and automatically opening and closing the gates ready for travel (as

above). The lift car button stations would have four possible buttons: up, down, emergency stop and alarm. The up and down buttons would have to be activated once to operate continuous control.
(3) Replace existing landing station buttons with stations using Dewhurst US85 pushbuttons with LED-illuminated halo:
  (a) Top landing having two buttons. The top button to be engraved with 'Call Lift' infilled in black with lettering no smaller than 15 mm high. The lower button to carry the legend 'HELP' engraved and filled with red in lettering no less than 18 mm high. This button to be connected as a momentary 'push to make' and wired to the existing cable provided by the Arts Council. The push station to be mounted so that it is supported within the knurl post, at approximately 1000 mm AFFL, with a brushed steel surround. The knurl post to be hollowed, with cabling chased into the centre and led down away from sight in the centre of the post. The post stained and polished to match existing. The enclosure to comply with all British Standards on lift safety and fully earthed.
  (b) Bottom landing to have one button engraved with 'Call Lift' infilled in black with lettering no smaller than 15 mm high. The push station to be mounted so that it is supported within the knurl post, at approximately 1000 mm AFFL, with a brushed steel surround. The knurl post to be hollowed, with cabling chased into the centre and led down away from sight in the centre of the post. The post stained and polished to match existing. The enclosure to comply with all British Standards on lift safety and fully earthed.
  (c) The car to have four buttons in a horizontal station. The buttons to be Up arrow ↑, Down arrow ↓, an alarm bell and the legend 'STOP'. The arrows to be engraved and filled in black, with height of no less than 30 mm, a body width of no less than 5 mm and a tail. The alarm bell to be no less than 30 mm high, engraved and filled with yellow. The legend 'STOP' to be no less than 20 mm high, engraved and filled in red. The push station to be mounted so that it is supported on the metal section housing the existing push station, pre-

senting the buttons towards the user but leaving the platform clear. The enclosure to comply with all British Standards on lift safety and to be firmly affixed to the lift car so that the call button is no more than 1000 mm AFFL, and fully earthed. The fixing mechanism and supports to be finished as per lift columns. The push station face plate to be finished as per existing.

(4) Button housings to be prepared off-site with fixing on-site. The lower gate to be provided with a support bracket to take the rear unit pivot. The gate operators should be affixed either by drill and tap or by means of bolting through the main uprights. White plastic end caps to be provided to bolt and nut heads. The rod pivot point to be fixed to a metal plate which spans the glass door infill.

All works to be carried out under 'clean' conditions with the minimum disruption to the client. Where possible, the work to be carried out 'out of hours' subject to agreement with the client.

The use of lifts to facilitate access is probably best illustrated by the following case studies.

Case study: Through floor lift

Client: Royal Court Young People's Theatre

This is an example of a lift that makes use of the European Standard ISO 4000, which allows wheelchair platform lifts up to 4000 mm as opposed to the British Standard that only includes specifications of platform lifts up to 1980 mm AFFL. (However, there is a strong move currently within the British Standards Institution to revise the Standard to include guidance for lifts up to 4000 mm.) It is important to note that detailed discussions with the building control department and the building insurers should take place before a lift like this is installed.

In this building, which is a two-storey (ground floor and basement) building, with flats above, there was a requirement to install a lift so that wheelchair users could enter from the ground floor and have access to the basement. Because of occupants above the building, and a concrete slab below, there was not the room to install a hydraulic passenger lift. The floor-to-floor height was approximately 2460 mm, which would be the lift travel.

A screwdrive lift was ordered from the distributor of an American product in the UK because there was no UK manufacturer of lifts of this travel. This lift would now be a hydraulic lift supplied by Imperial as the hydraulic lift has superior performance and is almost silent in use, while the 'screw' variety is extremely noisy.

An opening was cut in the floor, the lower partition built to one-hour fire separation and the lift dropped into the resulting shaft. The ground-floor partition was constructed to one-hour fire separation and the doors also built to the same specification (see Figures 11.13–11.17).

Figure 11.13
Basement of a building which required wheelchair access via a lift

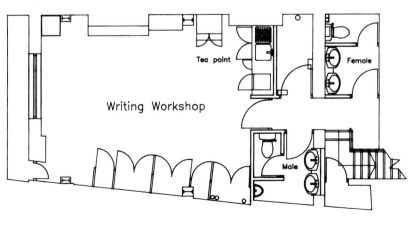

Before

Figure 11.14
Conversion of the building with a lift and toilet and reworked writing space

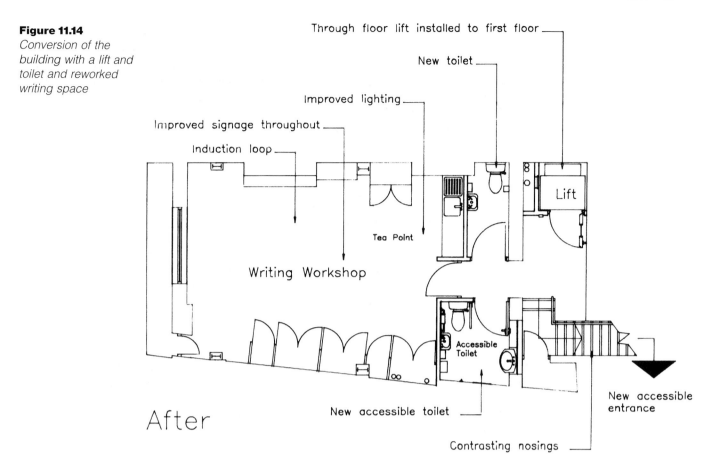

Through floor lift installed to first floor

New toilet

Improved lighting

Improved signage throughout

Induction loop

Lift

Tea Point

Writing Workshop

Accessible Toilet

After

New accessible toilet

New accessible entrance

Contrasting nosings

Figure 11.15
Section through the building showing the lift platform shaft

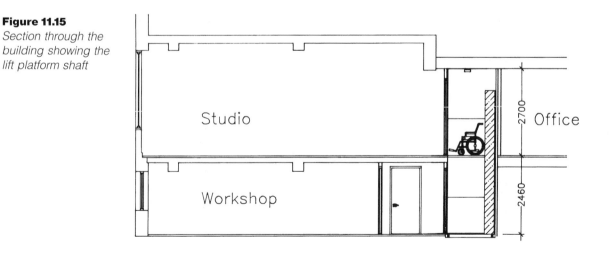

Studio

Office

2700

Workshop

2460

Figure 11.16
Plan showing the lift layout on the basement and ground floor

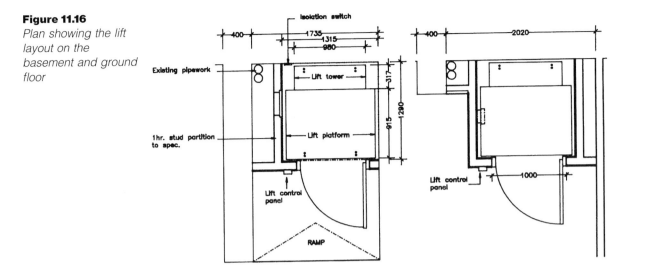

Lift Plan at Basement Level   Lift Plan at Floor Level

Figure 11.17
Section through the newly created lift shaft

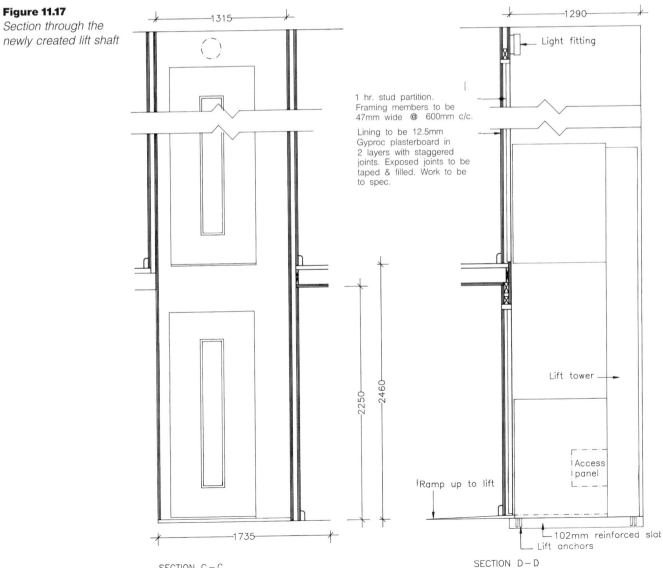

1 hr. stud partition. Framing members to be 47mm wide @ 600mm c/c.

Lining to be 12.5mm Gyproc plasterboard in 2 layers with staggered joints. Exposed joints to be taped & filled. Work to be to spec.

SECTION C – C   SECTION D – D

It is important to note on a lift of this type that the inside shaft should be *completely* free from any surface obstructions, including signage. This requires the doors to be constructed like safe doors and to produce a flush surface when closed (see Figure 11.18). Fire-resistant glass such as 'Pyrostop' from Pilkington should be used for vision panels and fixed according to manufacturer's specifications.

This type of lift should not be seen as an alternative to a passenger lift. It can be usefully used where there is limited headroom and a low traffic usage. This lift is intended to allow only two wheelchair users into the basement, as more would not be evacuable. (The battery back-up is supplied as a safety measure for blackout, rather than for use in an emergency.) It is also important to note that a lift like this must be accompanied by a 'Management Procedure' which shows the use of the lift, emergency procedure and the fact that it should be key-controlled to comply with the limits on the number of wheelchair users in the basement.

However, in these conditions it can provide an extremely effective and low-cost solution – £9000 for the lift and approximately £4500 for the shaft, with fees contributing another £3000, giving an approximate figure of £16 500 (plus any VAT applicable) for a lift.

Case study: Lift alternatives

Client: Kingsgate Workshops

There are many ways to lay out a space using wheelchair stair lifts and platform lifts. This example is taken from a small gallery space in north London. As can be seen in Figure 11.19, the existing gallery has a split level, with the upper floor being at street level and providing access to the toilet area and the lower level containing a large viewing space with the height of hanging space preferred by the artists.

Options 1 and 2 (Figures 11.20 and 11.21) create a larger gallery floor space and move the steps to allow toilet access from the entrance level. The choice between a platform lift and a wheelchair stair lift in this example depends on

Figure 11.18

Details of door construction to give one-hour fire separation floor to floor

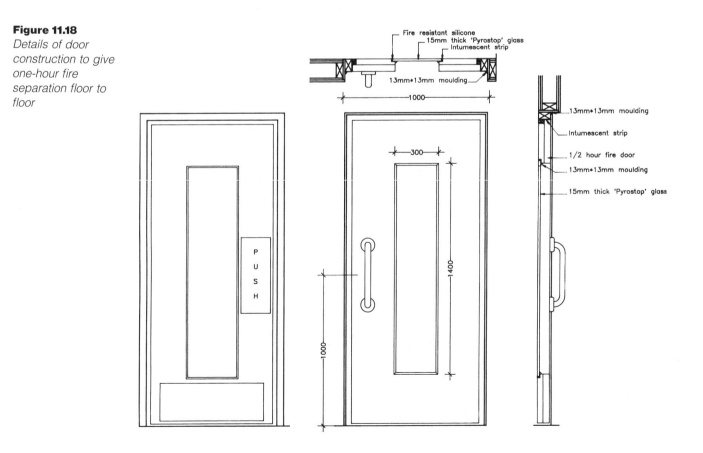

Figure 11.19
Small gallery space requiring wheelchair access

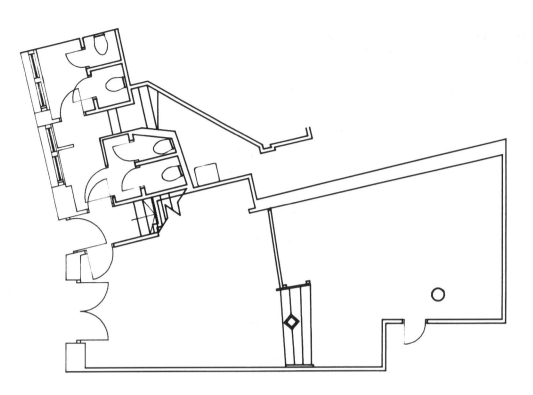

Figure 11.20
Option 1 moves the floor and uses a wheelchair stair lift for access

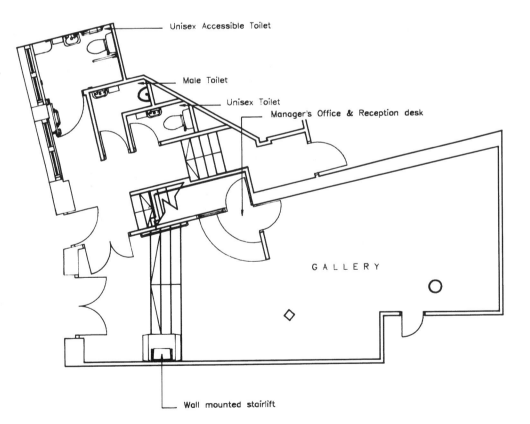

Figure 11.21

Option 2 uses a platform lift and floor move but ties up considerable floor space

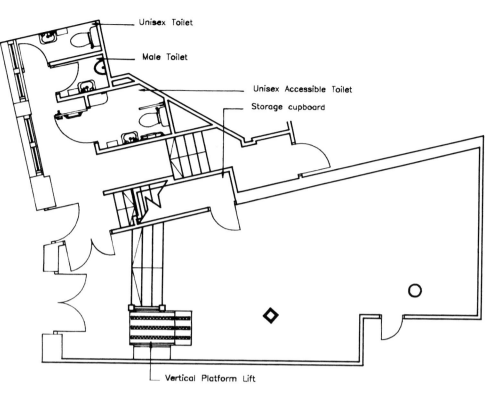

Unisex Toilet

Male Toilet

Unisex Accessible Toilet

Storage cupboard

Vertical Platform Lift

the frequency of use of the space by disabled people. The cost of the two options is approximately the same (using either a Wessex stair lift or an Imperial platform lift), but the permanent space taken up by the platform lift would argue in favour of the use of the stair lift. If the gallery was larger, and there was a higher expected attendance of wheelchair users, then the platform lift would be preferred for its ease of use, and the real-estate would be tolerated.

Options 3 and 4 (Figures 11.22 and 11.23) illustrate the difference more clearly. Figure 11.22 shows the movement of the stairs and the creation of a full-height hanging wall by the column and the use of a wheelchair stair lift, which is folded against the wall when not in use. Figure 11.23 shows the use of a platform lift in the same location, with the result that the stairs have to remain in their existing location and there is a net reduction in the hanging space. Option 3, Figure 11.23 proved to be the preferred and lowest-cost option.

Recommended reading

1 British Standards Institution, BS 5588: Fire precautions in the design, construction and use of buildings: Part 8: 1988 Code of practice for means of escape for disabled people.
2 British Standards Institution, BS 6440: Code of Practice: Power lifting platforms for use by disabled persons: 1983

Figure 11.22
Option 3 uses a wheelchair stair lift and adds a wall for hanging space

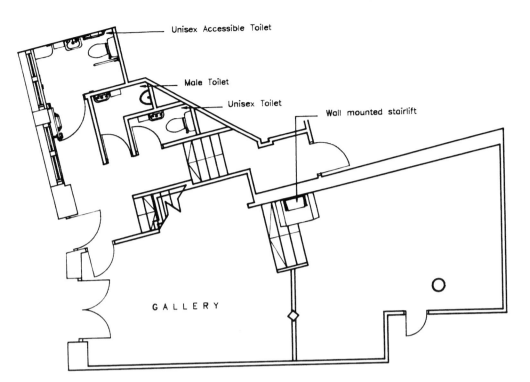

Figure 11.23
Option 4 uses a platform lift which occupies a large amount of floor space

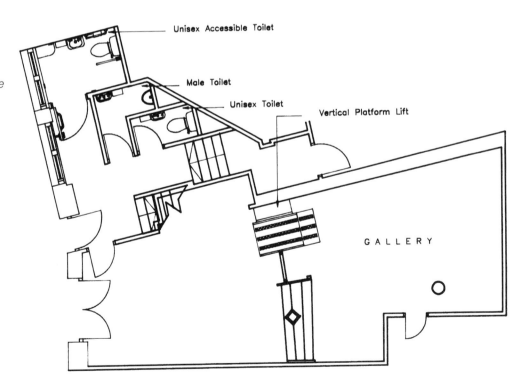

12 Signage and labelling

Signage is a consistent theme across all areas of a building and the built environment. Signs need to answer the differing needs of language, comprehension, literacy, colour perception, visual ability, cost production methods and aesthetics.

Large volumes have been written on small fragments of these features. This chapter does not intend to be comprehensive but rather indicates some of the requirements of some of the features of the signage needed to facilitate use by disabled people.

Signage is an expensive business. A smaller organization may make extensive use of laser-printed and stencilled signs. Many of the features discussed in this chapter can be applied to this type of sign.

Signage in a building and leading to the building has more of an impact on disabled people than may be at first realized. As stated in earlier chapters, people with hearing and visual disabilities make up the largest group of disabled people in the community. Signage affects both groups. Good signage can prevent people with a hearing disability having to ask questions to which they cannot get the answers, and large clear signs can assist people with a visual disability to navigate the built environment.

The design of signage in a building – or 'wayfinding', as it is more commonly called – is a professional occupation in its own right, and a feature that is most noticeable when it is not present. These cues to the environment are continually searched for and assessed in order to orientate ourselves and plan our next steps. This chapter deals, in the main, with the principles for signage layout and, in particular, how signage can be improved for people with visual disabilities. However, in buildings where these principles have been applied, feedback from other users has stressed the usefulness of clear signage.

Signage is more complicated than it at first appears. The following features affect the accessibility of a sign:

- Choice of easily recognizable typefaces
- Height of lettering
- Colour of lettering and backgrounds
- Location of sign (height)
- Clarity of information
- Light level on the sign
- Use of symbols
- The incorporation of tactile information.

The last feature is one of the most recent developments of signage and assisting people with a visual disability, and is included towards the end of this chapter. More detailed discussions on lettering and the presentation of printed material can be found in Chapter 6.

It is strongly recommended that specialist publications on the design and layout of signs, in conjunction with the corporate identity of the building, are consulted, as well as employing specialist designers. Many of the large signage companies such as Spandex or Modulex have staff that specialize in advising clients on the specification route (free of charge) and who are skilled in the 'hand-holding' process.

Information in signs

There are four basic types of information contained in a sign: typeface, colour, location, and pictograms.

Typeface

Typefaces have several features which make them accessible or 'legible', i.e. easier to read:

1 *Case*   The issue of signage which uses both upper- and lower-case lettering has been researched to assess the speed at which people can interpret escape signs when they are in an emergency. Most data have shown that signs which use upper- and lower-case lettering are easier to read and assimilate more quickly than those which utilize only UPPER-CASE lettering. This is thought to be due to the fact that we learn to recognize 'word shapes' rather than literally read every letter to build the word. With upper-case lettering each letter has to be read in turn and takes longer to recognize. Therefore, in general, signs are more effective when they employ both upper- and lower-case lettering.

2 *Font*   One of the key factors in the legibility of a font has been found to be the ratio between the height of the lower-case letter 'x' and the capital letters of the same typeface. This ratio should be approximately 75 per cent (i.e. the 'x' is 75 per cent of the capital height). There is little difficulty concerning stroke width and capital height unless the letters become excessively bold, in which case they become more difficult to read. Typefaces which have these features, and are therefore recommended for the majority of signage work, include Helvetica Medium and Light, Univers, Century Schoolbook Bold, Clarendon Bold and Goudy Extra Bold.

3 *Lettering height*   The height of lettering in a sign is important. Apart from the basic feature of a larger letter being easier to read for someone with a visual disability, the height can be used to indicate the nature of the information that the sign is imparting. The feature that lets one know that a headline is different from body text is the height of the lettering and sometimes the boldness.

- *Internal signs*   The Canadian Standard for Orientation and Wayfinding states that, as a general principle, letter heights for orientation, general information and identification purposes should be at least 25 mm (capital height) and letter heights for directional signs at least 37 mm (capital height). Door signs and directory signs fall into the category of information signs. However, it should be borne in mind that these specifications assume a viewing distance of approximately 5 metres. In buildings where there is less viewing distance the size of the lettering can be scaled down proportionately. When designing a directory board recently with a viewing distance of only 2 metres and a floor-to-ceiling height of only 2100 mm a directory board designed to comply with the lettering above exceeded the floor-to-ceiling height in which to hang it! In this case a floor indication letter height of 25 mm was used, with each floor indicated in 17 mm high lettering. The signage was made from cast vinyl applied to the Spandex 'Slatz' signage system.

- *External signs*   Similar considerations apply to internal as well as external signs. Lettering for directional signs should be no less than 75 mm high. The yardstick to use in determining the required letter heights (for Helvetica Regular lettering), in ideal conditions with perfect vision, yields a viewing distance of 15 metres per 25 mm letter height (capital letters). For example, a 25 mm high letter can be seen 15 metres away, and a 100 mm high letter 60 metres away. However, where signs are being provided which are visible for people with partial vision the yardstick changes to approximately 7.5 metres per 25 mm of letter height (capital letters), translating into 100 mm high lettering being visible 30 metres away.

Colours

There are two basic principles to be considered when choosing colour: the information conveyed by the colour of the lettering and the brightness differentials between the letter and background colours. Safety signs largely use the three main information colours: red, yellow and green.

The brightness differential is determined by the differences in the reflectance of the colours of the type and the signface. There is a large range of optimized colour combinations, which are determined by the colours' relative reflectance differentials. A large difference in the reflectance generates a good contrast and improves visibility.

Optimum combinations of colours include white and black, yellow and black, yellow and blue, white and blue, red and white, and dark-grey and white. The surface treatment of the colour should be low-gloss in nature. There is an opportunity to contrast the finish between the lettering and the typeface, but care should be taken to avoid glare.

It should also be noted that the definition above does not refer specifically to 'colour'. The concept of reflectance is sometimes difficult, but the aim of the lettering is to provide a contrast between the lettering and the background. This contrast can be provided using the same *colour* but a different *hue* (light-blue lettering and dark-blue signfaces can produce an effective sign).

Environment

The choice of colouring on a sign is dependent not only on communicating information but also on the sign's background. Locating the information within the sign is dependent on detecting the sign itself. The ability to detect a sign is determined by a feature called 'target value'. A black sign on a black background will have a low target value, whereas a white sign on a black background will have a high target value. The decision to use positive or negative form (i.e. positive equals black lettering on a white signface) is largely determined by the colour of the general background. However, this feature does not need to determine the colour of the sign. The target value of the sign can also be increased by using a contrasting border to the wall. Thus a white sign on a white wall will have a high target value if it has a contrasting border on its outside edge. The degree of the target value will then depend on the width of the border and the contrast of the colour.

Layout

Layout considerations exist both within the sign and the location and placement of the sign in the built environment. They are concerned with the 'readability' of a sign. These become obvious when discussing directional signs and, at the most basic level, involve whether the messages are displayed flush left/ragged right, flush right/ragged left, or centred.

Figure 12.1
Example of a sign which makes good use of large lettering and symbols

Arrows

If signs are to contain arrows, layout of arrows, words and directions must be considered, with the preference being for left-pointing arrows and text to be flush left and be displayed first, and for right-pointing arrows and text to be displayed next and flush right. Where there is text and arrows also referring to straight ahead they should be placed at the top and the arrows displayed on both sides pointing straight on (see Figures 12.1–12.3).

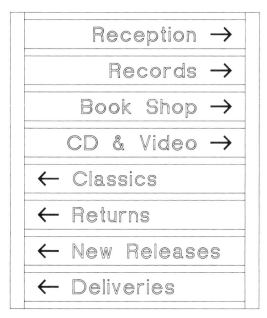

Figure 12.2
Sign showing the justification of arrows and text making reading easier

Figure 12.3
Innovative use of signage slats to create a large floor number and directory board

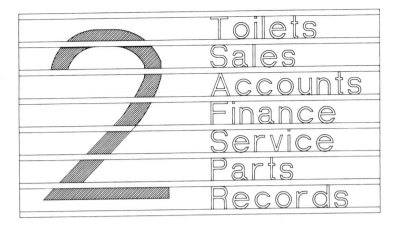

Location/placement bands

Consistent sign location/placement bands should be established throughout the building. The need for a placement band is that the location of the sign is often as important as being able to read the information on it. The development of a consistent approach will also help in the drawing up of a signage schedule for the building.

There is no 'perfect' place for such an information band. What might be optimum for a partially sighted wheelchair user may be uncomfortable for a partially sighted ambulant person of average height. Such placement also has to take into account the available placement areas within a building to fix the signage.

There are broadly two 'bands' that are useful to place signs in. The main band is for close viewing of signs and the upper band for viewing of signs over the heads of other people. This is because the lower 'viewing' band can be obscured when people are standing in front of or are using the signs in this band. An example of upper band use is the placement of fire exit signs so that they can be seen when people are escaping from a fire.

A compromise has identified the lower band height to be placed between 1300 mm and 1600 mm AFFL. This is not the thickness of the band – signs are placed at the top of the band (i.e. at 1600 mm AFFL) and additional elements of the sign are displayed below the sign to a maximum total depth of 300 mm (see Figure 12.4).

Directory board

Directory boards in medium-sized buildings will often exceed this information band. Where space permits they should not be designed like a tower block, but rather arranged by floor along the band. Exceptionally, the band can be extended down by a further 300 mm and the title of the sign extended above the band.

Door signs

Door signs should be located on the latch side of the door, on the wall, with the top of the sign 1600 mm AFFL and 25 mm away from the door frame. Signs that would traditionally be found on the door should ideally be positioned on the wall to the side of the door. Where this is not possible then the sign should be centred on the door within the information band.

Toilet doors are ideally signed centrally in the door using a tactile sign. Toilet signage is discussed in more detail in Chapter 15.

Lift floor and stair floor signs should have 100 mm high lettering indicating the floor number on a sign that is located with the top at 1600 mm AFFL. Signs in lift wells should be located so that they can be seen from the lift on the opposite wall. Supplementary signs should also be placed within the door opening of the lift, so that it can be seen without leaving the lift and when the lift lobby is full of people. This sign should be located approximately 1800 mm AFFL (see Figure 12.3).

Light level

The light level on a sign should be between 100 lux and 300 lux depending on the surrounding light level. An attempt should be made to maintain

Figure 12.4
Corridor showing the features that improve its layout for people with visual disability

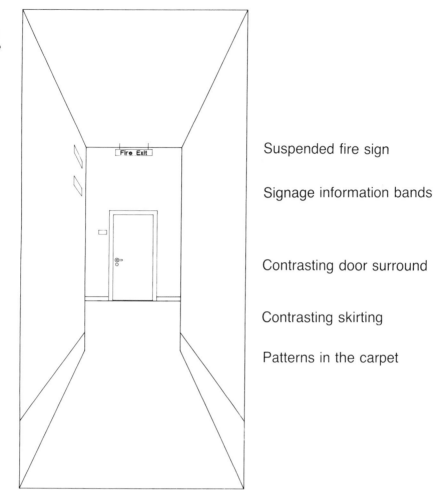

Suspended fire sign

Signage information bands

Contrasting door surround

Contrasting skirting

Patterns in the carpet

illumination of the sign to approximately 50 lux above the surrounding light level to ensure that the sign stands out from the main area (Figure 12.5).

Surface finish

To a certain degree, positioning of light source(s) in relation to the viewer and the sign contribute to glare problems, with light reflecting off the surface of a sign. The more glossy the surface of the sign, the less desirable from a legibility viewpoint. Surface finish of signs should be either matt or semi-gloss in order to reduce such glare. Most of the sign manufacturers such as Spandex and Modulex now offer matt and semi-gloss finishes as a standard part of the range, and the vinyls that are supplied with them can also be provided with low-glare finishes.

Figure 12.5
This sign uses a 100 mm high numeral to indicate the floor, with 20 mm high text

Tactile signs

Incorporating touch into signs is a new development in the UK, but has been law in the USA for over a year. The RNIB and the Sign Design Society are putting together a design manual for signage in this area which was not available at the time of going to press – they should be contacted directly. Further guidance is available in the Americans with Disabilities Act (ADA) which specifies the requirements of tactile signs.

In the UK it has been difficult to get tactile signs as a standard specification, and was only offered by Modulex who can produce raised lettering and Braille on any of a range of signs. Modulex use a process of nylon waste where the photosensitive nylon is exposed to a bromide of the sign artwork. Where the light touches the sign the nylon becomes brittle. When this is subjected to a jet wash the nylon is washed from the sign leaving a positive of the desired sign information. The sign is then painted with a solid background colour and the upper areas of the sign are screen or roller painted to differentiate them from the signface colour. The process offers an excellent sign with hard-wearing properties and the raised section is almost impossible to remove from the signface. An advantage of this process is that the Brailling on the sign is integral to the signface and is left in the background colour, and therefore does not distract the sighted user, while providing an extremely tactile Braille for users.

The Modulex process has a few disadvantages – the colour on the lettering is a paint, and therefore liable to scraping, and the process is rather expensive at present, as the signs are made in Denmark. For an example of the type of sign produced you can visit the Photographer's Gallery where the signs were designed in conjunction with The Partners graphic design company and All Clear Designs (see the case study) or at the headquarters of the Bristol Royal Society for the Blind.

For three years All Clear Designs has been trying to introduce a second system into the UK using the Rowmark signage system. This is a self-adhesive plastic appliqué which is treated in a similar fashion to vinyl cutting, except that it uses an engraving machine. The appliqué is placed on the substrate and is engraved using an extremely fine cutter (ground to a point). The cutter is positioned to penetrate the appliqué but not the substrate. Once the lettering has been cut, the remaining appliqué is weeded from the signface and the sign is left so that the adhesive can cure. Once cured, the lettering is permanently stuck to the signface.

The advantage of the Rowmark system is that both the appliqué and the substrate are of solid plastic and will not be worn off by touching or scraping. The substrate can be from any substance that can be positioned under an engraving machine and can form the sign in its own right or be fabricated from thin sheet that can then be used as part of a signage system.

The Rowmark appliqué is imported by Spandex and available to their signmakers (lists are available from Spandex) as well as from Recognition Express who have the capability to fabricate the signs themselves. (See case study below.)

Many of these engraving systems can also incorporate Braille into the sign. This will depend on the signface as the Braille is mainly engraved as a positive in a 'well' which is engraved into the signface.

Braille

Braille is the system by which people with a visual disability and total blindness can read. A series of dots that are proud of the signface are read using the fingers passing across them. Braille has a reputation as being as difficult to learn to read as Russian and is currently read only by 4 per cent of registered blind people. However, there is a movement among blind people and their organizations to increase the use of Braille, and it is important to note that the low use of Braille may be due to the low frequency of Braille in the built environment. Every opportunity should be taken to incorporate Braille into signage systems and in the USA the use of Braille in signage is a legal requirement. A limited selection of Braille signs are available from Seton Limited, imported from the USA. The signs are available in a range of colours and are self-adhesive or frame-mounted. Alternatively, signs are available from Tactyle and have a dark legend, Brailled message and 'locator' to assist people in finding the centre of the sign. Again, they are self-adhesive.

Tactile maps

Tactile maps are graphic representations of the layout of the building or the environment. These maps are extremely useful to people with visual disabilities who wish to understand the layout of the building or to use the map.

There are several manufacturing methods for producing tactile maps which are broadly similar to the systems used for the production of raised lettering on signage. However, what is more important is the design of the graphic image before it is made into a raised sign, as the information on the sign that is useful to a person with vision and a person with a visual disability is very different.

It is important to reduce the information on a tactile map to the minimum information that is necessary to someone with a visual disability. Doors are represented by gaps in walls and walls by lines of a standard thickness (unless there is important information contained in the change of a wall thickness).

Production

Once the graphic has been produced, a low-cost tactile map can be made with 'pearl' paper – better known as 'blister' paper. This paper has small glass beads of alcohol under a plastic membrane. The graphic is applied to the paper using a low-temperature photocopier. The paper with the image is then placed under an ultra-violet heat source. The black area of the image absorbs the heat which causes the glass balls to burst and raise the plastic membrane. The areas of the paper which do not have the black image on them do not rise. Thus a positive image of the graphic is produced in a raised format.

The blister paper is a low-cost but low-durability product. The RNIB raised diagram service in Peterborough can produce the raised diagrams from A4 artwork and normally take a few days. The cost (1995) is approximately £0.60 per sheet. Sheets larger than A4 are available, but the paper becomes rather flimsy.

In order to increase their durability the papers can be encapsulated in clear material after they have been raised. The encapsulation is done in a vacuum pressure format where the laminate is applied under pressure and heat. The lamination process does reduce the tactile sharpness of the image, but greatly enhances its durability. It is advisable to have both sides laminated to balance the sheet. The lamination costs approximately £1.00 per side, resulting in a total sheet

cost of approximately £2.60. Some care should be taken if large numbers of sheets are to be laminated. A recent variation of the paper has produced a blistering effect where the lamination does not take properly, so a test is strongly advised. (See case study below.)

Case study: The Arts Council of England; Signage project

As a part of the Arts Council's strategy for making its building accessible to disabled people the whole issue of signage was examined. An opportunity presented itself when the corporate identity changed and new signage was specified throughout the building.

The small viewing distances in the building allowed use of a smaller type size than recommended for larger buildings. (When the signs were mocked up in the sizes recommended in the Canadian standard of 37 mm and 25 mm the directory board would not fit in the floor-to ceiling height.) (See Figure 12.6.)

Figure 12.6
Directory board using large lettering in an attractive layout

Spandex slat systems were chosen as they offer an economical and adaptable signage system with a space in between the slats which gives separation of the lettering. A white cast vinyl with a low sheen was used on a matt-black slat system as the signs were predominantly being used on white walls. Lettering of 25 mm was used for the main floor slats with 17.5 mm high lettering for the directory slats. Floor signs were generated using 100 mm high lettering on black slats.

Tactile

At the same time as looking at the general signage (tactile signs were not available at this time in the UK), a project began to consider the use of tactile signs for people who were visiting the building. The first step was to design the artwork. As the building had been entered onto the CAD (computer aided design) system it was a simple process to edit the drawing to remove all but essential information. However, as there is no standard symbol set for items such as toilets that are also tactile a project was developed to

design these and testing was carried out among people with a visual disability (see Figures 12.7 and 12.8).

Eventually symbols and artwork were produced. These were translated into the raised paper format discussed above. Both plain paper and laminated booklets were produced. With over ten sheets in each booklet the plain paper version is intended to be sent to a visitor to the building, but is then relatively disposable (at a cost of £6.00). The laminated versions are intended to be kept at reception and distributed to frequent visitors and members of staff (at £23 per book).

Tape guide

A sign on its own can be used to tour the building, but this is not recommended. Signs like these should have a tape guide that walks the user through the building using the signs. Thus users can familiarize themselves with the layout and location of the departments before they arrive. The guide to the building was done in conjunction with a partially sighted consultant.

Figure 12.7

The client wanted a tactile plan of the building – this is the original building floor plan

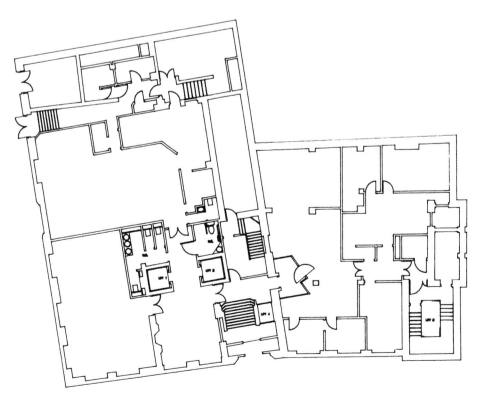

Figure 12.8

Redrawn plan ready for production as a tactile map for people to feel

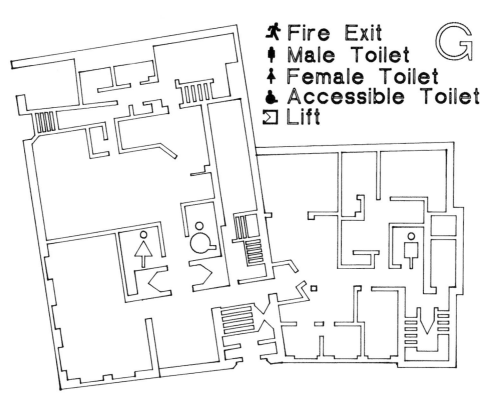

Permanent signs

At the beginning of the project there was no technique for producing permanent versions of the sign in the UK. Three years after the commencement of the project there are now a range of production techniques available – some of which are discussed above. The one that is being used for the production of these signs is the Rowmark appliqué system, producing a unit cost of approximately £150 per sign (including design and installation).

The signage in this building has now been designed to cater for a variety of needs that have been expressed by the partially sighted users of the building and has received extremely good comments.

Symbols

Symbols represent a powerful addition to the battery of signs. Large numbers of users have a low literacy or complete inability to interpret written signs. The use of symbols also introduces an international element into the sign and can allow a shorter sign than text alone.

The ability to recognize a symbol is quicker than the recognition and interpretation of text. However, symbols should always be complemented by text to define the symbol more clearly. (The wheelchair symbol can mean accessible toilets, lift, etc. The partially sighted user will require the symbol to be more clearly defined.)

The same colour considerations as textual signs apply to symbols (e.g. colour/hue contrast with the door surround or mounted on a plate with a contrasting border/surround) and they should also be raised 1 mm from the surface of the signface (see the production methods discussed above).

Symbols should be at least 100 mm high along their main axis. They should be located in the same information band as discussed above and the text should be no smaller than 25 mm high (capital height).

The correct symbols should be used to indicate *independent* use of the facility. Some of the symbols are illustrated in Figures 12.9–12.20.

Figure 12.9
Symbol to indicate accessible parking

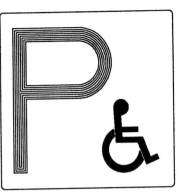

Figure 12.10
Symbol to indicate an independently accessible entrance

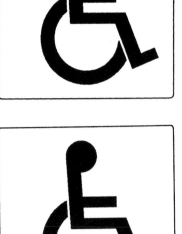

Figure 12.11
Symbol to indicate a ramped entrance

Figure 12.12
Symbol to indicate level access throughout the building

Figure 12.13
Symbol to indicate that assistance is available

Figure 12.14
Symbol to indicate that guide dogs are welcome

Figure 12.15
Symbol to indicate a wheelchair-accessible toilet

Figure 12.16
Symbol to indicate a wheelchair-accessible lift

Figure 12.17
Symbol to indicate an induction loop

Figure 12.18
Symbol to indicate the sympathetic hearing scheme

Figure 12.19
Symbol to indicate an infra-red system

Figure 12.20
Symbol to indicate a wheelchair-accessible telephone

Fire exit signs

Fire exit signs are discussed in more detail in Chapter 13 and should use white lettering on a green background. Lettering should be no smaller than 75 mm, using 100 mm where possible. Signs should indicate whether the escape route is accessible or only accessible to ambulant people, using the layout shown in Figures 12.21 and 12.22.

Where possible, the signs should be suspended directly beneath light fittings, so that an even illumination is provided to both sides of the sign. In any case the sign should be illuminated to 50 lux above the general light level.

Figure 12.22
Fire escape sign indicating the route to wheelchair users

Notice boards

Location

Notice boards should be hung to have their base at approximately 1000 mm AFFL, with headings located at approximately 1800 mm AFFL. These headings should be in upper- and lower-case lettering no less than 37 mm high in a colour which

Figure 12.21
Signs indicating wheelchair-accessible fire escapes

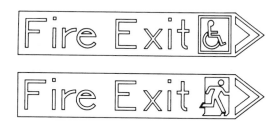

contrasts with the notice board, which in turn contrasts with the background colour.

Notices

A standard specification for notices should be issued to all people using the notice boards. This specification should suggest a *minimum* size print of 14 point (or lettering no less than 5 mm high). Black type against white or yellow backgrounds represents an optimum visual contrast. Notices should primarily be positioned on the notice board between 1000 mm and 1600 mm AFFL so that they are visible to people using wheelchairs and with partial vision.

Lighting

Notice boards should have an illumination level of no less than 100 lux on the notices, and preferably between 300 and 400 lux.

Museum and gallery labelling

The labelling of exhibits and pictures in galleries and museums needs to address the requirements of people with visual disabilities. Exhibits behind glass cases are particularly important because they are normally farther removed from the user.

There are some extremely high-tech solutions to labelling in the form of CD-ROM (compact disc read-only memory) players which detect the exhibit that the user is looking at and give a description of the exhibit in the language that has been suggested. There is also a 'talking wand' version of this device, which operates on a similar basis. The conventional taped guides of a museum or gallery operate in a less high-tech manner and are cheaper to set up and change, but do not allow people to wander in a random way around the exhibits.

However, there are lower-tech solutions – labels should ideally use lettering no less than 5 mm in height (upper-case lettering) and the same contrast requirements that are discussed above for signage. Titles should be in sans serif typefaces and the body of the label can be in either sans serif or serif. However, the size of the type depends upon the distance of viewing for the user. The further the distance, the larger the type should be.

There is obviously a trade-off between the amount of information that can be placed on a label using a larger type size and the relative size of the display area and encroachment of the labels on the display. Where these requirements are going to severely conflict, or where relabelling of the exhibits would be too time-consuming, it is advisable to supplement the labels with a numbering system. The numerals should be no less than 15 mm high and the colours should conform to the discussions above. These numbers can then be used against a key, which can be printed in large print and hold the labelling information.

Rather than having numbering moving from 0 to 1000 it is advisable to divide the numbering into floors, galleries and cases, so that the system would have, for example, 1st, Long Room, Cabinet A, exhibit number 1. This will reduce the impact of changes in the layout of the exhibitions on the list production and minimize the amount of duplication and reproduction. Lists for separate galleries can then be distributed on request, and should be produced using 5 mm high (14 point Helvetica Regular) upper- and lower-case lettering, on white paper. (Most laser printers and word processors can produce this lettering.)

Conclusion

Signage has a great impact on the use of a building. This chapter has related most of the discussion on signage to aspects of visual disability. However, signs also have a great impact on people who have a hearing difficulty or speak a different language, as asking directions to a non-signed location is extremely difficult for them.

Recommended reading

1 Federal Register (1991), Non-discrimination on the Basis of Disability by Public Accommodation and in Commercial Facilities, Vol. 56, No. 144 Rules and Regulations, Department of Justice, USA.
2 McLean, Ruari (1980), *The Thames and Hudson Manual of Typography*, Thames and Hudson, London.
3 Passini, R. (1984), *Wayfinding in Architecture*, Von Nostrand Reinhold, New York.
4 Public Works Canada (1987), *Orientation and Wayfinding in Public Buildings: A Design Guideline*, Public Works Canada.
5 Public Works Canada (1988), *Orientation and Wayfinding in Public Buildings: An Overview.*

6 Public Works Canada (1990), *1, 2, 3 Evaluation and Design Guide to Wayfinding.*
Note: These Canadian standards are extremely useful and well written. They are available free from the Public Works section at the following address:
Documentation Centre
Architectural and Engineering Services
Public Works Canada
Sir Charles Tupper Building
Riverside Drive
Ottawa, Canada, K1A OM2

13 Fire and emergency escape procedures

Associated information

For information on fire doors and electromagnetic holdback devices, refer to Chapter 14.

Introduction

Fire and emergency escape procedures are often cited by building managers and owners as reasons for the exclusion of disabled people. There are situations in buildings in which it would be unsafe to have people with reduced mobility, reduced sensory ability or with learning difficulties. It could be both unsafe for the disabled person and their presence could add increased risk for other occupants. However, it is rare that these situations could not be overcome with either a physical adaptation to the building and/or a change in the management of people and spaces within the building.

The building manager/owner may refer to the 'Fire Officer' who may not allow the changes suggested. What is more often the case is that the fire brigade would be more than willing to entertain suggestions for access for disabled people while maintaining the safety of the building's occupants. It is important therefore to check where the 'blockage' to access for disabled people lies. It is unlikely to start with the fire brigade.

The basic idea that all parts of buildings should be accessible to disabled people was legislated in documents such as the Chronically Sick and Disabled Persons Act 1976 and the Building Regulations 1985. However, the evacuation of disabled people is also covered by the Fire Precautions Act 1971, which places an obligation on places of employment to provide safe means of escape, suitable firefighting equipment and sufficient training for all employees (including dis-

abled ones). Also the Health and Safety at Work Act 1974 requires employers to maintain safety for their employees in their place of work. This is further amended by the Fire Safety at Places of Sports Act 1987. Regulations governing access for disabled people to buildings did not effectively come into force until 1984, and the guidance on how to get people out was not available until the publication of BS 5588: 1988: Part 8, Code of Practice for means of escape for disabled people. This is discussed further in this chapter, and gives examples of both the design and location of 'areas of refuge' for disabled people and means for the management of a building to facilitate a managed escape for disabled people. The Building Regulations 1991, Part B1 (1992) Fire Safety specifically makes reference to BS 5588: Part 8 and the means of escape for disabled people. In Appendix A BS 5588: Part 8 states that 'Non-compliance with all the recommendations in this code should not be used as grounds for excluding disabled people'.

So it seems reasonable to adopt the principle that people should not be encouraged to enter a building unless adequate means for escape have also been provided, and that there should be some limits to the numbers of people in a building. Where the escape requirements and the numerical limits affect the access and use by disabled people, the design and management solutions discussed in this chapter should be used to overcome the difficulties and increase those limits to an acceptable level. It is the responsibility of the management of a building to research the ways that access can be gained, with guidance and assistance from the fire authorities.

As a final rider to this section, it is worth stating that there are few buildings that cannot be made safe with some thought and expenditure of money. Saying 'It cannot be done' is more often than not a political statement which actually reads 'We do not have the money or the will'. The fire officer can only comment on what is presented to him or her.

Fire safety

Fire safety for disabled people falls into several categories which affect the following areas: general provision, means of escape, and management issues. General provision covers the installation of items such as fire extinguishers, notices, break-glass alarm points, emergency lighting and alarm warning systems. Means of escape includes issues such as the provision of areas of refuge and evacuation procedures, where management issues examine the use of Personal Evacuation Plans (PEPs) and other information such as fire information cards and signs.

General provision

This section deals with the aspects of a building that has no special adaptation but all the features that one would expect in a well-maintained and safe building. Small changes to the layout of statutory provision will achieve the inclusion of disabled people in the safe upkeep of the building and reduce the risk to life and property in it.

Fire extinguishers

There is a degree of confusion in buildings as to the type and use of extinguishers. Effective use of an extinguisher will considerably reduce the risk of spread of fire. There needs therefore to be a simple and clear explanation of the appropriate use of the extinguishers located in the building.

Extinguishers should either be labelled in lettering no less than 25 mm high, showing which extinguishers are suitable for which fires, or use self-adhesive labels such as those from Signs & Labels Ltd (e.g. FB26B). These should be located on both the wall and the extinguisher.

The location of an extinguisher is important to its use. Many extinguishers are located above the reach of a wheelchair user. The device is already at the heavy end of use for a wheelchair user, and may be unusable if located over 1200 mm AFFL. It is the case that most minor fires are extinguished within the first few minutes of alert, and that these

are done by the occupier rather than the emergency services. If a wheelchair user occupying the building has the capability to eliminate the fire then they have added to the safety of the building. During the establishment of a Personal Evacuation Plan (discussed later) with a large London theatre a wheelchair user was taught to use a CO_2 extinguisher and practised on a live charge. Her experience, apart from greatly increasing her confidence, made her more likely to be able to tackle a small office fire and reduce the risk to her building. Extinguishers should therefore be hung with their handles no higher than 1200 mm AFFL and with easy-lift brackets, rather than straps.

Fire blankets

Fire blankets should be located with pulltape no higher than 1200 mm AFFL. Care should be taken when the blanket is located above a work surface that it is within reach of a wheelchair user. Fire blankets should be labelled in lettering no less than 25 mm high.

Break-glass alarm points

Break-glass alarm points should be at a maximum height of 1200 mm AFFL (without hammer) and 1300 mm AFFL (with hammer). The ideal arrangement is at a height of 1200 mm with a hammer.

Fire call accepted indicator

A fire call accepted indicator is used in buildings where activation of the break-glass system does not immediately initiate an audible alarm for the first stage of evacuation (e.g. in television studios where false alarms can be eliminated within a few minutes of warning before a bell interrupts a broadcast).

Where employed, fire call accepted indicators should be at a similar height to the break-glass fire alarm points. Identification signs should utilize upper- and lower-case lettering, at least 10 mm high. The visual display should incorporate a high brightness filament or LED, be no less than 8 mm in diameter and red in colour.

Signs

Fire signs in a building which contains disabled people, and especially those that have areas of refuge for disabled people, should use fire signs to indicate their location. More importantly, the size and frequency of fire escape signs should be larger, to assist people with visual disabilities.

Fire escape signs

The size of lettering used on fire signs is dictated by the local fire authority. These sizes have been determined for people with good vision and in limited smoke conditions with adequate lighting. In most cases it is prudent to go to the next size up of lettering and *overspecify* the sign. For example, a suspended sign with the wording 'Fire Exit' on it in 50 mm high lettering will normally be marked as S 2 F. This should be altered for a sign with the code S 2 H (75 mm lettering) or, if there is room, S 2 K (100 mm lettering). In brief, the codes are as follows:

1 Exit
2 Emergency Exit
3 Fire Exit
4 Slide to Open (with arrow)
5 Push Bar to Open

The ideal for a push bar to open sign is one using at least 40 mm high lettering (e.g. 6 E). An example of a marked-up floor plan is given in Figure 13.1. Up-to-date lists of fire signs should be obtained from the local fire authority, and will be contained on the drawings of the building if there is a fire certificate.

Location of the sign

Many fire signs in modern buildings are suspended – either single-sided signs close to the wall or double-sided signs in a ceiling grid. The location of the signs is crucial to their viewing, and the lighting of the sign is particularly critical.

In a ceiling grid there is often the opportunity to use light provided by an existing luminaire. If the sign is double-sided and suspended on one side of the luminaire, there will be a side with extremely high illumination and a high degree of glare (see Figure 13.2) while the other side of the sign will be

Figure 13.1

Floor plan marked up with fire exit signs agreed by the fire officer to assist wheelchair users

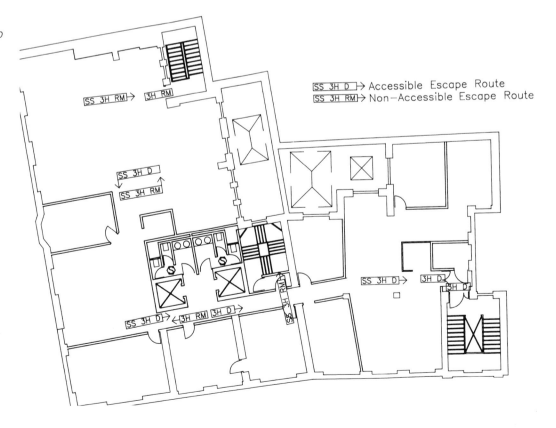

Figure 13.2
This escape sign is well lit by the luminaire as it is centrally suspended

in almost complete darkness (against the halo of the luminaire). Suspending the sign so that it straddles the luminaire will provide even, glare-free illumination to both sides of the fire sign. In any event, the aim is to provide a light level on the surface of the sign of 50 lux higher than the surrounding illumination.

Indicating escape for disabled people

In buildings where there are areas of refuge, emergency evacuation lifts or where there is a level escape as well as stepped escape, it is important to indicate the correct route to a disabled person. There is no specific method within the British Standard to insert a symbol into a fire sign to impart this information. However, in consultation with the local fire authority, signs can be made to include the disabled symbol and indicate the preferred route (see Figures 13.3 and 13.4). The sign with the running person is therefore taken to indicate routes that are not accessible.

The colours needed for signs according to BSO4E53 are Poppy Red, which is closest to 100-466 in vinyl, and Irish Green BS14E53, which is closest to 100-027 in vinyl. (These colours should always be checked with the local fire brigade.)

Fire point identification

Fire point identification signs are used to indicate the location of a fire point. The signs should be in white lettering no less than 75 mm high on a red background. Where the fire point is in a long corridor then the sign should also have a cantilevered version over the fire point, to allow visibility from further down the corridor.

Statutory fire and first aid signs

Statutory fire and first aid instruction signs should have large-body text using lettering no less than 8 mm high (capital size). These signs should be located at the fire points and hung between 1370 and 1525 mm AFFL (see Chapter 12 for details of locations).

Emergency instruction signs

Emergency instruction signs should use a 'bullet point', simple, step-by-step instruction, in black lettering no less than 20 mm high on a white background with a green surround. Signs should be located at fire points and near telephones in wording such as the following:

In case of emergency:

Fire
- Break glass alarm point.
- Dial 666.

Report
- Who you are.

Figure 13.4
Fire escape sign indicating the route to wheelchair users

Figure 13.3
Signs indicating wheelchair-accessible fire escapes

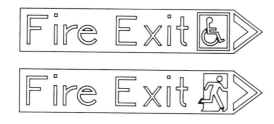

- Where you are.
- Location and nature of fire.

- Leave the building.

First aid
- Dial 2555.

Report
- Who you are.
- Where you are.
- Need for first aid.

- Keep patient warm.

Obviously the specific procedure for each building should be inserted here.

Fire procedure instruction sheets

Fire procedure instruction sheets, issued to staff and located on notice boards throughout the building, should have a large text size with good reproduction (no smaller than 5 mm high capital height (= 14 point), black-body text on a white background). The sheets should repeat the information in the emergency instruction signs and introduce the reader to all the relevant procedures.

Telephones

In some buildings where fire points include telephones for reporting incidents the handset and keypad should be no higher than 1200 mm AFFL. This height allows full use of the telephone by wheelchair users. The telephone extension number, which could be vital in locating the source of the fire and ringing the caller back, should be in the largest typeface possible, but no less than 10 mm high.

Telephone directory

There should be a short directory of important telephone numbers such as operator, nurse, security, etc., in black lettering no less than 10 mm high on a white background (or vice versa if the wall is light in colour). The directory should be positioned close by or on the telephone.

Fire alarms for people with hearing difficulties

People who have hearing difficulties or who are working in areas where machinery may mask the sounds of the alarm bells can make use of two different systems:

- High-intensity beacons attached to the existing fire alarm system and located at strategic visual locations
- Vibrating pagers worn by individuals to alert the user that the alarm has been activated.

Visual fire alarms

Visual fire alarms are designed to supplement the bell system and provide a warning to people with hearing difficulties or where machinery masks the bell system. The visual alarm is the most reliable of the warning systems as it is hardwired to the system and will have to be maintained to satisfy the British Standard and periodic inspection.

The beacons usually use a flash xenon tube to emit a bright frequent flash of light to alert the occupant and should be sited in locations where they are most likely to attract attention in the sight line. For instance, a beacon sighted directly above a desk will only attract the user by the reflection of the light, rather than being caught in the outer visual area. Location on a wall or in a corridor of an open-plan office is more likely to attract the user. Where closed-cell offices are used the beacon should be installed inside the office, preferably below approximately 2000 mm to attract the user's peripheral vision.

When installing a fire alarm system, or planning for an upgrade, care should be taken in the specification of the system's electrical capacity. Once the number of beacons per floor has been specified, the cable and battery back-up should be overspecified to allow the installation of an extra five full-power beacons per floor. The precise number will depend upon the size and layout of the floor. Open-plan offices may be converted at some point into cellular offices, which may house a person with hearing difficulties. This will prevent the replacement of expensive cables and batteries at a later date.

The power of the beacon should be 5 watts or greater (e.g. Delta Design LT 3x24/5C). Smaller 1 watt and 2 watt beacons (e.g. Menvier MXB124

Figure 13.5
Plan indicating location of visual beacons on a fire alarm system to alert people with hearing difficulties

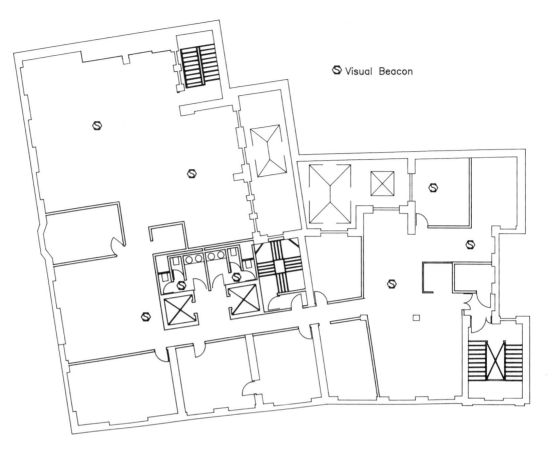

⊘ Visual Beacon

and MXB224) can be used, but only for extremely small areas, such as toilets, where the beacon should be located in the user's line of sight. Alternatively, combined sounder and flash units (e.g. RS Components RS 566-162) may be specified for small buildings and located in corridors, etc. (see Figure 13.5).

Alarm beacons should be sited in high-use areas and located to alert people in office areas. Fire panels and cabling should allow for the installation of extra beacons in offices when specially required. Further information can be found from the Royal National Institute for the Deaf.

Vibrating pager systems

Vibrating pagers are used in a similar system to personal pagers. A central system can be used to alert people with a hearing difficulty in the building (e.g. Micropage 90 from Sound Advantage). The vibrating system should *not* be used as an alternative to the visual system. The system incorporates a pager which vibrates and a central call station which transmits to the pager. The pagers are all alerted by the security/reception area in the event of an alarm.

At present, pagers are not capable of being wired into a building's fire alarm system. They have to be activated therefore by an operator who detects the alarm situation and triggers them. For this reason there is the possibility of human error and cases have come to light (in false alarms) where the pagers were not triggered and the deaf users failed to evacuate the building. Further information can be found from the Royal National Institute for the Deaf.

Domestic use

For domestic use there are a range of smoke warning devices and other devices that will flash lights to warn people with hearing difficulties. It is not recommended that these are used in a commercial or public building. They are available from Connevans Ltd by mail order.

Emergency lighting

Regulations stipulate an emergency lighting level of approximately 0.1 lux at floor level on an emergency escape route. Where the escape route is in a room the lighting level is increased to 0.2 lux. It is recognized, however, that these levels are much too low for certain specialist areas such as old people's homes.

It is also worth noting that these levels will leave people with sensory disabilities without a clear view of the escape route. As a minimum it is recommended that main escape routes be illuminated with a minimum of 10 lux at floor level in emergency situations. As Chapter 15 emphasizes, a toilet should be provided with an emergency light system with an output greater than 1600 lumens.

Personal evacuation plans (PEPs)

Personal evacuation plans are needed for disabled people because their escape from a building is not as straightforward as that for the able-bodied. Perhaps when buildings are designed for *all* people the concept of a 'personal' evacuation plan will not be needed.

A Personal Evacuation Plan is a document and a process that formalizes the escape arrangements that a disabled person and the management need to agree. The document fulfils several roles:

1   It acts as a medium for the disabled person and the management to discuss escape arrangements for that disabled person in different circumstances and locations.
2   It allows the nomination of assistants and people within the area who might assist a disabled person in the event of evacuation and formalizes this arrangement.
3   It acts as a permanent record for a disabled person to refer to if he or she is unsure of his or her escape arrangements and details.
4   It alerts management to any potential areas of difficulty that the disabled person will have before they arise in an emergency.
5   By having a renewal cycle the document ensures that both management and the disabled person are up to date on the escape arrangements.

The last point is essential. While carrying out a fire drill in a large company that had a department with seven disabled employees the employees were asked about their fire procedure. 'We have been told to return to our office and security staff will come and assist us from the building.' When the management were asked they said, 'There is a list of office staff who have been allocated to get them out – we cannot now allow security staff to re-enter a building when it is in a state of alert'. When the list was eventually found it was discovered that over 90 per cent of the staff on the list (by now a few years old) had moved on to other departments in remote areas of the building.

There are several methods for assembling a Personal Evacuation Plan. The Northern Officers Access Group have issued a booklet and questionnaire to assist in the compilation of a plan and recommend involving the local access officer. This is certainly to be recommended where there is any degree of uncertainty. Large organizations would be well advised to employ an impartial adviser to liaise between the management, employee(s) and the fire authorities.

A process that has been found successful in the past is to assemble a small group for a tour of the building and discussions with staff members. The group should consist of the employee(s), the building manager, safety/fire officers and a note taker to record the decisions made.

It is important to recognize that a disabled employee has a right to access all parts of the building (excluding security restrictions). This tour is not to demarcate limits but to record the actions needed to ensure safe escape. All the parts of the building that the employee will use should therefore be toured and at each point the actions for evacuation should be considered: 'What if the alarm goes off and you are here?'

In the office, if there are going to be nominated members of staff to assist disabled people then they should be made aware of this and asked by management, not the employee. Training should then be provided as well as regular programmes of awareness and retraining in methods of assisting. If the member of staff leaves then his or her responsibility must be passed to new members or other members in the office.

A procedure needs to be considered when the disabled employee is likely to be working at times when these members of staff are not present (working late, meal breaks, etc.). The Northern

Officers Access Group recommend five headings:

1 *Location* If the disabled employee uses several different sites, then he or she will need a PEP for each.
2 *Awareness of procedures* The fire procedures must be explained to all employees and, if necessary, made accessible to people with sensory disabilities (e.g. in Braille or tape). The RNIB can give advice in this area, or refer to Brailling in Chapter 6.
3 *Emergency alarm* This section examines the needs of the employee to both hear and trigger an alarm. The issue of sensory disability discussed under visual fire alarm systems is relevant here, as is the ability of a disabled person to activate the break-glass alarm call points as discussed above.
4 *Assistance* This section formalizes the assistance needed and the arrangements made by the management to provide the assistance. This will incorporate the method and type of evacuation, such as whether Evac chairs are to be used, and the training of the necessary staff on them. This section can also alert the need for general principles, such as the procedure in meetings that the disabled employee attends out of the office, and the nomination of staff at the beginning of the meeting.
5 *Getting out* Here the physical nature of the evacuation is discussed in each of the areas of the building and resource implications will be noted. These may include the need to provide areas of refuge, evacuation chairs, escape lifts, etc. It will also point out the need to locate signage to indicate the facilities that do exist. In the past it has proved invaluable for the disabled employee to practise the proposed suggestion to test its feasibility.

If a plan is put together under these headings it should be reviewed at least every six months for the first year after employment and perhaps yearly after that.

Evacuation methods

Assisted escape is often the only way that a person with a mobility or sensory disability can successfully escape from a building. There are broadly two methods of assisted escape for wheelchair users – carrying by others or the use of an evacuation chair.

Evacuation chairs are largely supplied by two companies, Gimson Tendercare and Paraid. Both products work on the principle of transferring the disabled person from his or her wheelchair or walking device and placing him or her into the evacuation chair. These chairs are also recommended by the manufacturers for pregnant women and older people.

There are several difficulties with these devices. They will be likely to be used by people inexperienced in their use; transferring a disabled person from a wheelchair may cause injury to both the disabled person and the assistant; there are grey areas of insurance if an injury is caused while trying to implement this method; the equipment is expensive to purchase, liable to vandalism and removes the independence of the disabled person. Once the safe area has been reached, the disabled person is left without his or her own means of transport.

In buildings that have already installed these devices regular training and consultation must be carried out to ensure their safe use and that the people for whom they are intended are happy about their use. In discussions with many disabled people the reaction has overwhelmingly been in favour of people carrying them either with or without their chair. They were generally not comfortable about the use of evacuation chairs, even in the event of an emergency.

However, there are many buildings where evacuation chairs have been installed. More critical in the effective evacuation of disabled people is the regular training of the people who are going to facilitate their escape. Research by the University of Portsmouth (in *Design for Special Needs 42*) has shown that training and familiarity are critical. During an exercise in evacuating wheelchair users they discovered that evacuation speeded up as the evacuation progressed, reaching speeds of 0.41 metres per second, compared with 0.5 metres per second for ambulant people. This research emphasized the need for regular refuges where the people carrying the wheelchair user can rest without blocking the flow of ambulant escapees. Regular training in the preferred method of escape will improve the speed of evacuation and reduce the likelihood of interfering in the smooth evacuation of the building. Where the user has a power chair it is preferable to remove the batteries and initiate the carrydown procedure.

Research has also emphasized that disabled people are the most knowledgeable about the best means for their evacuation. They should be taught how to communicate this to willing participants so that they are assertive in emergency situations.

Areas of refuge

Areas of refuge are crucial in the modern management of safety for disabled people in buildings. BS 5588 1988, Part 8, Fire precautions in the design and construction of buildings has introduced the concept of escape for disabled people, and the use of areas of refuge, management procedures and evacuation lifts:

> The limitation of distances of horizontal travel for means of escape purposes means that most disabled persons should be able to independently reach the safety of a protected escape route or final exit. However, some disabled persons, for example those who are wheelchair bound, will not then be able to use stairways without assistance, and for this reason it is necessary to provide refuges on all storeys other than those in buildings of limited height.

The key *political* implication of this statement is that disabled people should be given back their own ability to enact their escape procedure from a building, rather than being dependent on other people in the building. (This is discussed later as part of a Personal Evacuation Plan.)

Principles

The basic principle of BS 5588: Part 8 is that an area of refuge is used where people can wait for a brief period, protected from fire and smoke, before receiving assistance to get to a place of safety, usually the exterior of the building. It is an area that is both separated from fire by fire-resisting construction and provided with a safe route to a storey exit (a protected escape route leading to a place of safety), thus constituting a temporarily safe space for disabled persons to await assistance for their evacuation (see Figure 13.6).

A refuge needs to be of sufficient size both to accommodate a wheelchair user and to allow the user to manoeuvre into the wheelchair space without undue difficulty. The *minimum* space provided for a wheelchair user in a refuge, excluding manoeuvring space, needs to be at least 700 mm × 1200 mm, and ideally 900 mm × 1400 mm after including an allowance for manoeuvring and the space needed by the facilitator, if there is one.

The following are examples of satisfactory refuges according to BS 5588: Part 8:

- An enclosure such as a compartment, protected lobby, protected corridor or protected stairway. Figure 13.7 shows a refuge in a complete room, Figure 13.8 the use of a stair lobby to provide a refuge, and Figure 13.9 a lobby being used as a refuge area.
- An area in the open air such as a flat roof, balcony, podium or similar place which is sufficiently protected (or remote) from any fire risk and provided with its own means of escape.
- A protected lobby to a protected evacuation lift, in which the protected lobby is capable of accommodating at least one wheelchair.

The position of a refuge should be such that it does not interfere with the flow of persons escaping (as shown in Figure 13.10). There are many areas that can be converted into areas of refuge. The diversity of the refuge concept means that corridors and stair landings can be used and nominated for areas of refuge, making the concept ideal for installation as a retrofit in a building. (See the case study.)

Figure 13.6
Principles of fire evacuation to BS 5588 Part 8

Figure 13.7
Rooms acting as refuge area to BS 5588 Part 8

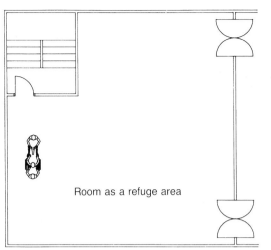

Room as a refuge area

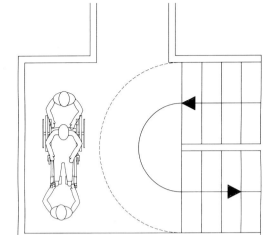

Figure 13.8
Stair lobby acting as a refuge to BS 5588 Part 8

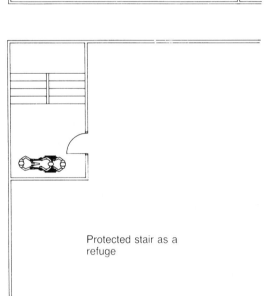

Protected stair as a refuge

Figure 13.10
Refuge area on a stair indicating a clear fire escape route. Scale 1:20

Smoke protection

Smoke is the biggest killer in the event of a fire. The doors surrounding a refuge should be given added protection from smoke as people might be expected to wait in a refuge for up to 30 minutes after activation of the fire alarm.

In a well-constructed doorset, with adequate smoke brushes, the most likely source of smoke will be from under the door. Dropdown smoke seals are installed on the underside of the door so that in the open position the seal is retracted into the door but when the door closes the seal drops down to form a barrier against smoke. These devices do not add to the force required to open the doors, as they retract when the door is opened.

Sound insulation is also provided by the 'Athmer' range from Strand Hardware Ltd, with the double seal DB350 being used to seal a gap in a fire door. These products do not reduce the fire rating of a 30-minute door.

Figure 13.9
Lobby acting as a refuge to BS 5588 Part 8

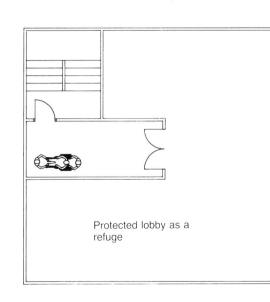

Protected lobby as a refuge

Communications

In addition to the above, BS 5588: Part 8 recommends that all refuges be provided with intercom/handset systems that put them into direct contact with the rescuing agency and/or a central control point. There are several reasons for this:

- The person in the refuge can alert the building management and the fire brigade to his or her presence in the area of refuge and therefore effect the evacuation plan.
- Knowing that the evacuating authority has been alerted is more likely to encourage the disabled person to stay in the refuge, rather than enter the flow and cause a blockage.
- Where there is two-way communication the evacuating authority can provide assurance and updates on how the evacuation is proceeding to the occupants of the refuges, and can prioritize the rescue effort.

At its simplest the communication device can be a hardwired switch system, which illuminates a light next to the fire alarm panel indicating the location of the refuge and the fact that it is occupied. It is important to note that the base station should have the capability to cancel the call so that new calls can be received. When the button is pressed in the refuge there should be a response to indicate that the call has been accepted – either a mild alarm or a visual light. It is important to note that the cable run for these devices should be protected from fire for at least one hour.

More complicated alarms can use wireless systems – e.g. where a toilet alarm system already exists in the building (e.g. the Tunstall Telecom 'Nursecall'), with a base station in the fire control room. These can provide two-way voice communication and automatically indicate the location of the refuge.

Specialist systems are not expensive to create, using the components from door entry systems. The following performance specification illustrates a system retrofitted to an East London community-based building during access improvements over three floors and a basement.

Area of refuge intercom system: performance specification (to be read along with drawings)

Aim

The purpose of the system is to provide warning that the area of refuge is occupied by a disabled person in the event of a fire and two-way communications to coordinate his or her evacuation.

Operation

A person entering the area of refuge may not have enough manual dexterity to continuously operate buttons. Therefore the action of pushing the large pushbutton will activate three features:

(a) Illuminate a high brightness 10 mm LED, preferably flashing, that indicates the floor which is activated on the base station and on the remote station
(b) Activate a warning buzzer in the base station to alert people to activation of the system
(c) Allow communication without further pressing of buttons from the remote station to the base station speaker. However, the base station will only allow two-way communication when the talk button is pressed.

Base station

The action of pressing the push to talk button will cancel the sound and allow two-way communication with the remote station. Pushing of the talk button will not cancel the floor indication button. Activation of another remote station or of a previously activated station will reactivate the call sound and floor light.

Pressing of the reset button on the base station will cancel all calls and reset the lights on the base station and the remote call stations. The schematic design for the refuge system is shown in Figure 13.11. This specification was translated into an 'Aiphone' system adapted by Access Consultants which uses a 10 watt amplification system to allow for the fact that the user might have difficulty in talking close to the intercom, and the fact that the fire alarm bells may be sounding. This intercom is normally used in car park areas, and will therefore serve well in the average building.

Specification

All components and enclosures should give protection to adverse conditions to IP67 because of the likelihood of dribbling and cleaning. All enclosures should be fully grounded and use low-voltage systems (12/24 V).

Figure 13.11
Purpose-built refuge communication system to BS 5588 Part 8

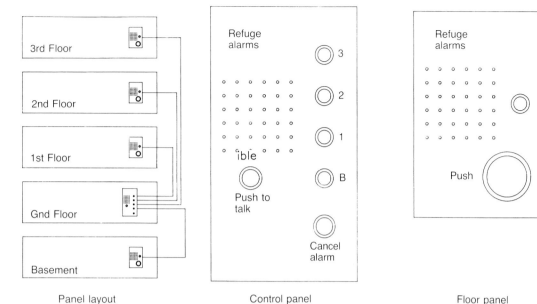

Panel layout   Control panel   Floor panel

Cable

To be provided, approximately 100 metres needed.

Numbers

One base station
Four floor stations, including one outside (basement).

Why create a refuge?

Areas of refuge will protect a disabled person from a fire that has spread throughout a building. The route from the refuge to escape from the building is also protected and this allows the fire brigade or the building's management to use means to evacuate disabled people.

The alternative to this is a disabled person attempting to escape by a normal escape route. The nature of an escaping flow of people is that the flow moves at the pace of the *slowest* person in the escape. At best, this means that the people behind the slowest person are held up in their escape – sometimes with fatal consequences. At worst, people will be held up, in the panic they will force their way past the slow person, causing crush injuries, perhaps death, block the escape route and contribute to the deaths of a large number of people.

Escaping people are often in a state of panic. There are normally large amounts of noise, possibly smoke and fire and generally pandemonium. It is wise therefore to remove slower people from the flow of escaping people but, at the same time, keep them safe and in a location where they can be safely evacuated.

Fire cards

Fire cards/instruction sheets are used to inform disabled people in a building about the facilities that are available to protect their safety and the location of areas of refuge. The cards can be a diagrammatic map of the building to indicate the location of the refuges and simplified instructions for the emergency escape procedure.

Cards such as these can be used in the induction procedure of all staff, fire wardens, first aid personnel and disabled visitors to the building. It is suggested that disabled staff have laminated versions that will have a longer lifetime and that visitors to the building be given the paper version.

Evacuation lifts

Evacuation lifts are not widely in use but reduce the level of physical handling of a disabled person in tall buildings (or anything over two floors).

Details of the design of such a lift can be found in BS 5588: Part 8. An evacuation lift has the following essential features:

1 It is always associated with a firefighting stairwell.
2 Duplicate power supply. Fires are often caused by power supplies. The second supply must be from a separate source that is not likely to be broken by a fire in the primary source. An electrical switch will automatically transfer the lift to this second supply in the event of failure of the primary supply.
3 A switch for transfer of control to the evacuating officer. This switch prevents the lift from responding to the landing pushbuttons. The lift will only respond to the internal control panel buttons. If the lift is not at the ground floor, activating this switch will automatically return it to the ground floor.
4 A communication system (except in two-storey buildings) that informs the car attendant which floor has been activated. The operator can then go to the floor where the person requires evacuation.
5 A fire-resisting shaft to at least 60 minutes should enclose the lift and any accompanying stairway.

The lift should be installed next to or in the core of a stairway to allow the design of refuge areas. The effect of such lifts can be seen to good use in tall buildings such as Canary Wharf at One Canada Square, Isle of Dogs.

The following is an edited excerpt from a talk given by Ms Carla Picardi, Project Executive for Olympia & York Ltd.

This building has 50 floors in total. One central lift, a goods lift, has been nominated for the evacuation of disabled people. The lift is pressurized, to prevent the shaft filling with smoke from the fire. The management of this building illustrates how a lift can be used to ensure the evacuation of disabled people:

Fire wardens know of disabled people in the building as well as those having 'temporary' disabilities. One warden on each floor is solely responsible for disabled people. The wardens will direct disabled people into the area of refuge by the goods lift and communicate with the command centre in the basement of the building to notify their location. Floors immediately above the fire floor are evacuated, with the remaining 48 floors being instructed to await instruction. The two floors on the highest state of alert are evacuated next. The two lifts measure 9000 mm by 3000 mm and the other 3000 mm by 2000 mm. They move at a speed of 1800 mm per second, moving from top to bottom in a time of 52 seconds!

Once the floor is ready for evacuation the lift will be sent from lobby level to collect disabled people. From the lobby they leave the building to a place of safety. All occupants of the building are given a 'Fire and Life Safety Plan'.

This excerpt is used to illustrate that even the tallest buildings can successfully evacuate disabled people using existing guidance material and an effective escape management procedure.

Case study: Fire safety

Client: The Arts Council of England

The Arts Council of England moved from its offices in Piccadilly to a modernized building in Westminster. The move highlighted the needs of its disabled employees and visitors, and especially the requirements for effective escape procedures.

As a part of a large project (see other chapters) the design and functioning of the building was examined to improve the emergency escape for disabled people. The following design adaptations were carried out:

• Installation of visual fire alarm beacons on all floors
• Installation of an area of refuge on the fifth floor
• Installation of electromagnetic holdback devices on large-circulation doors and widening of the doors
• Installation of smoke seals on the doors protecting the evacuation lift
• Uprating of a goods lift to a full escape and evacuation lift, including the installation of a communication system
• Design and implementation of a fire card.

These areas are discussed in more detail below:

- Visual fire alarm beacons were installed as part of an upgrading of the fire alarm system. This necessitated rewiring the whole building and upgrading the power capabilities of the battery back-up and board. It is important to oversupply the power capabilities of the system to allow extra beacons to be installed at a later date and for deaf people to move offices. During the process it was discovered that the 1 watt beacons that had been recommended were not sufficient, and that 5 watt beacons were the minimum power for office areas (see Figure 13.5 for location of alarm beacons).
- At the beginning of the project the fire officer would not allow occupation of the fifth floor by wheelchair users. His reasoning that there were no acceptable routes of escape, despite the low occupancy of the floor, was accepted and a solution sought. Despite the fact that the emergency evacuation lift at the far right of the building penetrated the fifth floor, it would not be advisable for wheelchair users to use this lobby as a refuge, as the stairwell surrounding the lift did not continue to the fifth floor. There was therefore no non-mechanical route to the place of safety. It was therefore decided to create an alternative area of refuge on the far side of the building. The location was housed within the well of the stair which eventually exited to a place of safety. A simple switch was placed within the area of refuge and terminated with a buzzer and light in both the reception area and in a panel installed next to the fire alarm panel. (Figure 13.13 shows the area of refuge with the instruction signs and switch to signal the presence of a disabled person in the refuge.) Wheelchair users are now allowed to use the fifth floor of the building and participate fully in the activities on that floor.
- The installation of electromagnetic holdback devices on large-circulation doors and widening of the doors was necessary to improve the circulation of wheelchair users during normal use of the building. The proximity of the first step and the entrance of the lift, along with the heavy door closer, had been found difficult by the building's users. In consultation with the fire officer the doors were widened and holdback devices installed,

Figure 13.12

Signs for an area of refuge giving instructions on use

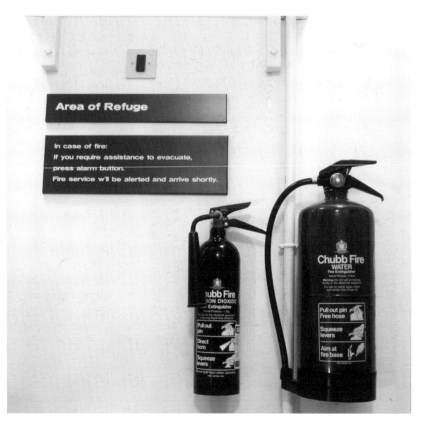

along with their smoke detectors on either side of the door, and wired into the alarm system. When there is a fire alarm in the building, these doors automatically release to provide protection to the lift and stairwell.

- Smoke is the biggest killer in the event of a fire. The doors surrounding the lift well would be protecting an area where people might be expected to wait for the lift for some minutes. It was decided therefore to install dropdown smoke seals to the door so that in the open position the seal is retracted into the door. When the door closes the seal drops down to form a seal against smoke. These devices do not add to the force required to open the doors as they retract when the door is opened. The models used were from the 'Athmer' range from Strand Hardware Ltd, with the double seal DB350 being used to seal the 15 mm gap. These products do not reduce the fire rating of a 30-minute door.
- Uprating the goods lift to a full escape and evacuation lift, including the installation of a communication system, had been partly

achieved by installing lift doors with a one-hour fire rating and the fact that the lift was already enclosed in a one-hour firewell. The lift needed a second power supply, which was taken from a neighbouring substation. This is connected to a 'fallover' device. It the power from the lift's usual source fails, the mechanism automatically switches to draw power from the second source. As many fires begin in electrical areas, the second source must be protected from the first.

Critical to the success of this lift was the installation of a communication system to the lift. An evacuation lift comes under control of the escape landing station and the car. Calls to the lift from floor landing stations have no effect. It is necessary therefore to communicate the presence of disabled people needing to evacuate. In this instance this was provided by means of intercom stations on each landing (see Figure 13.14), and a call indicator/communications panel inside the lift (see Figure 13.15). The important feature of the panel was the facility to merely dislodge the

Figure 13.13
Intercom located 1200 mm AFFL and activated by knocking off the hook

Figure 13.14
Lift car refuge alarm intercom panel

intercom to activate the call light (indicating the floor occupied) and the two-way speech facility. This means that people without the manual dexterity for the use of an intercom handset can activate the panel and hear the response. This system has since been superseded by the type illustrated above, with a simple pushbutton and two-way speaker-box.

- The design and implementation of a fire card is critical to the success of giving disabled people the independence that they deserve, even in the case of emergency. The fire card should contain relevant escape information and any illustrations to help the person understand the escape procedure. It is important for disabled people to know where they can escape and how. This type of card is used in conjunction with Personal Evacuation

Plans to communicate an escape procedure to disabled occupants of the building. The fire cards are kept in the reception area and distributed as visitors arrive. They are also used by fire wardens and during fire escape exercises.

Recommended reading

1 CAE (1992), *BS 5588 Part 8; Part B; and Means of Escape for Disabled People*, Seminar report from Centre on Accessible Environments.
2 Council on Tall Buildings and Urban Habitat (1992), *Fire Safety in Tall Buildings*, McGraw-Hill.
3 Gartshore, Philip and Sime, Jonathan (1987), 'Assisted escape', *Design for Special Needs*, **47**, 6–9.
4 *Guide to Fire Precautions in Existing Places of Entertainment and Like Premises*, HMSO, 1990.

14 Fire doors and other doors

Doors play an important role in access for disabled people. At best, they can allow free movement for disabled people through an area while still providing protection against fire or the elements. At worst, they act as a considerable barrier to disabled people using the building. Not only is the door itself important but so is the arrangement of the door in a lobby set-up and its location on a wall or off a corridor.

This chapter deals with the basic features that make a door and lobby arrangement accessible, and will also discuss door furniture, security systems, electromagnetic holdback devices and the automation of doors to provide mechanical means of overcoming barriers.

Part M of the Building Regulations (1992 edition) states that 'disabled people should be able to use the principal entrance provided for visitors or customers and an entrance which is intended, exclusively, for members of staff'. The features that determine the accessibility of doors include the following.

a standard hinged door, then an approximate measurement can be taken by finding the length between the door stops and subtracting approximately 20–25 mm, i.e. if the between-stops size of the leaf is 765 mm, then the clear open width is likely to be approximately 740 mm. (This is only approximate because the door may be hinged in a way that does not leave the leaf in the door opening.)

There is no *absolute* width to which a door should conform. The sizes quoted are designed to take into account the increasing size of the electric wheelchair types and the greater use of electric doors.

Negotiating a door and the way that it is approached also determines the size needed from the clear open width. Wheelchair and electric trike users will find it easiest to approach a door 'head-on'. Where this is possible, the user will need a smaller clear open width to pass successfully. However, where the user has to turn and negotiate the door from the side he or she will

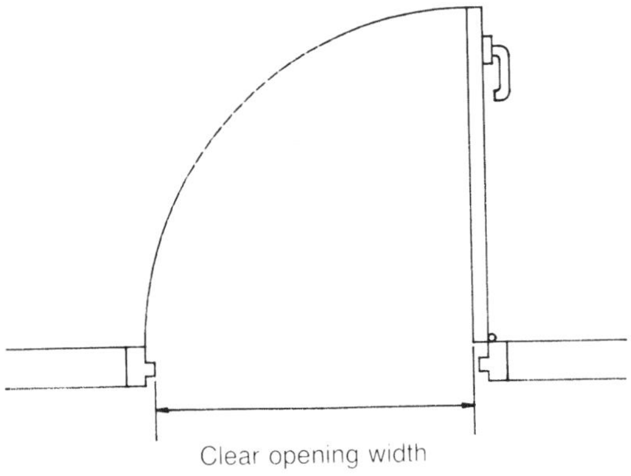

Opening width

Door sets are fitted into structural openings in the wall. The measurements that are quoted when discussing doors will deal with the structural opening, the leaf size, and the 'clear opening width'. It is the clear opening width that is the important factor in the accessibility of a door for people using wheelchairs. It is the actual width that is available to negotiate the door when the door is fully open, and taking into account the door leaf and features such as the door stop and the door furniture. When measuring a door opening, open the door fully and measure the distances between the door stop and the edge of the leaf (see Figure 14.1). If the door is locked, and is

Clear opening width

Figure 14.1

Measurement area for a clear open width on a door

Figure 14.2

Indicating the appropriate door structural opening widths depending on the approach

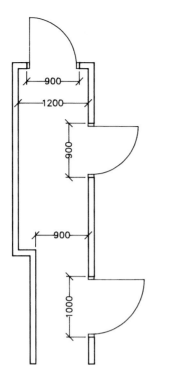

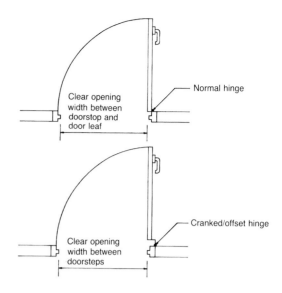

Figure 14.3
Use of a cranked hinge to increase the available clear open width

be part-way through the turn when negotiating the door opening. This door will therefore have to be wider to allow the user to negotiate the door opening successfully.

The critical distinction that determines whether a user is approaching a door 'head-on' is whether the corridor that the door is in equals or exceeds 1200 mm, which allows users to manoeuvre so that they are effectively approaching the opening head-on (see Figure 14.2). In corridors smaller than this there is not enough manoeuvring space to approach 'head-on', and the opening therefore needs to be wider.

Room doorways should have a *minimum* unobstructed opening width of 810 mm (obtained from a 1000 mm single-leaf doorset – actually generating an 850 mm clear open width) when they are in corridors less than 1200 mm wide. The clear opening width can be reduced to 760 mm where wheelchair users can approach the opening head-on or from a corridor wider than 1200 mm (obtained from a 900 mm single-leaf doorset actually generating a 770 mm clear open width).

Cranked hinge

Where a door is already approximately 20 mm below the required clear opening width it is some-

times possible to increase the width by up to 20 mm using a cranked hinge. This removes the door panel from the door opening and increases the width, as shown in Figure 14.3.

Part M

The Building Regulations, Part M specifies an external door width of 800 mm and an internal door width of 750 mm, but in practice these have not been found to be sufficient.

Double-doors

Double-doors in corridors or rooms should have at least one leaf providing a clear opening width of 810 mm *minimum* (provided by a 1.8 m double-leaf doorset). In many openings this means adopting a 'hospital' type of arrangement where one door leaf is larger than the other (Figure 14.4). It is generally preferred when these doors are in corridors that they have a double swing action. Wheelchair users find it much easier to open a door by pushing it with their kickplates or by 'crashing' it at some speed. If the door has an interleaf arrangement then they will have to pull from one direction, which is much more difficult (see Figure 14.5).

Figure 14.4
Door swing types

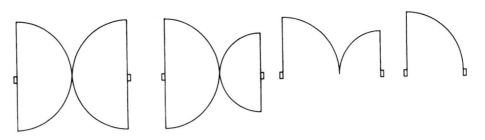

Figure 14.5
Layout of doors in a corridor to provide sufficient handle and opening space

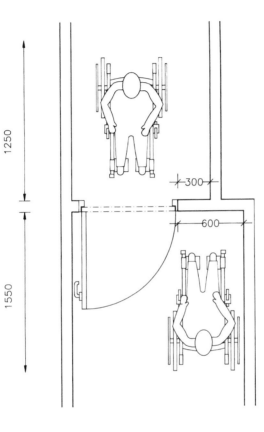

Door lobbies

The dimensions for door lobbies are laid down in Part M of the Building Regulations. They vary depending on the number of doors and the direction of the swing and are designed to allow a wheelchair user to get past the first door before he or she has to attempt to negotiate the second.

Where doors are directly 'in line', or there is a 90° turn, the width of the lobby conforms to the requirement of a 1200 mm corridor. The length of the corridor, between doors, is a minimum of 2000 mm to allow one to get through one door before reaching another. (This is where one door opens into the lobby and one opens out.) Where the two doors open into the lobby more distance is

required between the doors with a lobby of 2400 mm. This length can be reduced by widening the lobby to 1500 mm, giving more circulation space, and reducing the lobby length needed for circulation to 1700 mm.

An important feature of the positioning of the doors in the lobby is that the handle side should have a 300 mm clear space before the wall to allow a wheelchair user to reach the handle. This is because pulling a handle to open the door is easier from the centreline of the wheelchair, and this also allows an easier manoeuvring action to pull the door open than when the handle is next to the wall. See Figure 14.6 for external door lobbies and Figure 14.7 for internal lobbies, which are taken from Part M of the Building Regulations.

Vision panels

Vision panels originally were introduced to fire doors to allow people escaping to see fire and smoke through the fire door and allow them to choose an alternative route. However, they have been found to be advantageous in helping people to avoid collisions when travelling rapidly through doors. Double-vision and single full-length vision panels allow people approaching a door to see wheelchair users and children on the other side at a low level. Providing only high-level vision panels will not allow a person approaching the door to see people below this level, and can cause injury. Vision panels that are centred on the handle side of the door are preferred to the 'porthole' type that are centred on the door, as they offer a greater possibility of seeing people on the other side. Where portholes are important for the design of the building, they should be large enough to provide a good view, and located in the upper and lower halves of the door. (See Figure 14.8 for a summary of vision panel types.) Glass should be

Figure 14.6
*Minimum dimensions
for internal door
lobbies*

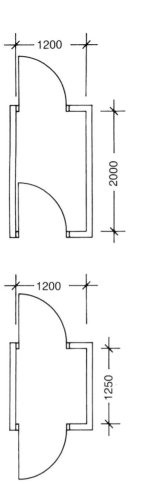

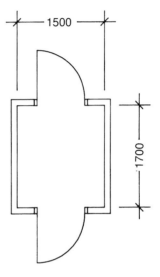

Georgian Wired glass or fire-resistant 'Pyrostop' from Pilkingtons.

Height

Where vision panels are located only in the upper half of the door they should be at least 900 mm AFFL at their lowest point.

Door closers

Time-delay closers

With some doors it is important for a person to be able to negotiate the doors without the doors closing immediately on him or her. This can be achieved with either a slow-closing mechanism, a restraint device, or a delay built into the closer which is configurable. A door closer such as Dorma TS 83 has a built-in delayed closing mechanism. Alternatively, it may be advisable to install a mechanism such as 'Door Dwell' holders. These are suction pads which are fitted to the door and when the door is pushed completely open the suction cup engages. Within a short period of time the suction reduces and the door closer closes the door. These allow the user to open the door and travel through unhindered by the full spring strength. They are particularly recommended where there may be high trolley or wheelchair traffic. On non-critical doors a self-closing hinge will use the weight of the door to provide a gentle closing force and a low opening force to the user. These are not suitable for fire doors or where positive security latching is required.

Opening forces

The force required to open a door is often the single most important barrier on a door once any latching mechanism has been overcome.

Figure 14.7
Minimum dimensions for entrance door lobbies

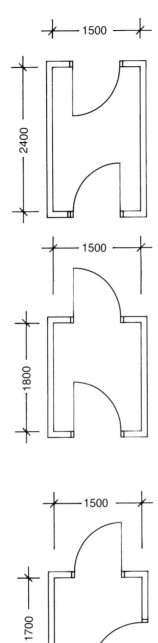
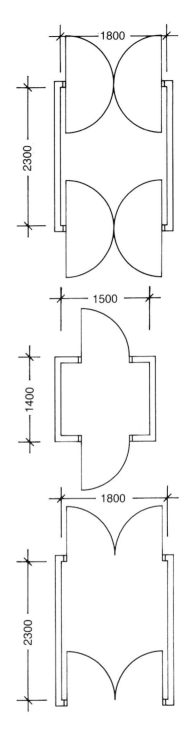

Most disabled people are able to exert approximately 25 newtons both pushing and pulling from a stationary position. Forces lower than this are desirable, but this is considered to be a maximum force for everyday operation of a door. A high spring force on a door closer can render the door unusable by a disabled person. Door springs can be set to well over 100 newtons,

and are frequently installed at their factory settings, which are normally high. Snagging of the door, badly set hinges and improperly fitted smoke seals also add to the initial force required to open a door and may cause significant difficulty to the disabled user.

The recommended force for a door closer should be 25–30 newtons or less. Door closers

Figure 14.8
Door vision panel arrangements

are normally installed for fire protection and security reasons. Where they are installed for fire purposes, the force of the operator should be set at the lowest possible setting while still allowing the door to operate *effectively* as a fire door. Where doors require an opening force of more than 30 newtons to operate effectively (e.g. because of air pressure differentials or the mass of the door), they should be automated or considered for hold-back devices.

It is important to note that a door with a high force, or snagging and rubbing, will earn abuse from its users, and may have to be replaced more frequently than a well-maintained door with a low opening force.

Door furniture

Door furniture normally incorporates a pull handle, a lever latch or a locking mechanism, or a combination of all three. The first difficulty with door furniture is making it visible. The colours chosen should provide a good visual contrast with the door and background colours. Door handles and pull handles should be located at a comfortable height for both ambulant and wheelchair users.

While most door furniture in buildings has a metal component, the nylon- and powder-coated finishes are preferred for their ability to provide a variety of colourways and the smaller 'thermal shock' of use. Older and arthritic hands can seize when they come into contact with cold surfaces. Metal fittings in buildings are extremely 'cold' to the touch, whereas nylon fittings are 'warm'.

Lever handles

Lever door handles are easier to turn and grip than round knobs, especially for people with arthritic hands or limited manual dexterity. These handles can also be operated by elbows or the edge of a hand when carrying bundles. Lever handles should have a return towards the door at the end of the handle, which helps prevent a person's hand from slipping off (e.g. the Hewi zg SR 1113UK). It is preferable with a door handle such as this to specify a rose fitting as this will increase the visual target that indicates the location of the door handle.

Integral locksets inside the door should use as large a twist mechanism as possible for activating the deadbolt from inside the door. Many designs use a small twist knob which is extremely difficult for people with a manual dexterity difficulty. Thumb turns such as those provided on the Hewi '217.31' and '306 NR' should be used. Lever handles should be located at a height of approximately 1000 mm AFFL, and have a minimum cross-section diameter of approximately 20 mm.

Pull handles

Vertical pull handles should be located with the bottom end at 900 mm AFFL with a *minimum* handle length of 250 mm (e.g. Hewi '111.250G'). On doors where no external handle is fitted a door pull should be provided so that the door is not closed using the key.

Pull handle cross-sections should have a minimum diameter of approximately 25 mm, although 40 mm is recommended, and be at least 300 mm long. Handles such as the Hewi '550.33' (300 mm long, 33 mm diameter) or '550.40.360' (360 mm long, 40 mm diameter) are suitable. It is preferable with a door handle such as this to specify a rose fitting as this will increase the visual target which indicates the location of the door handle.

Finger plates

Finger plates should be located between 1000 and 1350 mm AFFL and can incorporate the 'Push' sign at the top of the plate.

Keyhole and lock guides

Guides to assist in the location of keyholes can help people with a visual disability or limited manual dexterity. Products such as the 'Lockmate' from Nottingham Rehab assist in locating the keyhole and holding the lock open. Using lock units that project from the door such as Euro Profile cylinder or Union cylinders will help people with a visual disability to locate the keyhole.

Escutcheons

Brightly/contrasting coloured escutcheons help people with a visual disability to locate the keyhole on a door such as the '306' range from Hewi.

Emergency bolts

Where offices are used as through passageways in a fire route, and an emergency bolt is required, then 'break glass/dome' types should be avoided. 'Slam Locksets' are preferred (e.g. Wellington's Exodus or The Emergency Bolt Company's Cooper Bolt). These systems have large push pads, require no hammer, and can be alarmed for extra security. They offer much less of an obstacle to disabled people than the break-glass type.

Panic pads

Panic pads operate on a similar principle but can make use of existing installations of Yale locks. These are most useful where a Yale lock has been used for security and escape, but the small twist knob is not easily used by people with a disability. The Normbau '9200 Panic Push Pad' has been specifically designed for this purpose, with a 'push' sign on the paddle, and costs approximately £50.

Kickplates

The majority of wheelchair users open doors using the footrests of their wheelchairs. Kickplates not only protect the door but also make opening it easier by providing a surface that the footrest can easily slide along.

Kickplates should be fitted across the full width of a door, made from either aluminium or a tough plastic (such as nylon), and be at least 200 mm high above the floor (as this is the height that kickplates are above the floor), and fitted to the leading edge of the door. Kickplates can be cut to size, such as the Hewi 55 PSB, which is a solid nylon plate and therefore less likely to show scuff marks. Plates should be either drilled and screwed (with countersink dome-head screws) or glued using an adhesive over the complete surface of the plate. Self-adhesive pads will leave the plate proud of the door finish and the plate will eventually loosen.

Rubber surfaces are not recommended as they do not allow the sliding action required by trolleys and wheelchair users, and will show marking from scuff marks. The kickplate should be used to provide colour contrast with the door or the surrounding area.

Signage

Interleaved doors should have signs (i.e. 'Push' and 'Pull') indicating which one to open first on both sides of the door. These signs should be in lettering (upper and lower case) at least 20 mm high. The colour of lettering on the signs should contrast with the background colour, which in turn should contrast with the door colour.

Glass doors

The transparent elements of a structure (e.g. glass doors and full-length windows) are often indistinct to visually impaired people and therefore present a hazard. Large glazed areas should be clearly marked at eye level (around 1600 mm AFFL) to warn people of their presence. Glass doors should be clearly distinguishable from adjacent glazing and also be marked with warning strips around 1600 mm AFFL.

Visual doorbells

When people who are deaf are working in offices they may be unable to detect a knock at the door. Either a hardwired doorbell-activated light can be installed or a portable system, such as the 'Visual Indicator' from Connevans, will alert deaf people to the presence of a knock.

Security systems

Security systems to prevent unauthorized access through a door are becoming more frequently installed. Security devices can be provided from the control of a single door opening to the large-scale systems that take care of upwards of 100 doors across a large site. Broadly, systems divide into those that require physical contact with the security system, card swipes and numerical keypads, to those that operate at some distance, such as proximity sensing devices. The devices that require no contact with the sensing area offer the best alternative for disabled people, as they can be used by people with limited manual dexterity. Other methods should be optimized for

people with physical and visual disabilities to ensure that they can be easily used.

Keypads

Where electronic keypads are used for entering a PIN number they should be of the computer keyboard type (e.g. low-profile Radio Spares RS 664-575). Membrane keypads should be avoided because of their lack of feedback when the button is used. Keypads should be located no higher than 1200 mm AFFL, and utilize keycaps with either white legends on a black cap or black legends on a white cap. Where necessary, specialist keypads can be made up to order by companies such as Access Control who designed the keypad used in the case study below. Keycaps with removable covers were used and laser-printed numerals were placed beneath the keycap. Pressing the key gives positive feedback in the form of a beep.

Proximity sensing access

Proximity sensing access devices operate on an electronic key system where the key is waved in front of a reading pad and activates the door device. New systems can detect the key from several metres away and can operate through glass or even brick. This means that vandal-sensitive electronics can be embedded inside a brick wall or mounted inside a glass area to reduce the likelihood of vandalism. Units that detect for some distance can be used to operate electronic doors without any need to 'show' the key. Wall-mounted sensors should be located approximately 1200 mm AFFL and the colour of the unit should contrast with the background wall.

Card keys

Card keys such as those used in hotel rooms and some office complexes, requiring considerable manual dexterity, high visual acuity or sustained pressure on the key, should be avoided.

Mechanical digital locks

Mechanical digital locks (e.g. 'Unican') should be positioned so that the top button is located no more than 1200 mm AFFL and utilize a lever handle as opposed to a knob. There are a range of easy-to-install electronic door locks such as the 'Omnilock' from Abloy Security, the 'Access-Code lock' from eff-eff available from Viking Security Systems or the lower-cost 'AL200 single door access control', again from Viking, or the 'Electronic Door Lock' from J. E. Reynolds.

Door openers

Automatic and semi-automatic door-opening devices can assist disabled people and remove barriers to others. Automatic sliding doors are preferred to swing doors as they use less circulation space. Sliding doors are preferred for high-traffic entrances, while swing-door openers are preferred within the building. Swing-door openers can be simply retrofitted to most hinged doors. It should be noted that sliding and swing glass doors should not have large expanses of unmarked glass. There should be a warning strip on any glass located at approximately 1600 mm AFFL. The warning strip has to warn clearly of the presence of the glass, but this does not mean that it has to be intrusive. A subtle sandblasted or etched effect can be used with a welcoming message, logo strip or abstract patter. The strip should have an effective depth of approximately 30 mm and span all areas of unbroken glass panels. Applied vinyl such as 3M 'Scotchcal' 'Dusted Crystal' can be used to imitate sandblasting or etching at low cost.

Automatic openers

Fully automatic openers always open the door when the presence of a user is detected. The openers should be capable of high cycle loads over an extended period of time and should have an override switch fitted to maintain them in the open position. Automated doors must be fitted with devices which protect the users from accidental damage and such devices include pressure mats and infra-red sensors. There is a wide range of manufacturers of sliding and swing-door systems, none of which appear to offer any advantages over the other as far as disabled people are concerned.

Semi-automatic openers

Semi-automatic doors are useful in locations where a high force is required for operational rea-

sons (e.g. studio door with magnetic seal), for entrance doors where there is an air pressure differential, or just to facilitate the entrance to an area of the building. In this case large pushbuttons are used, located either side of the door. When optionally activated the door opens, allowing unhindered passage, and closing a short time afterwards.

When specifying semi-automatic closers attention should be paid to the following:

1   Buttons should be located no higher than 1200 mm AFFL, with a press plate no less than 30 mm × 30 mm with the text 'Press' in lettering no less than 10 mm high (caps height). Where possible a larger button, e.g. Lendrums 150 mm diameter pad, with the text 'Push to Open Door' (see Figure 14.9) or the Dorma large 'elbow switch' or 'wall switch', which is a switch up to 800 mm long (variable), should be installed.
2   In the case of fire the operation should automatically revert to door closer function with no automatic operation. This will normally require a fire sensor both sides of the device or connection to the fire alarm.
3   In the case of power failure the opener should automatically revert to the door closer function.
4   Safety devices to prevent accidental injury should be installed (e.g. sensors and barrier rails).

Figure 14.9
Automatic door activation button (150 mm in diameter)

A 'performance specification' is important in the specification of automatic door opening equipment. If a specialist contractor is being used then a specification as in the following case study should be used to ensure that the fittings will perform the function that is desired.

Case study: Automatic door installation

Client: Arts Council of England
(see Figures 14.10–14.12)

Brief: The entrance to the library area also acted as fire separation for two buildings that had been joined into one. When the building was refurbished a set of doors with a lobby had been installed, and infilled with 'Pyrostop' glass from Pilkington. The designer had considered their use by wheelchair users, but had made the 'commonsense' observation that the doors should be as large as possible. Unfortunately, increasing the size of a door with this glass also considerably increased its mass, and therefore the strength needed in the floor spring to return it to its fire-resisting position. This resulted in the doors requiring an opening force in excess of 120 newtons, which is well above the force that can be exerted by a wheelchair user. This pair of doors therefore required automation and needed to provide: fire separation; security separation; and an emergency breakout facility.

Figure 14.11
Large automatic door with an entry keypad and clear signage

Figure 14.10
Automated door lobby system

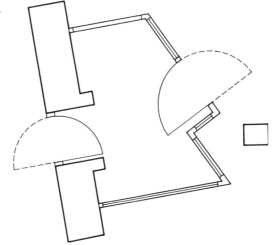

Figure 14.12
Two doors which open simultaneously and use radio-activated buttons

The specification for the automation of the doors was as follows:

Supply and install the following:

1   Two no. Tormax 'TB' swing-door operators with common controls.
    (a)   One unit to be fitted on reception side of outer door (nearest to reception area) with normal power operation into lobby and emergency breakout operation into stair-well.
    (b)   Second unit to be fitted to lobby side of inner door, again with normal power operation into lobby.

2   *Outer floor security*
    (a)   Magnetic fail-safe lock to be fitted to top rail of door, with door pushbutton release to be sited on wall in lobby adjacent to door.
    (b)   Coded digital keypad to be sited (on panel to be provided by others) fixed to glazed screen in stairwell area adjacent to outer door, in exact position to be agreed. The digital keypad to use keycaps with numerals of 10 mm high, black on white background. Pressing of any key to provide acoustic feedback. (See Figure 14.13.)

3   *Safety*
    (a)   Green door release break-glass points to be sited fixed to glass adjacent to items

2b.   This item to be monitored via local low-level audible alarm unit with key override.
    (b)   Fire alarm input connection to be allowed for to cause direct release of outer door lock on fire alarm operation.
    (c)   Two presence detectors to be fitted at high level in lobby area to prevent doors closing on a body or object within lobby.
    (d)   Wireless touch switch to be provided on glazed screen adjacent to inner door to allow normal egress, operation of switch will open both doors.
    (e)   Wireless touch switch to be provided on wall inside the lobby area to allow normal egress from the lobby, operation of switch will open both doors.

Operation sequence of system

Entry
Entry from stairwell via authorized code entry on keypad will cause both doors to open into lobby. If no entry is made into lobby area doors will close after preset period. Once entry is made into lobby both doors will be held in open position by presence detectors. Once lobby area is clear both doors will close simultaneously.

Exit
Operation of wireless pushbutton sited on office side of inner door will cause both lobby doors to open into lobby area. If no entry is made into lobby area doors will close after preset period. Once entry is made into lobby both doors will be held in open position by presence detectors. Once lobby area is clear both doors will close simultaneously.

Emergency
During power failure both doors can be pushed open in direction of escape to front entrance stair lobby. If power has not failed outer door lock will be released by:

1   Operation of green break-glass point.
2   Operation of fire alarm.

This specification has produced extremely effective, if complicated, automation of an extremely difficult lobby arrangement. The design and installation was carried out by Access Control Services from the above performance specification. It is always recommended that a specialist

Figure 14.13
This keypad was specifically made with large, clear, 10 mm high numerals

access control consultant is used for the detailed specification of the automation.

Low-frequency automation

For doors where there will be a low frequency of automation (e.g. a person's office where automation is required) the full power automation device may be excluded because of expense (the average single swing door is approximately £1500). There is a new product on the market called an 'ezi-enter' from Ezi-Line Ltd. This product is a small friction wheel located at the base of the door. Operation of the unit spins the wheel which pulls the door open. Once open, the unit will wait, and then reverse direction to close the door. The unit is powerful enough to overcome most latches and will work on most floor surfaces. In 1995 the unit costs in the order of £195–£495 and for installation, which gives an automatic opener for approximately £700. These units are not, however, recommended on doors where a high traffic level is expected.

Electromagnetic holdback devices

Fire doors are one of the largest barriers to the free movement of people with mobility disabilities. It is desirable, where possible, to restrain the doors in the open position with a mechanism that will release the doors into their fire protection position in the event of a fire.

Electromagnetic door releases are accepted by the Home Office and local authorities and comply with the Building Regulations, Approved Document Parts B2, 3 and 4, Appendix B, 1992. The document states that all fire-resisting doors should be fitted with an automatic self-closing device which is capable of closing the door from any angle against any latch fitted to the door. It also states that where a self-closing device would be considered a hindrance to the normal use of the building, fire-resisting doors may be held open by electromagnetic or electromechanical devices susceptible to smoke.

Electromagnetic door closers should always be connected to the fire alarm system and provision should be made for smoke detectors to be mounted in both of the compartments separated by the door to which the door closer is fitted.

Electromagnetic releases should not be fitted on stairwell doors.

BS 5588: 1988: Part 8 also makes provision for the installation of hold-open devices with the following wording:

> Means of holding any door open or of overriding the self-closing device may be provided by a hold-open system incorporating an automatic release in compliance with BS 5839: Part 3. The automatic release should release the doors to close automatically in the event of each or any of the following:

1 The detection of smoke by suitable automatic apparatus
2 Failure of power supply
3 Operation of the manual fire alarm system or automatic fire alarm system
4 If the facility is provided, manual operation at a central control point.

The mechanisms are available in two forms; independent electromagnetic holders with a catch plate located on the door, which hold the door in the open position, such as the Tamtec FSDH24 door release unit, the Menvier MDR24L door release unit or the Dorma 'EM' range; as an integral part of a door-closing device which permanently holds the door in the open position, such as the Jebron 'Series 7000' door closers. Dorma offers a comprehensive range of door closers with electromagnetic hold-back features that allow the closers to work with rebated meeting stiles and door selectors such as the 'EMF/S' range. They also have a 'swing-free' device, which is a door closer that allows the door to operate without any closing force until the door-closing unit is activated by the fire alarm or the smoke detection units, when the spring power is restored (e.g. the Jebron 'Series 7000' door closers and the Dorma 'EMF' range). Dorma also offers a unit (the 'EMR') that has an integral smoke detector built into the unit. These will operate as a hold-open, swing free and can also coordinate another door closer on a second closing leaf.

In the case of a fire, when doors automatically close, it should not take more than 25–30 newtons to reopen a door. Thus door springs should be adjusted to accommodate this while allowing for effective closure of doors.

Door thresholds

Door thresholds exist to provide a weather barrier to sound, air or fire, but may also effectively provide a barrier to disabled people. The most difficult barriers are large, sudden thresholds or deep and invisible weatherbars. The ideal threshold is a completely flush entrance.

Where there is a desire to prevent water penetration a 1:60 fall is recommended in front of the door, with a slotted drain in severe conditions. The maximum door threshold recommended in most guides is 15 mm. However, even a 10 mm threshold can effectively bring the modern sports chairs to a halt and tip out the occupant. There are several products on the market to provide a completely clear threshold. The Wellington 'Visitability Threshold' has a mechanism which flips up when the door is open, leaving a clear threshold, but the action of closing the door seals the underside of the door, preventing any water penetration. The 'Raven RP3' lifting flap seal from Lorient Polyproducts (see Figure 14.14) also provides a low-cost seal that comes into contact with the ground only when the door is closed. This will work on a door up to 1200 mm wide. Threshold seals that are designed to keep out driving rain include the Sealmaster 'BD' range which caters for inward- and outward-opening exposed and sheltered doors. Lower-tech seals provided by the Athmer TS 205 are designed to seal against the door and are a rubber blister construction which seals up to 13 mm high gaps. For a more positive seal the Athmer Threshold Tilt Seals TSA 380 and the TSV 381 provide a positive sealing action.

Obviously all these seals will only perform well if they have been located in a relatively sheltered area, so the design of porches and canopies as well as effective drainage should be considered in conjunction with seal design.

Acoustic seals

Studio doors which require an effective studio seal are traditionally sealed with magnetic strips similar to fridge magnets, which increase the opening force required for the door to approximately 120 newtons. The magnetic seals also cause noise as they positively act to seal the door.

The alternative to the magnetic seal is to use a 'crush' seal and a dropdown acoustic-type seal. The mechanisms are noiseless in operation and offer a good acoustic performance. The 'Raven' RP47 and RP10 from Lorient provide the crush seal element of the design, with the RP8 and RP38 self-lifting seals providing a barrier-free acoustic seal from within the door or surface-mounted on the edge of the door for retrofitting.

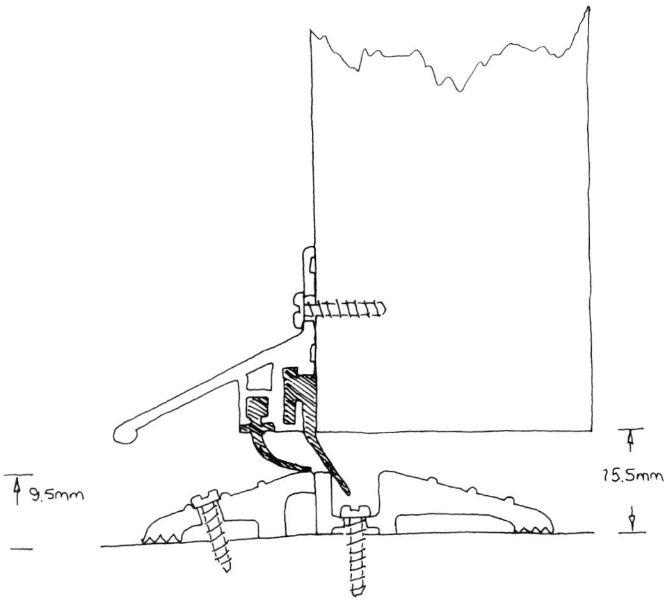

Figure 14.14
Door threshold system allowing wheelchair access and keeping out water

9.5mm

15.5mm

Surface-mounted doors

Occasionally, where there is an existing opening that will not allow the installation of a doorset and provide adequate clearance, it is possible to install a surface-mounted door. This may exist in buildings where thick walls would have a prohibitive cost attached to widening the opening. The opening must comply with the clear width that is required of the clear open width of the doors as above, and the door frame is then built onto the door opening to provide the full opening of the structural opening. (See Figures 14.15 and 14.16 for the layout of surface-mounted doors.)

It should be noted that the fire officer should be involved in agreeing the design of the door, and that the door frame and door may need to be fitted with intumescent strips.

Figure 14.15
Surface-mounted door arrangement making use of the full structural opening width

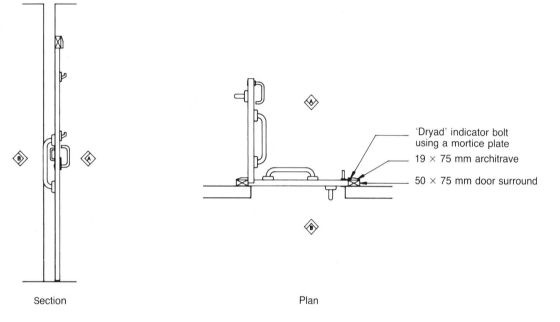

'Dryad' indicator bolt using a mortice plate

19 × 75 mm architrave

50 × 75 mm door surround

Section   Plan

Figure 14.16
Surface-mounted door elevations

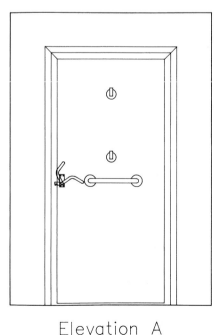

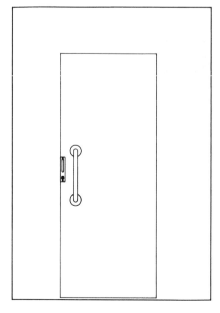

Elevation A   Elevation B

15 Accessible toilet, bathroom and shower design

Introduction

This chapter provides a guide to the design and fitting of accessible toilets to comply with the Building Regulations 1991, Approved Document, Part M 1, 2, 3 and 4 which came into effect in June 1992. The second half of the chapter deals with extension from the principles of the general toilet area to look at shower/bathrooms in bedrooms and shower/bathrooms in theatre dressing rooms.

The toilet facility in a building is extremely important – it may determine whether a building is truly accessible to a disabled person or not. This chapter is one of the longest in the book. This emphasizes the importance of the design of toilets, and in particular the attention which needs to be applied to detail, as it is this that makes the toilet accessible.

Toilets for disabled people should be referred to as 'accessible' toilets rather than 'disabled' toilets as the latter all too often refers to the functionality rather than the target user group. Part M of the Building Regulations gives the basic dimensions for the layout of an accessible toilet. However, in the many toilets that have been seen in the process of making buildings accessible to disabled people, the majority of which complied with the basic requirements, few were accessible to the group of people at whom they were aimed.

This chapter will examine how disabled people use the toilet, which determines the design and the 'performance specification' of the products that are selected for the design. It should be remembered that the spatial layout implies that these toilets are used only by wheelchair users. These toilet areas are, in fact, used by people with extremely wide-ranging disabilities, and our conventional view of a wheelchair user is not the correct target user.

Distribution

There is no standard for the numbers of accessible toilets per hundred of building occupation as there are with able-bodied people. The only reference to the distribution of accessible toilets is in Part M of the Building Regulations which states that the number and location of accessible toilets should allow *horizontal* travelling distances of no more than *40 metres* from the workplace. Single-sex toilets can be on alternate floors, as long as lifts are available and the *total horizontal distance* does not exceed 40 metres. This is often satisfied by a single unisex accessible toilet located on the ground floor next to the lift lobby, regardless of the numbers of people that occupy the building or the effectiveness of the lifts.

Gender

Where there is only a single accessible toilet then it is important that it is unisex to allow a facilitator of the opposite sex to enter the toilet with the disabled person. The person facilitating a disabled person is often a spouse or friend of the opposite sex who would find it difficult and embarrassing to have to enter a toilet area for another sex. The ideal situation is to have a number of unisex toilets as well as accessible cubicles integrated into the main toilet facilities in a building.

As a guideline, there should be at least one unisex accessible toilet in a building, with another one sexed toilet per hundred staff, i.e. if there are a hundred staff, fifty men and fifty women, there should be one unisex accessible toilet and one male and one female toilet. The toilets should be logically located on the floors where the main toilet facilities are located, with a unisex toilet in the

Figure 15.1
Most common transfer arrangements for wheelchair users onto toilets

lobby area at reception to serve visitors to the building.

To complicate this slightly, toilets are left-handed and right-handed (depending on the location of the pan and the transfer space – this is discussed in more detail later). There is a preference in the UK for right-handed toilets, but, where possible, it is worth installing both a left- and a right-handed toilet in the building to cater for people's preferences.

The aesthetics of accessible toilets is as important as that of any other toilet, although for some reason this tends to be forgotten. There are many hotels with the most sumptuous of toilets and bathroom suites, high-quality finishes and gold-plated taps – yet a journey into the accessible toilet in an equivalent suite reveals a toilet bowl perched on an enamel plinth in a sea of quarry tiles, with enough chromium grabrails and padded cushions to fit out a gymnasium. The small sink is normally fitted with an inadequate spray-head tap and an undersized bar of soap. Accessible toilets do not have to appear 'medical'. They can, with thought and attention to detail, have the same standard of finish as the rest of the facilities in order to achieve integrated use.

Where space allows, a full range of baby-changing facilities can be incorporated into the toilet area. This will, no doubt, earn the condemnation of some groups of disabled people who wish to reserve accessible toilets for disabled people only. The issue of a 'RADAR' key is discussed later, but the basic principle is that all toilet facilities should offer some level of access, and that any feature that encourages a greater usage by a wider range of people will ensure that the facility exists, that the door will not be locked, that the facility will be clean and well stocked, and that it is less likely to end up as a storage space (this is the favourite resting place of the majority of 'disabled' toilets). More of this discussion later.

Basic principles

This chapter will discuss the basic principles that determine the layout of a toilet designed for disabled people. The information is intended to inform designers so that they can understand the functional layout of the toilet and can adapt the design to cater for the installation of toilets in non-uniform spaces. (It is rare to find the spaces drawn in books like this in real buildings!)

Use

The use of the accessible toilet is what determines the layout of the cubicle. Figure 15.1 summarizes the types of transfer that are used by a wheelchair user to get onto the toilet. Bear these manoeuvres in mind as you read the information on the layout of fittings and fixtures.

Dimensions

Layout requirements are largely determined by wheelchair use and the ability to manoeuvre. This produces a toilet with the minimum internal cubicle dimensions of 2000 mm × 1500 mm. (**Note**: these dimensions are minimum and should not be reduced.) There are many types of wheelchairs and wheelchair users with a wide range of mobility and muscle strengths. Wheelchair users may also have facilitators to assist in the use of the toilet, and they need the space to move around the wheelchair users.

Users

The choice and layout of fittings is arranged to facilitate transfer from a wheelchair onto and off the toilet *independently*, or allow room for the facilitator to manipulate the person onto and off the toilet, or allow an ambulant, but unsteady, user to stand and use the toilet.

Layout

The layout of the space and fittings around the pan should enable users to wash their hands and themselves *from the pan* and dry their hands or themselves *from the pan*. This is important; if the user has become soiled on the pan, then he or she does not want to remount the wheelchair to get to a handbasin thus soiling the wheelchair. Nor does the user want to push a chair, with wet hands from the sink, to the hand drier on the other side of the room. Achieving the correct location for all these requirements requires careful and precise thought, and is the reason for stressing the degree of detailing that has to go into making a usable toilet area.

The handbasin should therefore be within reaching distance of the pan (200–300 mm) with hand-drying towels close by. Hand towels are the principal method for drying hands that should be reached from the sink – there simply is not enough room to install a hand drier in this space. (Figure 15.2 shows how the positioning of the hand towel too far forward can unbalance the disabled user – possibly causing them to topple off the toilet.) The electric hand drier should be positioned so that it can be used by the person resting their elbows on the handbasin. This will primarily be used once the user has re-entered his or her wheelchair or by ambulant users of the toilet.

Doors

The entrance to the toilet area is important, in size, method of opening the door and location within the room. Further and more detailed information on door designs is located in Chapter 14.

Lobbies

Lobby entrances to toilets may be required to protect the inside of the cubicle from the view of passers-by and to act as sound and smell barriers. Where used they should comply with the minimum dimensions specified in the drawings, with a minimum lobby dimension of 1500 mm by 1800 mm. Where possible, the external lobby door should be replaced by an offset entrance/vanity wall arrangement, so that there is only one door to pass but clear vision of the cubicle is restricted.

Vision panels

The outer door of the lobbied area should have a full-length or double-vision panel to avoid the danger of collisions, as specified in Part M of the Building Regulations.

Types

Doors present the disabled user with a serious barrier to the toilet. Heavy and heavily sprung doors require a pull strength which many wheelchair users do not possess. Sliding doors, on the other hand, offer a wide and unobstructed pathway, but glide rails require a fair level of maintenance and never really provide a feeling of security which is a vital component in a successful toilet. The sliding door also creates a large amount of noise and in general presents more difficulty to the user than a hinge swing door.

Door swing

The direction of door swing has implications in respect of fire, space and emergencies. From the space and emergency point of view it is beneficial that the door opens outwards from the cubicle area. The door swing does not then restrict the amount of internal circulation space, and if someone falls inside the toilet they will not block the opening of the door.

Where the door is going to open into a corridor it will be necessary to discuss this implementation with the fire officer responsible for the building. The general rule of thumb is that the accessible toilet has few combustible hazards contained in it, and will have, at most, two occupants who will be escaping through the door. It is advisable to hang the door so that it swings shut with the flow of escaping people.

Inward swing

Where the door is designed to open into the cubicle there is a danger that the user could collapse behind the door and prevent the door from opening. In this case a door pivot set and removable door stop should be used. The door stop is removed from the outside of the door and the

Figure 15.2
Reaching for a distant hand towel can overbalance the user

lock activated using the coin release. The door can then be swung out of the toilet area, releasing the occupant.

Door pivot sets and removable stops are available from the 'Helping Hand Hardware' by Wellington, reference 8080 for the pivot and 8081 for the removable door stop (see Figures 15.3 and 15.4).

Size

A 1000 mm wide doorset is highly desirable to generate a clear open width of 810 mm minimum (in fact 850 mm generated by a 1000 mm doorset). This can be replaced by a 900 mm/914 mm wide doorset (generating a clear open width of approximately 770 mm), but only where the external and internal circulation spaces exceed the minimum specifications. To allow a wheelchair to make a 90° turn, the door should open fully into a corridor which has a minimum clear width of 1200 mm.

Door symbols

Symbols should be at least 100 mm high and positioned on the opening face of the door at 1370–1525 mm AFFL. Raised symbols are ideal and should contrast (in hue) with their background. Symbols such as those available from Hewi, '710.150.1.skz Male'; '710.150.2.skz Female' and the '710.150.3.skz Disabled', have a 'plump' Germanic appearance, but are the only raised symbols that clearly differentiate the toilets and can be felt by people with a visual disability. They are available in a wide range of colours. (See Figure 15.5.)

At present there are no adequate symbols for indicating unisex or family facilities. It is suggested that a group of symbols, male, female and wheelchair, be used to indicate that the facility is available to all, as shown in Figure 15.6.

Door signs

Symbols should be supplemented with text (e.g. 'Toilet', 'Female', 'Male', 'Unisex', etc.) in upper- and lower-case lettering, at least 25 mm high. The colouring of lettering on signs should contrast with the sign background colour which in turn should contrast with the wall/door upon which it is hung. Signs should be located 1300–1600 mm AFFL.

Kickplates

The majority of wheelchair users open doors using the footrests of their wheelchairs. Kickplates not only protect the door but make opening it easier by providing a surface that the

Figure 15.3

Specialist removable door hinge system for use in case of collapse in a toilet area

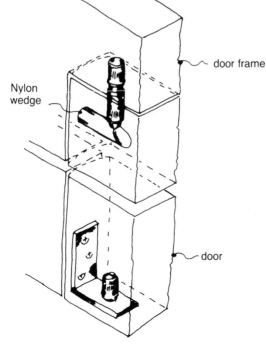

Figure 15.4

Removable door stop to open the door in the case of collapse in a toilet area

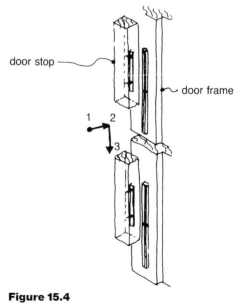

footrest can easily slide along. Where possible, the kickplate can be used to colour contrast with the door. Kickplates should be made from either aluminium or a tough plastic (such as nylon), be at least 200 mm high and fitted to the faces of the door that will be used for opening (e.g. Hewi 55PSB cut to size).

Door closers

In general, accessible toilet doors are unlikely to require door closers from a fire point of view, as there is seldom a risk from inside the toilet area – this should be discussed with the fire officer. However, as most accessible toilets open straight onto public areas it is recommended that door closers be installed. Where a lobby arrangement exists then door closers should incorporate a timed delay into the closing mechanism. This allows the user to open the door and pass through unhindered. Without such a delay the door closer can prevent the user from entering the toilet. Models on the market such as the Dorma TS 83 have this function. Spring pressure should be set to the lowest adjustment needed to close the door (i.e. no more than 30 newtons required to open the door) and the latching function of the closer should be disabled, as there should be no latches on the door to overcome.

Figure 15.5
Accessible toilets should be available to all and use all toilet symbols

Figure 15.6
These tactile door symbols contrast with the door and signface

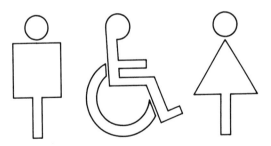

Pull handles

A pull handle is used to open the door against the closer. It should be of a contrasting hue to that of the door colour and located at a height which is comfortable for both wheelchair users and ambulant people (i.e. approximately 300 mm long and located between 900 mm and 1200 mm AFFL).

A vertical pull handle is physiologically easier to use than one positioned horizontally (e.g. pull handles such as the Neaco DF 5781 or the Hewi 550.33 or 550.40.360 with a BA1 or BA6 fitting). The handle should be fitted with roses to increase the visibility of the handle and improve its appearance. The Hewi handles are preferred because their nylon coating has a better feel for people who are sensitive to cold surfaces, and is resistant to a harsh environment (such as found in pub toilets) and attack from cigarette burns.

Door locks

The lock to the toilet door is often cause for concern for disabled people, as many of the locks used on conventional toilets require a large amount of manual dexterity and strength to operate. Disabled people often find themselves locked into cubicles through poor specification of the locks.

There are locks on the market produced by the 'RADAR key scheme' and available from Nichols and Clark. It is worth stating at the outset that these locks have not been found to be beneficial in use. They are designed to reserve accessible toilets specifically for disabled people, who can obtain keys directly from RADAR (a national charity for disabled people). The lock itself is not easy to use, having a stainless steel finished handle with no return into the wall, a difficult locking mechanism and low reliability with extended use – for the high price of £70. However, the main objection is that a large percentage of disabled people who could benefit from the toilet do not have a key and have to find someone to open the toilet. Because the toilets are used by so few people they tend not to be cleaned, maintained or restocked with paper and soap on a regular basis, and are eventually reclaimed for storage cupboards. The aim of this chapter is to produce a design of toilet that can be used by disabled people, parents with babies and others, which will be well used, cleaned and maintained, and available at all times. While it is recognized that there are difficulties and shortages of disabled toilets it is felt that an integrational response is to pressurize management to provide a larger number of better-designed facilities rather than reduce the use of the few that currently exist. There are exceptions to this – primarily where it is likely that the toilet will frequently be occupied by people for the purposes of changing or other activities.

There are few door locks which fulfil the performance specification for the wide range of people that will be using this toilet. There is a need for the door lock to be simple, have large, easily moved lever handles, as opposed to the small knobs and levers, and be operable by elbows, hands and chins. There should also be a coin release and a model in the range to cope with sliding doors where they are used. There are two which do: the 'Facility Indicator Bolt' (Ref. 37651) from Albert Masterson/Wellington which has the required functionality but not the aesthetic appeal (being brushed steel with sharp lines); and the 'indicator bolt B67 MP or RP' from Dryad Simplan. This product offers all the functionality required and is available in a wide range of powder-coated colours. A warning to contractors, though: the bolt must be ordered in good time as delivery times can be variable from Dryad Simplan, who deal direct rather than through a distributor (see Figure 15.7).

Colouring

The decoration in the toilet area is important for people with a visual disability. Many toilet areas have a strong approach, with dark wall tiles and light fittings that produce a dark area for other users and inadequate design for people with visual disabilities. More subtlety can be employed using 'bands' of dark tiles against a light background to assist such people. The key element of the 'banding' is to use the coloured band of tiles to indicate the location of the fittings. Particularly successful has been the design illustrated here, where tiles from H and R Johnson are used with the main white tiles being 'SF 17A Satin White Glaze' and bands of 'MG 76 Cobalt Blue Plain Gloss' size 152 × 152 × 5.5 mm. The blue tiles are used to indicate the location of the floor and the fittings, so that white fittings are used against this blue band. The satin glaze is impor-

tant to reduce the level of glare, and the gloss finish on the blue tiles accentuates the difference from the white. This tile arrangement is illustrated in Figures 15.8 and 15.9, showing the location of the coloured tile bands. Figure 15.10 shows an effective use of contrasting tiles and flooring. Figure 15.11 shows a more subtle approach to contrasting colours and an accessible vanity unit, Figure 15.12 the use of contrasting fittings in a bedroom bathroom with a shower tub, which is not as effective as contrasting tiles. The alternative is to use a dark grabrail against a light tile background, although this does not provide as effective a visual contrast for people with visual disabilities and the tile band is preferred.

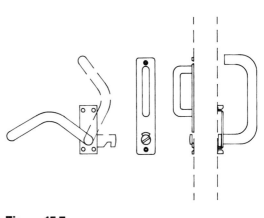

Figure 15.7
Dryad Simplan indicator bolt door lock is easy to use

Flooring

The flooring in an accessible toilet should provide a non-slip surface in a wet area. The floor surface colouring can provide further guidance to people with a visual disability by providing an inlaid strip of a contrasting colour. Vinyl flooring such as the Altro 'Designer' range can be used, with colour contrast produced by using the light colour 'Marguerite ASD25 415' inlaid with the darker-coloured strip made up with 'Midnight ASD25 421'. The flooring should be hot-welded and laid according to the manufacturer's instructions. The floor should be formed into a cove to allow better cleaning and a clear indication of the barrier between the floor and walls.

Sanitary ware

The sanitary ware used in the toilet area is again important. The WC needs to be well fitted to provide stability for people transferring their full weight across and onto the toilet pan. There is not a wide range of colours available in the pans that are recommended, and these should be selected for the aesthetic appeal of the toilet – to match other suites in the hotel or building and

to work well for people with visual disabilities. Where white is used (which is by far and away the most common colour, and therefore the easiest to obtain), note should be taken of the colours recommended for the wall and floor tiles and coverings.

Figure 15.8
Toilet layout showing tile arrangement to improve access for people with visual disability

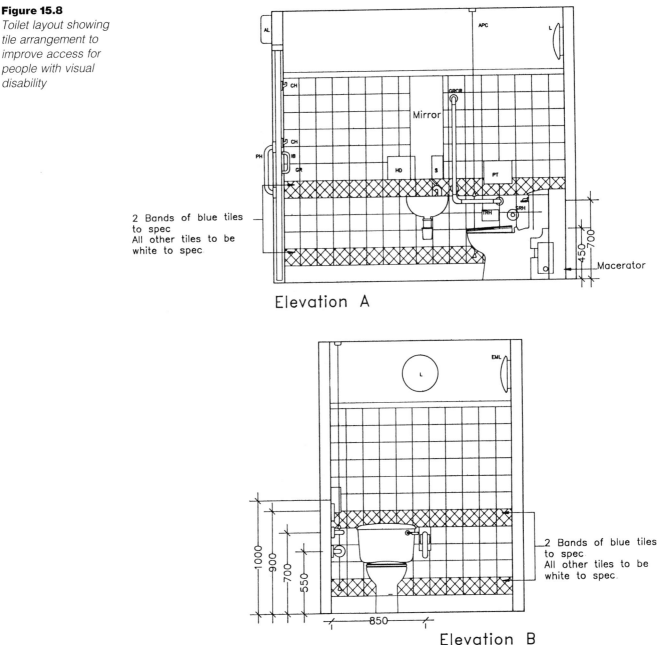

2 Bands of blue tiles to spec
All other tiles to be white to spec.

Elevation A

2 Bands of blue tiles to spec
All other tiles to be white to spec.

Elevation B

Figure 15.9
Toilet elevation showing arrangement to improve access for people with visual disability

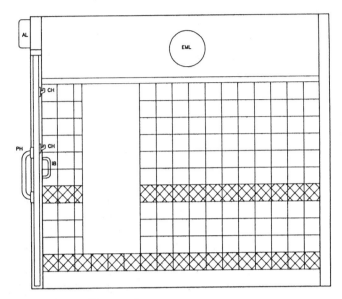

Elevation C

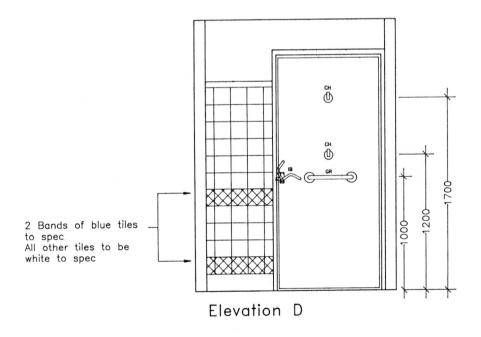

2 Bands of blue tiles
to spec.
All other tiles to be
white to spec

Elevation D

Figure 15.10
This toilet illustrates how a strong use of colour can assist people with visual disabilities

WC pans

The revised version of Part M of the Building Regulations (1991) has changed the minimum required pan height, to the top of the china, from 425 mm AFFL to 450 mm AFFL. However, there are currently no toilets on the market which satisfy this requirement. (**Note**: The Department of the Environment have agreed that the seat height can range between 450 and 475 mm as an amendment to the 1992 edition of Part M.)

The only product which complies with (pre-1991) the requirement of 450 mm to seat height is the Twyfords Avalon WC Suite. This product appears considerably more expensive than other alternatives. However, the screwdown cistern lid saves on the installation of grabrails and has vastly superior aesthetics to the alternatives. The 'Avalon' also has the capability of being fitted with seat heights that vary up to 3 inches and are easily removed with a coin from the top of the pan for thorough disinfecting and changing seat heights.

Figure 15.11
This composite of an accessible toilet shows the use of subtle colour

Figure 15.12
This slipper bath uses contrasting handrails to give the space contrast

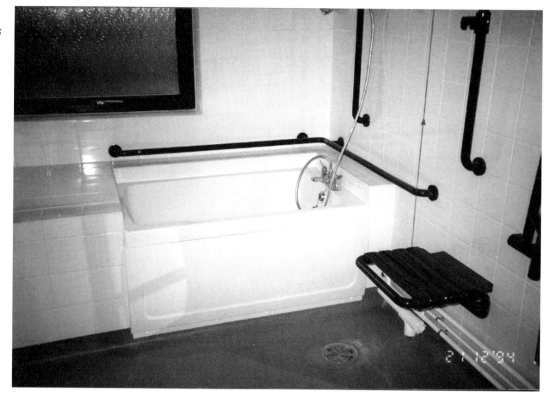

This toilet suite is strongly recommended, but the alternatives are outlined below for consideration and a demonstration of impartiality. However, it should be clear that none of these solutions fulfil the full requirements of an accessible toilet area, whereas the 'Avalon' does. The toilet types are illustrated in Figure 15.13.

Twyfords Avalon WC

A recent addition to the Twyfords range, in the shape of the Avalon suite, presents a good option. The Avalon is a close-coupled WC, obviating the need for a backrest. The white version comes with a screwdown cistern lid, which is recommended in accessible toilets. It is not recommended that the Part M pack is purchased (unless the budget is *extremely* tight), as this contains unsuitable hinged support rails, sink and tap. (**Note**: when ordering the white cistern with the screwdown lid, the lid and bracket must be specified – part No. 12986 WH9 for the lid and 64920 XXO for the bracket.)

Wall-hung pans

Wall-hung pans (e.g. Armitage Shanks 'Melrose') will achieve a variable seat height. These pans are an 'off-the-floor' type and the user may experience movement in the frame as the seated position is adopted. Reports from disabled people using this solution are that they feel insecure, and heavy use can lead to breaking of the seat, which is then difficult to replace. Therefore, if the toilet is going to be heavily used by disabled people a floor-mounted pan is recommended.

Pedestals

Alternatives to the above include the mounting of a pan, which does not have the desired seat height, on a pedestal. The pedestal should be constructed so as to fully support the pan and be durable enough to withstand any movement of the pan and a damp environment. In any event, the pan should be elevated to achieve the specified seat height of 450 mm AFFL. It should be noted that the Armitage Shanks 'Contour 2' is shown achieving the correct seat height in their 'Blue Book' section on accessible

Figure 15.13

Toilet pan types showing their relation to a wheelchair height and width

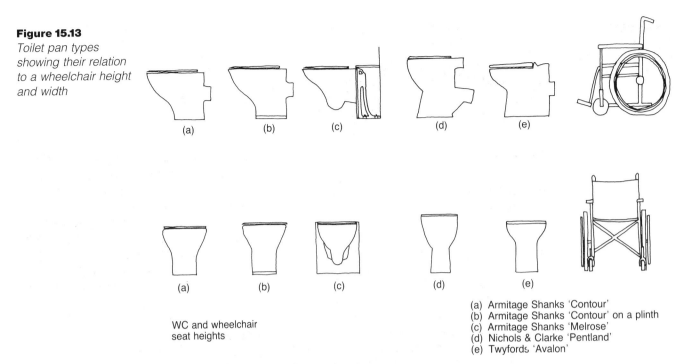

(a)   (b)   (c)   (d)   (e)

(a)   (b)   (c)   (d)   (e)

WC and wheelchair
seat heights

(a) Armitage Shanks 'Contour'
(b) Armitage Shanks 'Contour' on a plinth
(c) Armitage Shanks 'Melrose'
(d) Nichols & Clarke 'Pentland'
(e) Twyfords 'Avalon'

toilets. However, in their catalogue it is clear that this height can only be achieved using a plinth of some sort. As this normally only becomes apparent on-site the toilet is either installed too low or with a 25 mm piece of marine ply cut roughly to the plinth shape. This is not recommended. The rear boxing required by the Armitage Shanks solution produces a toilet of low aesthetics and a cleaning problem, as well as increasing the cost of the installation.

Cistern

The cistern should be low-level and preferably close-coupled to the toilet. Where the cistern is low-level a back-support rail should be used. Cisterns should be front-mounted, as this offers up the flush lever in an optimal position. Concealed cisterns are not recommended, except where aesthetics dictates.

Flushes

Lever flushes should be of a spatulate nature, e.g. those by Nichols & Clarke P.68308.11, or more highly recommended is the Thomas Dudley Dimple Lever (as supplied with the Twyfords Avalon suite). The lever should be positioned where it can be pressed by the user from his or her wheelchair, i.e. located between 700 and 900 mm AFFL on the wheelchair side of the pan (see Figure 15.14). Figure 15.15 shows the degree of flexibility needed to access a toilet flush that is located on the wrong side of the cistern and uses a high-level cistern.

Lids/seats

Seats should not incorporate lids, as they may interfere with transfer from the wheelchair to the pan (and vice versa), and generally get in the way (except in the case of the Twyfords Avalon). Open front seats are not recommended, nor are seats which have pronounced contours. These may present difficulty in rising from them and tend to squeeze the buttocks closed – hindering defecation rather than helping. They are designed to stop the user from falling off, but they are also uncomfortable for other users and are likely to discourage people from using the toilet.

The seat should be easy to remove from the toilet top (as in the case of the 'Avalon') so that it can be thoroughly cleansed, and should be well secured to be able to take the sideways forces that result from someone transferring across onto the seat.

Figure 15.14
Toilet lever handle from Dudley's which is extremely easy to use

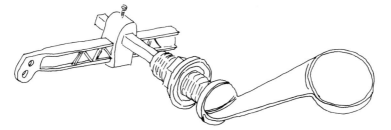

Position

Positioning of the pan is crucial to the operation of the room as a whole:

- The front edge of the pan should be positioned 750 mm from the rear wall. This dimension remains the same whether the cistern is concealed or front-mounted. This dimension allows for effective side, oblique and assisted frontal transfer.
- The pan is set centred 500 mm from the side wall, leaving a clear 300 mm between the wall and the pan (to allow for assisted transfer). This space is effectively reduced to 215 mm by the depth of the grabrails on the wall (grabrails project approximately 85 mm from the wall). This is illustrated in Figure 15.16

Figure 15.15
Placing a toilet flush behind the user makes it extremely difficult to flush

where the facilitator is being pushed forward by a badly fitted toilet dispenser and toilet pan. (**Note**: The use of a large toilet roll dispenser on this wall is not recommended because it reduces the standing space for an assistant between the wall and the pan. With this arrangement the assistant has no space to distribute his or her weight and may drop the user, or suffer injury.) (See below.)

Transfer space

There should be approximately 900 mm between the pan and the far side wall. This space is vital for effective lateral (side) transfer from a wheelchair. This area must not be occupied by bins, which the user would have to move before he or she could manoeuvre into the space.

Handbasins

In general, it is preferable to specify the handbasin from the same chinaware manufacturer as the cistern and pan. This will ease the ordering, delivery and discount process for the contractor. The requirements for the sinks are discussed below.

Position

The handbasin positioned close to the toilet is expressly for washing from the pan. It should be located 900 mm from the rear wall of the cubicle. Part M of the Building Regulations specifies that it should be 1000 mm from the rear wall, which is too far for someone with anything but the highest mobility to reach but is designed to protect the assistant's space. However, if the products specified here are used and located correctly the sink can be positioned close enough for comfortable use and ample space provided for the facilitator.

Figure 15.16
Large fittings mean that a facilitator has to bend dangerously over the toilet pan

Size

These handbasins are not required to be large as there are likely to be other washbasins in the area for general washing. Handbasins may be partially recessed (e.g. Twyfords 'Parmis') although these should be rarely used as they cannot take the taps recommended.

Waste plug

Because of its singular function, it is normally recommended that the handbasin does not have a plug or pop-up waste, so that it will not overflow in the case of accidental filling or slow tap control.

Tap holes

Handbasins are normally recommended with a single tap hole on the side closest to the pan. Suitable basins include the Armitage Shanks Dorex Code 12015L and 12014D (the right-hand-only version has been discontinued, therefore use model 12015N and block off the extra tap

hole with a sealed-in ceramic plug – Twyfords (VC 4907 WH)) and the Twyfords Sola 380 (WB 2515 WH or WB 2516 WH) with a plastic 'P' outlet (WF 8439XX). The basin should be sealed all round to the tiles with silicone sealant. It is not recommended to use a central tap hole sink, as the tap will be too far to be reached from the toilet. Moving the sink close enough to be reached will then reduce the space needed for an assistant next to the toilet.

Taps

The taps used for the sink are important so that people can use water from the toilet pan. They should clearly indicate the hot and cold selection and preferably be a mixer type so that both the hot and cold water are available from the seated position.

Ideally, control of the tap should be with a lever, such as the KWC Vita-Duo Code K12 T1 21 A150 and the RWC 'Starmix Taps MIXT 120 001'. Where there is a high level of vandalism the mixer lever is probably at risk. In this case it may be wise to use a hot and cold water tap. The hot water tap should be located closest to the pan (subject to the temperature control discussed below). The tap head should be of a short lever type such as the RWC 'Galaxy LTAP120' range or the Nichols & Clarke 'Phlexicare Novaturn tap P.63490.11'. These are one-quarter-turn ceramic block taps which will be easier to operate than a standard tap head.

Water temperature

It is essential that water should not be delivered hotter than 40°C. Because of concern over the threat of *Legionella* in hot water systems, and the consequent increase in the storage temperature of hot water, scalding from high-delivery temperature hot water has become increasingly likely. Scalding can occur from water delivered at the 55°C that is required for protection against legionnaires' disease. In fact, water temperatures up to 80°C have been measured in buildings, and the water is delivered through the taps at this temperature. Health Note No. 48 recommends that the delivery temperature of the hot water be considerably below that of the storage temperature. Although there are no legal guidelines to the delivery temperature, any scalding from the water could bring a prosecution under the health and safety legislation. Placement of a sign reading 'Beware Hot Water' is not sufficient.

For these reasons, it is important that the mixer tap has some form of temperature control built in to avoid the possibility of scalding. Both the mixer taps KWC Vita-Duo Code K12 T1 21 A150 and the RWC 'Starmix Taps MIXT 120 001' have a temperature control built in. The RWC is British-manufactured and costs approximately £80 and the KWC is Swiss and costs approximately £150. However, it should be noted that neither of these taps have a no-flow protection on the cold supply. Therefore if the cold supply fails then the hot water will be delivered at full temperature. Care against such a failure should therefore be taken in the building or an in-line temperature controller as discussed below should be used. Both taps are in heavy demand and should therefore be ordered early to avoid delay.

Where several sinks are involved or the design necessitates the use of hot and cold delivery taps an in-line mixer should be used as long as the distances to the basins comply with Health Note No. 48. A product such as the RWC 'Heatguard Highflow' will protect the taps against failure of the cold water supply and should be set to deliver the temperature to approximately 40°C. This unit can supply more than a single basin as long as the regulations governing the supply distance are followed.

Spray taps

Spray heads to restrict the flow of water are not recommended as they seldom allow enough water to flow to draw the hot water. They also provide insufficient flow for efficient washing of hands and tend to deposit water over the toilet area.

Fixtures and fittings

Fixtures and fittings found in the toilet area are more important in terms of functionality than aesthetics, although the latter is also important. The following discussion of fittings, and their selection for discussion, is the result of the assembly of a 'performance specification' and a search of existing equipment manufacturers. The products are measured against the performance specification and only those that provide the performance required are selected. At the same time, the pro-

ducts are considered against cost and likely lifetime expectations, which will be discussed later in this chapter.

Grabrails

Grabrails should project no more than 85 mm from the wall surface, allowing a hand to grip the rail well but not encroaching into the space required for assisted transfers and to avoid blocking access to the tap lever on the handbasin. IEE regulations (REG 471-35) state that: '. . . in a room containing a fixed bath or shower, supplementary equipopotential bonding shall be provided between extraneous conductive parts'. This is required in case the screw fittings for the rail penetrate electrical cabling, or come into contact with reinforcing rods in the wall that might be touching electrical fittings. Insulated rails, because they do not represent such a hazard, do not require earth bonding, thus saving cost on installation and reducing the likelihood of unsightly surface bonding where the cable is not hidden. Rails of this type include the Eclipse range of Southern Sanitary Specialists and Hewi's range of nylon grabrails. The Hewi range is particularly recommended because of the thickness of the nylon and the strength of the rails. Earth bonding is required where stainless steel or chromium-plated rails are specified. However, due to the clinical appearance of these rails, they are not recommended.

Incorrect fixing of grabrails is the most common cause of failure. When using rails, people place their full weight on them and fixings experience a large dynamic load. It is recommended that fixing be according to the manufacturer's instructions. It is important to note that different wall construction will require different fixing types. In a stud wall a support plate or extra studs may be required around the rail fixing points, while aerated blockwork may also need support plates and resinbonded anchors.

Hinged support rails

When selecting a hinged support rail, attention should be paid to the degree of wobble in the rail when in the lowered position. The rails are there to provide a feeling of security as well as support. Any 'wobble' will reduce the effectiveness of the rail.

Hinged support rails fall into two categories: those which require an upwards lift to activate the downwards action and those that are held by balancing springs or weights. Those requiring an initial upwards lift to activate are made from either aluminium (e.g. the Neaco Hinged Rail 750 mm DF6106) or steel (e.g. the Southern Sanitary Specialists Hinged Arm Support SSG26.3). The upwards lift is not achievable by a large number of disabled people, reducing considerably the use of the rail to those that need it most. Hewi (e.g. the 33.3081.80) produces a hinged support rail that is held in any position by a counterbalancing spring. The rail requires a light finger pull to lower it into the using position and a similarly low force to return it into its stowed position. Additionally, this rail can be twisted to the right or left to stow flat against the wall to create more room for a lateral transfer from the wheelchair located beside the pan. In this side position the rail is also locked in the upper position, acting as a substitute for the upright rail.

Hinged support rails are the most prone to breaking their fixings as they support a person's full body weight at the end of their length. Where the wall fixing is not strong (such as those built of lightweight, aerated or hollow blockwork) then systems such as the Southern Sanitary Specialists Rigibeam RB1 or Hewi Wall Mounting Plate 33.3081 WPN should be used.

Toilet roll holder

The toilet roll holder should allow effective use with *one hand* without the need for high manual dexterity (e.g. Hewi '450' or Neaco 'DF 5926') or long reach. Large industrial dispensers that use a plastic cover and a serrated edge for ripping the paper tend to leave the paper end high inside the dispenser, out of reach and surrounded by the sharp serrated plastic edge (a sort of mechanical Rotweiler!) illustrated in Figure 15.17. These large dispensers, positioned on the wall next to the pan, reduce the standing space for an assistant. With this arrangement the assistant has no space to distribute his or her weight and may drop the user or suffer injury to his or her own back.

Only the small individual toilet roll holders are recommended because of their functionality and lack of bulk. Toilet roll holders should be located on the side wall closest to the pan, within reaching distance of the pan.

Because these holders do not have a large capacity the use of a spare roll holder is essential. This should be located close to the toilet and be spring-loaded to allow use or storage of a spare roll (e.g. Hewi 455).

Soap dispenser

The type of soap dispenser used will depend on the company that supplies the cleaning and maintenance of the toilet area. Soap dispensers come in all shapes and sizes, and they all have different soap bag/pouch manufacturers.

Soap dispensers should take into account the fact that users of these toilets may have limited manual dexterity and therefore would experience difficulty in using a press button type dispenser. It is recommended that the dispenser either uses a pull lever type or has a large lever to allow the elbow or fist to be used (e.g. Nichols & Clarke P.68342.01). The Cannon Hygiene 'PressPack' has a large blue press and low pressure requirement and is available from Cannon even if you are

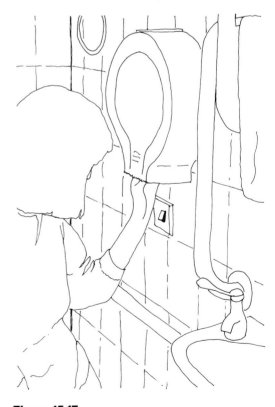

Figure 15.17
Toilet roll dispensers with sharp serrated edges are difficult to use

not a user of their services. The soap dispensers produced by DEB are good, except that they do not provide buttons that are colour contrasted from the body of the soap dispenser and a 'push' label is recommended to be stuck on the button.

Paper towels

Paper towels are important in an accessible toilet because they provide the means for drying hands from the toilet pan. The individual towel dispensers are preferred as they are easier to use than the large rolls of towels with the serrated teeth. The container needs to be of a slim design as the space where it is located is needed for the assistant during lateral transfer. Either the Mölnlycke 'Tork' range C-box dispenser or the Kimberly-Clark 'Kleenex Hand Towels' snap-shut controlled dispenser (No. 4403) in white should be used.

Alarms

There are four basic types of alarm:

- A *local unit* external to the toilet area which, when activated, emits sounds and light to attract attention from passers-by
- A system which is *hardwired* from the toilet area to a *centralized control point*
- A system which uses *radio transmitters* to activate a *centralized control point*
- Either of the *centralized* versions which offer the facility for *two-way speech*.

Local units, such as those available from KRS Electronics, CTS Security, and Impulse Engineering, offer the cheapest solution but have the least guaranteed response. The external unit, powered by either mains or battery, utilizes a range of flashing lights and sounders to alert passers-by. The nature of this alarm is that it relies on the goodwill/capability of passers-by to respond appropriately to an alarm call. There is a danger with these systems either that alarm calls will go unattended or they will evoke an inappropriate response. However, they are recommended in a small building where a caretaker or warden is within hearing range of the alarm. The unit by Emergilite 'helplight' has been found to be particularly successful and produces an acceptable

sound output with the possibility of a remote indicator added to the system. The reset button should be located near to the light switch no higher than 1200 mm AFFL.

Both the hardwired and radio systems feed into a staffed centralized area. Activation of the alarm will signal the toilet where assistance is sought. The alarm response procedure can then be put into action. With these systems it is essential that the staff are taught how to respond to an alarm call and that a protocol is developed. Without this, the alarm becomes ineffective.

Radio alarms, such as the 'Nurse Call' system available from Tunstall Telecom, allow swift, cable-free installation. The central base will indicate the location of the toilet alarm and a member of staff will be dispatched to investigate. Radio alarms offer the flexibility of being easily moved and supplemented with extra transmitters, and offer a reduced installation cost.

Hardwired systems, such as those available from Audio Communications, offer a low-cost, permanent installation, recommended where only a few toilet alarms are connected to a centralized alert panel. Centralized panels commonly have to be manufactured for the specific application.

Both radio and hardwired systems offer the opportunity for voice communication between the alarmed area and the centralized base. Therefore the base unit can ascertain the nature of the call and reset false alarms without dispatching staff and reassure the caller during the response period. Most manufactured alarm systems offer some of the facilities required but will, in most cases, have to be modified on installation – primarily in the use of activation switches listed below.

It is important when the alarm is activated from within a cubicle that there is both visual and auditory feedback. This could be from an announcer outside the toilet and an internal light indicator or from an internal buzzer (quiet) and light indicator (e.g. KRS Electronics Ltd Individual Alarm System).

Alarms should be located so that assistance can be summoned both from the pan and from the floor if someone has fallen from the pan or wheelchair. Alarms should be positioned on the side wall nearest the toilet pan at 900 mm AFFL, 750 mm from rear wall and on both side walls at 200 mm AFFL, 1600 mm from rear wall.

Alarms should be wired to slave switches around the toilet area, with the alarm mechanism acting as a base station. (Poorly designed alarm activation switches tend to be of the push-to-break variety, have a small visual target value and require a high pressure to activate.) Where pull cords are used the cord should be red with red acorns positioned at 900 mm and 200 mm AFFL on the cord (e.g. Crabtree Capital 6900/1RD cord and 7410/WH acorns).

Switches

Large, easy-to-push rocker switches are recommended (e.g. Tenby Multigrid 2005 and Harmony 7914 ranges). Clipsall offer a large rocker switch 'EP31A' which has a red switch unit inserted. This is a 'special' and should be ordered in good time. It is vital for people with a visual disability that the alarm switches are clearly marked and in contrast with their surroundings (e.g. MK Accent, which combines a choice of coloured front plates and coloured switches).

Light switches

Light switches are preferably the pull cord type located close to the front door and use white cord and white acorns. Where wall-mounted switches are used they should be located no higher than 1200 mm AFFL and should use contrasting switches. The switchplate should contrast with the wall colour, and the switch itself should contrast with the switchplate. This can be achieved with the black and white of the MK Accent which combines a choice of black front plates and switches, or the Clipsall range of light switches 'E31/1/25A' which come in a large range of colourways with the faceplates interchangeable with the switch mechanism. For example, the switchplate could be dark blue and the switch unit sparkle blue, giving an effective contrast from two blue components.

Reset button

There should be a reset button, or pull cord, for the alarm located within the cubicle (for local, radio and hardwired non-talking alarms).

Instruction signs

Internal

An important feature of pressing an alarm switch is to know the response and the likely response time. In order to comply with these requirements each alarm switch/pull cord should be clearly signed as follows:

Alarm
- Press/pull for assistance
- Bell will sound
- Help will arrive within 5 minutes
- Help will enter at your request

Lettering on the signs should be at least 15 mm high for the title and 10 mm high for the body text, upper and lower case, and either white on a red background or red on a white background (depending on the contrast with the wall). These signs should be located above alarm switches or next to pull cords as appropriate.

There should be an instruction sign outside the cubicle for people answering the alarm. Instructions should read as follows:

Toilet alarm
- If toilet alarm sounds
- Knock on door
- Wait for request before entering

Lettering on the signs should be at least 15 mm high for the title and 10 mm high for the body text, upper and lower case, and either white on a red background or red on a white background (depending on the contrast with the wall). Signs should be located immediately adjacent to doors at approximately 1370 mm AFFL.

Vanity units

Vanity units are frequently found in large toilet areas and supplement the hand-washing function of the handbasin in that they are used for other vanity functions. An accessible vanity unit is created by allowing a wheelchair user to get as close to the vanity unit as possible, ensuring that feet, knees, armrests and hand reach are taken into account. To achieve this, the following features should be incorporated (see Figure 15.18).

Washbasins

Washbasins should be located as close to the front edge of the counter as possible or semi-recessed into the counter-top, and incorporate pop-up waste and overflow (e.g. Twyfords Olympian 635 semi-recessed, Armitage Shanks Concept semi-recessed, Armitage Shanks Orbit counter-top).

Taps

Taps which limit the temperature of delivered water below 40°C present a large lever handle with the full range of water temperature and water pressure available throughout the lever movement (e.g. KWC Vita-Duo K12 T1 21 A150 and the RWC 'Starmix' taps).

Drinking-water taps

Drinking-water taps allow easy filling of vessels either through their location on the vanity unit or by use of an extending spout (e.g. KWC Domo and Vita-Duo ranges). These taps should be clearly indicated with a sign using 20 mm high lettering.

Soap dispensers

Liquid soap dispensers which conform to the discussions above should be located with the outlet point no more than 450 mm from the front edge and approximately 100 mm above the counter-top.

Vanity mirror

Part M of the Building Regulations 1991 recommends that a vanity mirror should be positioned to give an all-round view, with its bottom edge at 900

Figure 15.18
Details of vanity unit layouts for wheelchair users

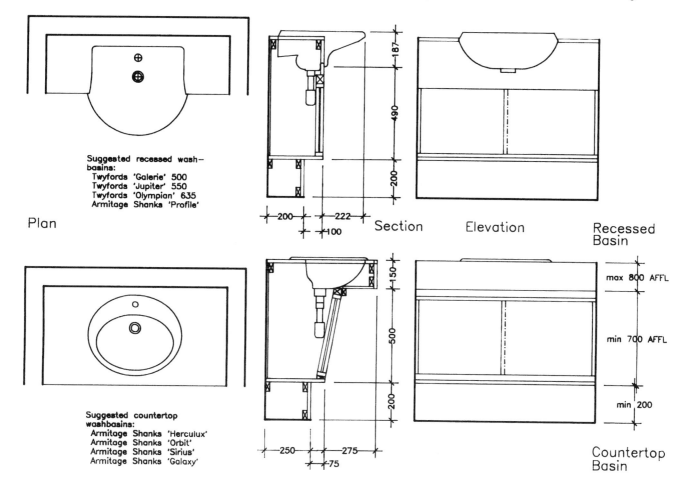

mm AFFL and top edge at approximately 1800 mm AFFL. However, the high positioning of the lower end of the mirror at 900 mm AFFL will not allow wheelchair users to view the lower half of their body. It is therefore suggested that a mirror 1500 mm long is installed, with the lower end located at 300 mm AFFL and the upper end reaching 1800 mm AFFL as recommended in Part M. The 300 mm clearance should allow safety from damage, for example, kickplates. Mirrors should be polished on all edges and filled with a moisture-resistant backing. For screw-fixed mirrors fixings should be capped with domed screw covers.

Miscellaneous

- *Coathooks* There should be coathooks available for both ambulant people and wheelchair users. They should be located at 1200 mm and 1700 mm AFFL (e.g. Hewi 520.50.1 or Neaco DF 5921).
- *Walking stick/crutches hooks* Such hooks are useful as a place to rest walking sticks or crutches while using the toilet to avoid the need for a person having to reach down to the floor to retrieve a fallen stick. Hooks should be located within reaching distance of a person seated on the pan but not interfere with the transfer space required around the pan.
- *Shelves* These should be at least 150 mm wide but no more than 600 mm wide (e.g. for baby-changing benchtop), ensuring that wheelchair access is not impeded by the shelf. They should be positioned between 700 mm and 800 mm AFFL. Shelf-support systems should be as concealed as possible to avoid snagging wheelchairs (e.g. Cliffhanger Shelf Grip). The colour of the shelf should contrast with the surrounding area.
- *Hand driers* These should be automatic in their operation when the hands are placed beneath them. They should be located no higher than 1200 mm AFFL. There are many products on the market, such as the Airstream '5000ST' and the Redring 'Autodry 100 – 56-750521'.
- *Bins/sanitary disposal units* Care should be taken to ensure that the smallest bin possible is used and that it is maintained in a position which does not restrict access to the toilet

from either side. Sanitary disposal units should be positioned as close as possible to the pan without restricting access to the pan.
- *Lighting* Light levels in the toilet area should be no less than 100 lux (measured on the seat of the toilet). The illumination should be even, and designed to avoid glare (e.g. diffused fluorescent or diffuse low-voltage lighting).
- *Emergency lighting* This should be provided in the cubicle, and in any lobby area, to provide a minimum of 10 lux of illumination for a period of no less than 1 hour. Where the emergency light is being added as a retrofit a non-maintained unit such as the Menvier 'Kwicklite 8 NM/3' or the 'Squarelight'. Where the toilet is a new fit-out then it is useful to install the emergency light as a maintained light which is switched to use as one of the toilet lights. The Menvier 'Squarelight' SPQ S/3 has a light output which will light a toilet if located centrally, or the Marlin Lighting 'Opaline' 325 mm diameter maintained emergency light can be used, but should be supplemented with a second, non-emergency unit for effective light levels.
- *Dispensing machines* These should be chosen for ease of use – as few levers as possible, electric operation, coin slots rather than trays, and delivery points and coin slots close together. Coin slots and delivery points should be located between 800 and 1000 mm AFFL.
- *Baby-change units* These facilities are becoming increasingly popular in toilet areas in hotels and restaurants, leisure areas and, more recently, in the workplace. Accessible toilet areas represent a useful place to install a baby-changing unit, as it will then also be accessible to parents who are disabled. There are few purpose-made baby-changing units on the market, but the one that currently satisfies the requirements is produced by Magrini, the 'Baby Nappy Change Unit' Model KBCS, which is only produced in beige. To ensure access for wheelchair users the unit should be located so that the lower surface of the unit, when opened, is located at 750 mm AFFL to give clearance to wheelchair armrests. The unit should be located close to the sink so that water can be reached without letting go of the baby.

Figure 15.19
Accessible toilet showing the layout of fittings and the use of coloured tiles with a baby change unit

All the above features are summarized in Figures 15.19–15.26.

Costs

As a part of a national costing exercise carried out for a client in early 1994 several specifications were put out to tender to suppliers such as Travis Perkins and Yannedis as well as the manufacturer. The point of the exercise was to justify the 'dream' specification combining Hewi and Twyfords products, as it was felt that they would probably be more expensive than other options.

Three comparisons were carried out using combinations of Hewi and Twyfords, Hewi and Armitage Shanks and Dryad Simplan and Twyfords. The comparisons surprisingly showed that the preferred 'dream' specification of the Hewi and Twyfords products was the lowest price, with a complete toilet fitting pack costing in the order of £1074.90. For large projects there were considerable discounts to be had for ordering multiples of ten of the products. These figures did not include the discounts that are passed on

to some account holders from different suppliers (see Tables 15.1–15.3 for figures).

More recent assessment and respecification of some of the products such as substituting the RWC tap for the KWC tap will reduce the cost further, as will substitution with other hand driers.

The general principles set out in the sections on the design and installation of accessible toilet areas can be extended to the design of combined toilet/shower bathrooms found in small bedrooms and theatre dressing rooms.

Bedrooms

Small bedrooms such as those found in colleges and halls of residence intended for wheelchair users should have en-suite bathrooms for disabled people. The bathroom should contain an accessible toilet, a shower tub and the facility to have a shower in a shower chair or seated on a fold-down seat.

Figures 15.27 and 15.28 illustrate the design of a small en-suite bedroom toilet/shower and 15.29 and 15.30 the general layout of a small shower/

Figure 15.20

Plan and elevation of an accessible toilet with Twyfords and Hewi fittings

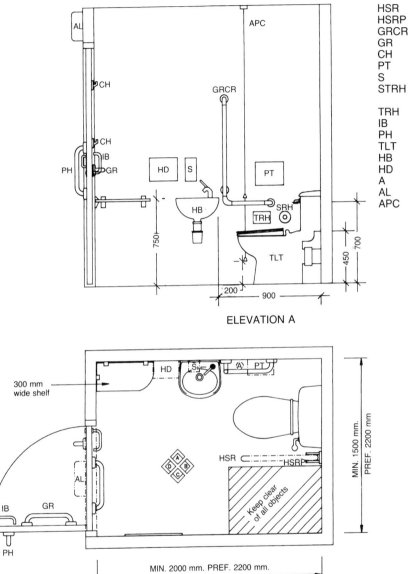

HSR	Hinged support rail
HSRP	Support rail wallplate
GRCR	Corner grab rail
GR	Grab rail
CH	Coat hook
PT	Paper towel holder
S	Soap dispenser
STRH	Spare toilet roll holder
TRH	Toilet roll holder
IB	Indicator bolt
PH	Pull handle
TLT	WC pan
HB	Hand basin
HD	Hand drier
A	Alarm
AL	Alarm light
APC	Alarm pull cord

ELEVATION A

FLOOR PLAN

Figure 15.21
*Elevations and plans
of an accessible toilet*

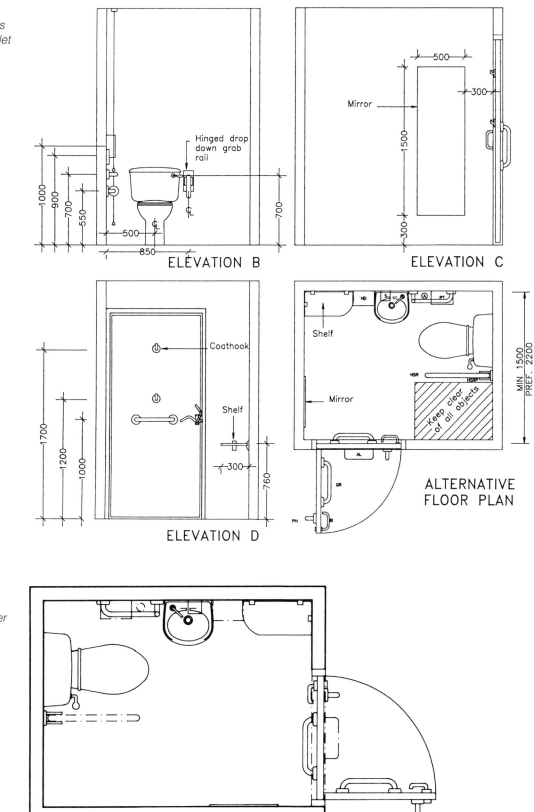

Figure 15.22
*Plan of a left-hand
transfer layout rather
than a right-hand
layout*

MIN. 2000 mm. PREF. 2200 mm.

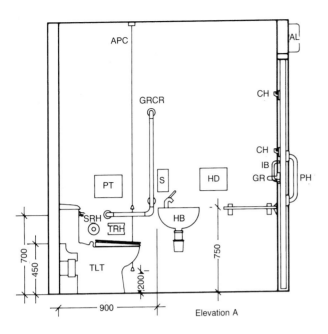
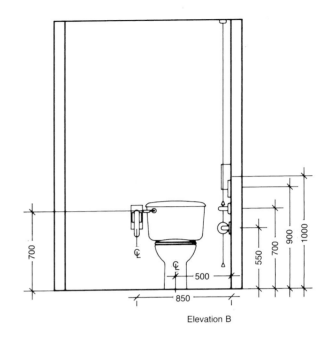

Elevation A

Elevation B

Figure 15.23
Elevations of a left-handed toilet

Figure 15.24
Plan of a unihanded accessible toilet which can be used on either side

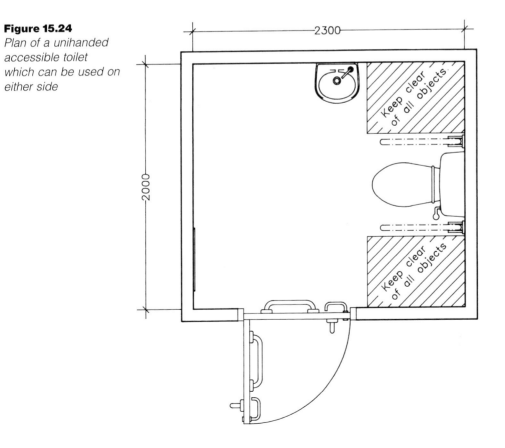

Figure 15.25
Elevation of an accessible toilet with a baby change unit

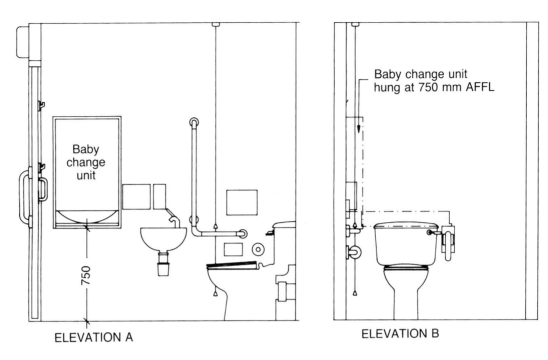

ELEVATION A

ELEVATION B

Baby change unit hung at 750 mm AFFL

Baby change unit

750

Figure 15.26
Plan of an accessible toilet showing a baby change unit which requires a larger cubicle

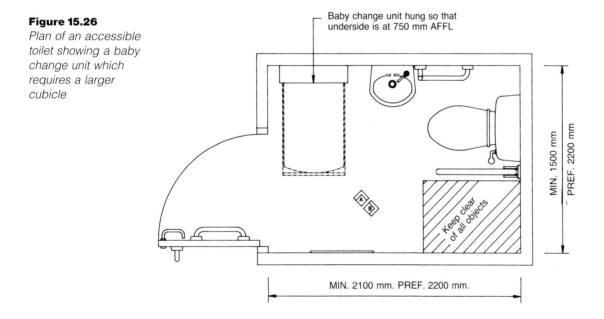

Baby change unit hung so that underside is at 750 mm AFFL

Keep clear of all objects

MIN. 1500 mm
PREF. 2200 mm

MIN. 2100 mm. PREF. 2200 mm.

Table 15.1   Toilet specification (Hewi, Twyfords)

ACD ref:	Description	Manufacturer	Order code	Price each (£)	Price per 10 (£)
SYM/HW1	Symbol male	Hewi	710.150.1.skz	3.30	3.30
SYF/HW1	Symbol female	Hewi	710.150.2.skz	3.30	3.30
SYD/HW1	Symbol disabled	Hewi	710.150.3.skz	3.30	3.30
KP1/HW1	Kickplate cut to 910 mm × 170 mm	Hewi	55PSB	9.30	9.30
DB1/DS1	Indicator bolt	Dryad Simplan	B67MP or RP	35.35	35.35
PH1/HW1	Door pull handle and BA1 or BA6	Hewi	550.33	26.58	26.58
HSR/HW1	Hinged support rail no toilet roll	Hewi	33.3081.80	188.82	188.82
HSRP/HW1	Wall mounting plate (for stud)	Hewi	33.3081 WPN	36.62	36.62
GRCR1/HW1	Corner support rail 785 × 400	Hewi	33.3020.90	100.90	100.90
GR1/HW1	Support rail 600 mm	Hewi	33.3010.60	43.53	43.53
CH1/HW1	Coat hook (×2)	Hewi	520.50.1	3.92	3.92
TRH1/HW1	Toilet roll holder	Hewi	450	7.44	7.44
STRH1/HW1	Spare toilet roll holder	Hewi	452.11	9.98	9.98
TLT1/AV1	Avalon WC bowl, horizontal outlet	Twyfords	AV 1158	87.98	83.58
CS1/AV1	7.5 litre cistern lid (screw-down)	Twyfords	AV 2711	64.58	61.35
SEAT1/AV1	Seat and cover	Twyfords	AV 7841	37.77	35.97
FL1/AV1	Dimple lever chrome-plated	Twyfords	CF 3009CP	17.23	16.41
SNK1/TW3	Sola 380	Twyfords	14660 WH2	26.01	24.71
MT1/KWC1	KWC Vita-Duo tap	KWC	K.12.T1.21A150	179.99	
HD1/AS1	Automatic hand drier	Airstream	5000ST	189.00	160.65
	Totals			**1074.90**	**855.01**

Manufacturer	Supply	Telephone
Hewi	Yannedis	0181 550 8833
Twyfords	Travis Perkins	0181 992 8001
KWC	KWC	0181 675 9335
Airstream	Airstream	0161 428 7544
Cannon Hygiene	Cannon Hygiene	01524 60894

bathroom/toilet area. The small shower tub by Armitage Shanks is used for its compact nature and the ease with which a facilitator can wash someone in need of assistance. The use of a dual shower rail, made to size from Hewi, allows the shower head to be used either in the shower tub or in the location on the rail. The KWC shower unit allows the shower or bath taps to be used and has water temperature control with a lever handle. This is intended to be used from both the shower tub and the floor shower. Figure 15.31 shows the main method for transferring into a bath, and therefore the need for the tiled 'shelf'.

The floor is *Altro* vinyl and the shower outlet uses a Harmer 'shower drain' which traps the vinyl floor and presents a low-profile flush drainage point to the shower. This is positioned at the lowest point in the fall.

Dressing rooms

Dressing rooms intended for wheelchair users should bear in mind the 1550 mm clear turning circle required for wheelchair users and, as well as ensuring that the space is provided for this, the floor surface should comply with the above specification.

Table 15.2   Toilet specification (Hewi, Armitage Shanks)

ACD ref:	Description	Manufacturer	Order code	Price each (£)	Price per 10 (£)
SYM/HW1	Symbol male	Hewi	710.150.1.skz	3.30	3.30
SYF/HW1	Symbol female	Hewi	710.150.2.skz	3.30	3.30
SYD/HW1	Symbol disabled	Hewi	710.150.3.skz	3.30	3.30
KP1/HW1	Kickplate cut to 910 mm × 170 mm	Hewi	55PSB	9.30	9.30
DB1/DS1	Indicator bolt	Dryad Simplan	B67MP or RP	35.35	35.35
PH1/HW1	Door pull handle and BA1 or BA6	Hewi	550.33	26.58	26.58
HSR/HW1	Hinged support rail no toilet roll	Hewi	33.3081.80	188.82	188.82
HSRP/HW1	Wall mounting plate (for stud)	Hewi	33.3081 WPN	36.62	36.62
GRCR1/HW1	Corner support rail 785 × 400	Hewi	33.3020.90	100.90	100.90
GR1/HW1	Support rail 600 mm	Hewi	33.3010.60	43.53	43.53
CH1/HW1	Coat hook (×2)	Hewi	520.50.1	3.92	3.92
TRH1/HW1	Toilet roll holder	Hewi	450	7.44	7.44
STRH1/HW1	Spare toilet roll holder	Hewi	452.11	9.98	9.98
TLT1/AS1	Contour 2 WC pan	Armitage	150701A	91.38	86.81
BOX1	Laminate-faced box	Armitage	7771000	82.00	79.32
CS1/AS1	9 litre surface mount cistern	Armitage	17651AA	28.20	26.79
SEAT1/AS1	Bakasan seat, rod and hinges	Armitage	68940B8	35.03	32.09
BSN/AS2	Dorex 365 mm basin 2 tap holes	Armitage	120015D	20.49	19.51
SNK1/TW3	Sola 380	Twyfords	14660 WH2	26.01	24.71
MT1/KWC1	KWC Vita-Duo tap	KWC	K.12.T1.21A150	179.99	
HD1/AS1	Automatic hand drier	Airstream	5000ST	189.00	160.65
Totals				**1098.43**	**877.51**

Manufacturer	Supply	Telephone
Hewi	Yannedis	0181 550 8833
Armitage Shanks	Travis Perkins	0181 992 8001
KWC	KWC	0181 675 9335
Airstream	Airstream	0161 428 7544
Cannon Hygiene	Cannon Hygiene	01524 60894

Dressing tables

The dressing table's lowest edge should be no lower than 800 mm AFFL, with the benchtop no higher than 850 mm AFFL. The benchtop should be no more than 600 mm deep.

Switches to activate the lighting and to control the socket outlets should be located no further than 650 mm from the seated position and clearly contrast with the surrounding surfaces. A preferable arrangement is to place the switches in the front panel of the dressing table to control the lighting and sockets remotely.

Wardrobes

Wardrobes should provide hanging at 1200 mm AFFL and 1700 mm AFFL, with door furniture at approximately 1000 mm AFFL. Lockable doors should avoid small keys. Full-length mirrors should be avoided in wardrobe doors.

Showers

Figure 15.32 shows a small dressing room which uses the Neaco 'neatdec' shower tray to provide a wheelchair-accessible surface that has a good

Table 15.3 Toilet specification (Dryad, Twyfords)

ACD ref:	Description	Manufacturer	Order code	Price each (£)	Price per 10 (£)
	Symbol male	Dryad Simplan	F40	9.96	
	Symbol female	Dryad Simplan	F41	9.96	
	Symbol disabled	Dryad Simplan	F43	9.96	
	Nylon kickplate 910 mm × 170 mm	Dryad Simplan	Kicking plate	25.73	
	Indicator bolt	Dryad Simplan	B67MP or RP	35.35	
	Door pull handle	Dryad Simplan	H92	19.27	
	Hinged support rail no toilet roll	Dryad Simplan	GH41/2	155.42	
	Corner support rail 815 × 405	Dryad Simplan	GH20/2	125.25	
	Support rail 450 mm	Dryad Simplan	GH11	36.36	
	Back support with cushion	Dryad Simplan	GH6PC	101.01	
	Coat hook (×2)	Dryad Simplan	H500	12.86	
	Toilet roll holder	Dryad Simplan	B710	29.98	
	Spare toilet roll holder	Dryad Simplan	B715	11.35	
TLT1/AV1	Avalon WC bowl, horizontal outlet	Twyfords	AV 1158	87.98	83.58
CS1/AV1	7.5 litre cistern lid (screw-down)	Twyfords	AV 2711	64.58	61.35
SEAT1/AV1	Seat and cover	Twyfords	AV 7841	37.77	35.97
FL1/AV1	Dimple lever chrome-plated	Twyfords	CF 3009CP	17.23	16.41
SNK1/TW3	Sola 380	Twyfords	14660 WH2	26.01	24.71
MT1/KWC1	KWC Vita-Duo tap	KWC	K.12.T1.21A150	179.99	
HD1/AS1	Automatic hand drier	Airstream	5000ST	189.00	160.65
	Totals			**1185.02**	**382.67**

Manufacturer	Supply	Telephone
Dryad Simplan	Dryad	01533 538844
Twyfords	Travis Perkins	0181 992 8001
KWC	KWC	0181 675 9335
Airstream	Airstream	0161 428 7544
Cannon Hygiene	Cannon Hygiene	01524 60894

water clearance and therefore allows 'wet' and 'dry' use of the toilet area. In a small dressing room this therefore means that a shower and toilet can be fitted into a small area.

Project planning

Figure 15.33 shows the type of timescale that could be expected to happen in the design of an accessible toilet. It is worth noting the extended period that is needed – a minimum of approximately 5 months between deciding to start the design of the toilet and the completion of the project.

Conclusion

The design and layout of the toilet area is critical to its success and the choice of the fittings is as important as their location. It is useful to gain an understanding of the use of the toilet area to help understand the design and layout of the space.

Figure 15.27
Plan of a proposed conversion of a bedroom for a wheelchair user

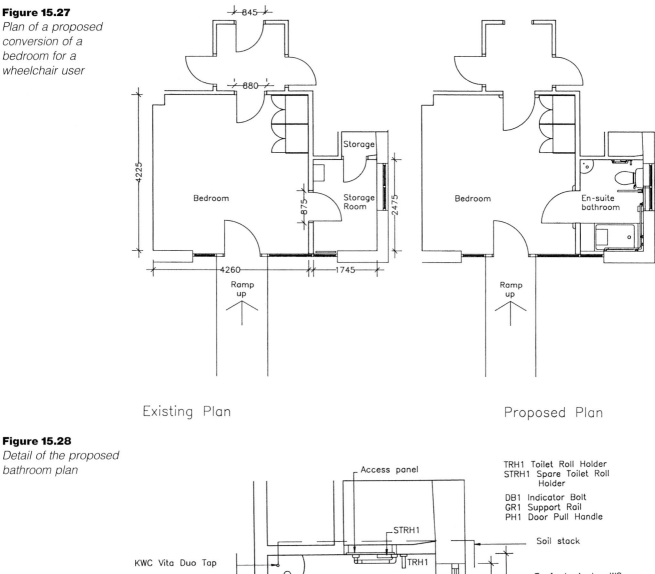

Existing Plan

Proposed Plan

Figure 15.28
Detail of the proposed bathroom plan

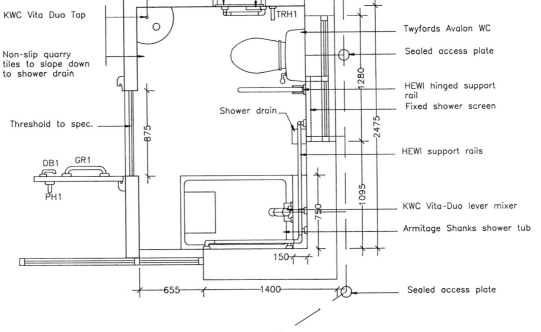

TRH1 Toilet Roll Holder
STRH1 Spare Toilet Roll Holder
DB1 Indicator Bolt
GR1 Support Rail
PH1 Door Pull Handle

Access panel

KWC Vita Duo Tap

Non-slip quarry tiles to slope down to shower drain

Threshold to spec.

Shower drain

STRH1

TRH1

Soil stack

Twyfords Avalon WC

Sealed access plate

HEWI hinged support rail

Fixed shower screen

HEWI support rails

KWC Vita-Duo lever mixer

Armitage Shanks shower tub

Sealed access plate

To manhole

DB1 GR1
PH1

Figure 15.29

Ideal layout of a purpose-built bathroom with a shower tube

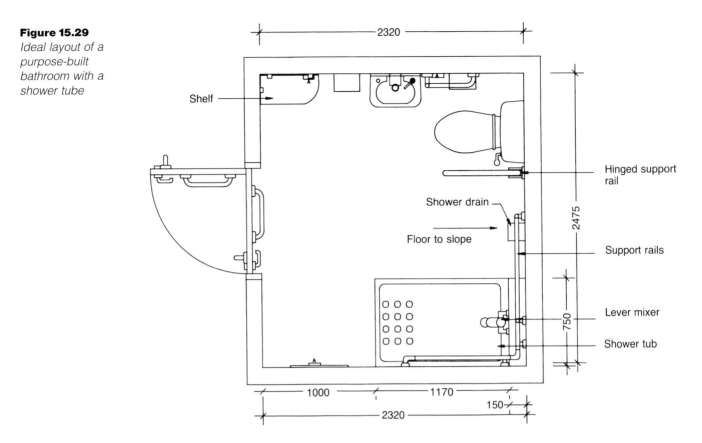

Shelf

Hinged support rail

Shower drain

Floor to slope

Support rails

Lever mixer

Shower tub

2320

2475

750

1000

1170

150

2320

Figure 15.30

Elevation of an ideal layout of a small bathroom with a shower tub

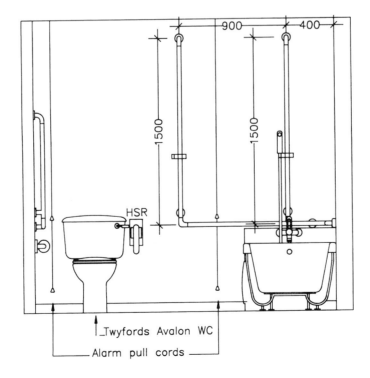

900

400

1500

1500

HSR

Twyfords Avalon WC

Alarm pull cords

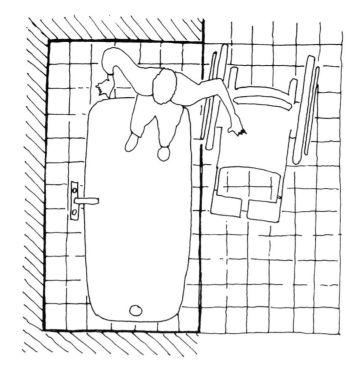

Figure 15.31
Transfer shelf being used in a bathroom

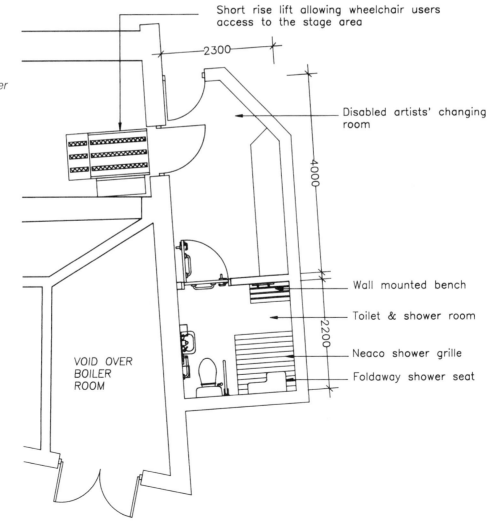

Figure 15.32
Plan of a proposed addition of an accessible dressing room on a theatre using a Neaco shower grille

Short rise lift allowing wheelchair users access to the stage area

2300

Disabled artists' changing room

4000

Wall mounted bench

Toilet & shower room

2200

Neaco shower grille

Foldaway shower seat

VOID OVER BOILER ROOM

Figure 15.33
Gannt chart showing the project stages and
timescales in the redesign and construction of an
accessible toilet

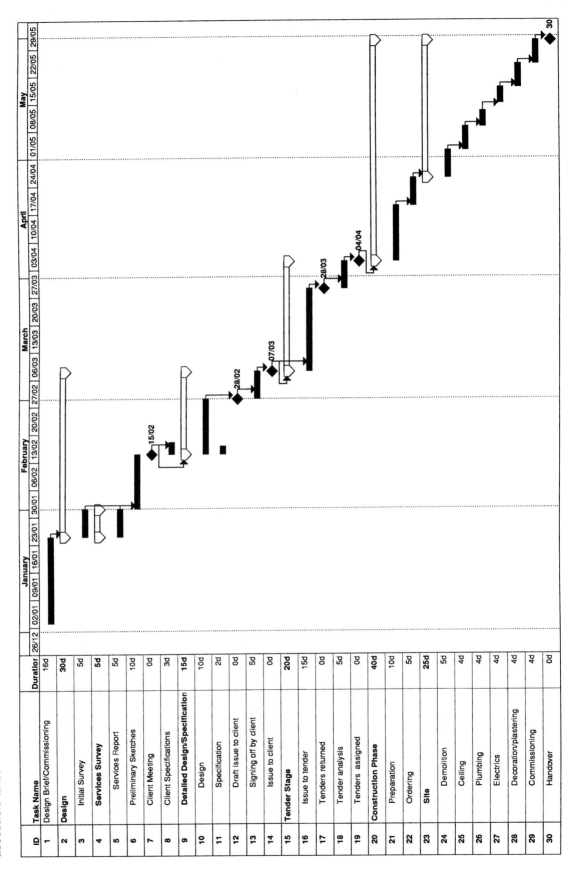

16 Circulation, décor, lighting, electrical outlets, furniture and fixtures and fittings

This chapter is designed to act as a 'catch-all' to deal with areas that span most of the other chapters and deals with decoration, carpeting, electrical fittings, furniture, and other fixtures and fittings.

Décor

The decoration of a space can have a large impact on its use by disabled people. People with visual disabilities look for bold indications of the layout of the space to guide them, and people who are blind use sounds and changes in floor surface to locate themselves within a building. However, the designs and colours used do not have to be 'obvious' in this respect, and even quite subtle changes in texture and contrast can be used to help guide people through the building.

Colour

Colour can be used in decoration to provide guides to building users, and is particularly useful to people with a visual disability. It is, however, not colour which is the most important feature in decoration but hue. The feature that helps people navigate around objects is the difference in contrast caused by the brightness differentials of two surfaces.

Brightness differentials are determined by the differences in the reflectances of the colours/hues of the surfaces. Optimum high-contrast combinations of colours include: white and black, yellow and black, yellow and blue, white and blue, red and white, and grey and white. However, equally strong contrasts can be generated using combinations of the colours themselves, for instance

using a dark-blue and light-blue surface next to each other.

Navigation

Key features in a colour scheme which help people navigate round a building are the skirting/door surround and carpet/flooring. The skirting and door surround give the viewer an idea of where the door openings are and the path of the corridor. The carpet or flooring does a similar job and can indicate where there are branches in the corridor. In large areas, depending on the floor and wall colour, the skirting should be a strong and continuous colour which contrasts with the floor and wall surround – for instance, where the floor and walls are light, the skirting should be dark, and vice versa. Door surrounds should similarly be differentiated from the wall colour to help the user to detect the door opening. If possible, the door should also contrast with the wall opening and the ironmongery contrast with the door colour.

At its strongest level people with learning difficulties find the use of strong colour to differentiate areas of a building extremely useful. In infant schools each classroom is traditionally painted with a different colour to help children to locate their class, and the same feature is now more commonly being used in places such as doctors' surgeries, where the patient can easily be directed to the coloured door. This technique can be subtly extended to the decoration of different areas of the building to great effect.

Corner and wall guards

Corner and wall guards can be used to guide people along corridors as well as indicate changes in the pathway by clearly indicating corners. The same colour considerations apply to the choice of wall guard colour, or the colour of paint applied to the mild-steel versions. On the whole, the plastic versions are preferred due to their wear quality, continuous colour, good collision absorption and warmth to the touch. Decoration schemes which accentuate these features will assist navigation through corridors.

Lighting

Colours applied to the walls reflect the light according to their reflectance. Lighter colours and hues reflect more light than darker ones and are therefore more appropriate for providing reflected illumination to an area from either daylight or artificial lighting. Considerable cost can be saved by using light-coloured decoration and reducing the amount of light that needs to be used to illuminate the space adequately.

Floor finishes

Floor finishes can provide useful navigational information which ranges from the type of finish to the inlay of a contrasting pathway to follow. The use of changes in colour and texture, for instance in lift lobbies, or using different-coloured floor surfaces and decoration schemes in different floors and areas of a building, can considerably assist people to differentiate between areas of the building.

Entrance matting

Entrances to buildings normally present difficulties to disabled people, which are often compounded by the entrance matting system in use. The primary function of the mat is to remove dirt and water from the feet of people entering the building. However, the different designs of matting affect the wheelchair users and other wheeled traffic in different ways.

It is always preferable that entrance mats are contained within a close-fitting well. Loose and surface mat systems should be well secured to the floor surface and will need a wedge chamfer to assist the entrance and exit from the mat.

Rubberized 'horsehair' and coir coconut types of entrance matting provide a great resistance to wheeled traffic, effectively trapping the wheelchair wheel and make traversing extremely difficult. The 'stopping' power of these mats is only equalled by their dirt removal. They are not recommended.

Matting which consists of aluminium channels with coir fibres or carpet pieces mounted in the channels is more accessible to wheeled traffic. The aluminium channels provide a firm surface for wheelchair users, prams and trolleys to traverse and provide adequate dirt and water removal. Examples of matting of this type include Neaco Neatgrille, Construction Specialities Pedigrid, Treadline and Pedimat, Jaymart Streetfighter and Competitor and Nuways Designate, Tuftiguard, Module 2 and Colourguard.

Where entrance matting precedes a high-gloss floor finish, the water-removing qualities of the matting are extremely important. Small-scale testing has indicated that the Neaco 'Neatgrille' matting is extremely good as well as having a good dirt-removal capability. However, it must be stressed that the rubber compound inserts should not be used where wheelchair users are expected to cross the matting, as these do not remove water and present an extremely bumpy ride to wheeled traffic.

Carpeting

The presence and type of carpet have great impact on a wheelchair user. Carpets with a deep pile require a wheelchair user to expend a significantly higher effort to traverse the space. A deep pile will also tend to lead the chair in the direction of the weave, so that even an electric chair will require continual directional adjustments. The basic principle is that the harder the carpet feels, the easier it will be to traverse in a wheelchair.

Carpets and carpet tiles should be securely attached and, where a cushion or backing is used, it should be firm. Piles should be of the level loop, textured loop, level cut or level cut/uncut pile texture. Low-pile looped or compressed-fibre carpets are preferred.

Exposed edges of the carpet should be fastened to the floor surface and have trim along the entire length of the exposed edge. Edge trim with a vertical rise does not require edge treatment, whereas vertical rises between 6 mm and 13 mm require a bevelled edge with a slope no greater than 1:2. Changes in level greater than 13 mm should be accompanied by a ramp and subject to the ramp specification guidelines.

Hard-wearing carpets with good wear and stain resistance such as the 'Unicare' range of contract carpets from Gradus have a relatively high installation cost but a low maintenance cost and long life. (**Note**: Installation of this carpet will be lower cost if a local carpet fitter is used rather than the manufacturer.) Other makes of carpet include the 'Escopallas' from Esco. Care should be taken with carpet tiles like this that installation is thorough and ensures that the tiles are well secured.

Bold patterns in carpets can be used to guide people through a building, with changes in colour serving to define administrative areas as well as contrasting building borders. However, swirling patterns which do not help in the directional guidance should be avoided as they tend to confuse.

Further information on carpet construction and suppliers can be found in the Disabled Living Foundation's *Information Service Handbook*, section 11 on Household and Environmental Fittings.

Linoleum

Linoleum is generally a good, though noisy, surface for wheelchair users. It should be firmly adhered to the floor surface, with the same edge treatment requirements as carpets. Polished linoleum can present a serious hazard when the flooring is wet. The risk can be reduced by using a non-slip flooring polish such as those supplied by Jebron.

Non-slip flooring

All floors should have a non-slip surface, especially in wet areas such as bathrooms, kitchens and toilets. Timber floors should be treated with a low-shine polish or with an oil that provides a non-slip surface.

Non-slip flooring surfaces fall into three types: grit applied to an epoxy carrier, abrasive vinyl sheet and rubberized tiles:

- The grit types fall into two categories: (1) the paint types like Carbo-Grip and Flowcoat, which are suitable for low-traffic situations where they will be renewed on a regular basis (yearly in some cases) and (2) harder-wearing and thicker polyurethane substrate with a grit,

such as Scotch-Clad or a faster-curing Acrydur which has an acrylic base and grit. These systems offer a more durable system that has the ability to flex slightly and therefore reduce cracking. New systems for internal use have recently been introduced by Altro.

- The welded abrasive vinyl sheets offer a hard-wearing flooring with a range of applications and colourways. They conform to use requirements in areas where hygiene is necessary (e.g. kitchens) and offer the opportunity to incorporate patterns into the floor surface as they come in a wide range of colours and surface patterns. They are adhered to the floor surface and hot-welded to form a seamless flooring. Such types of flooring are manufactured by Altro Ltd and Marley Flooring.

- Rubberized flooring presents a slightly lower-cost floor and wall covering and offers a larger colour range than the above flooring systems (except external UV-safe versions), and more variety in the surface textures available. The rubber systems, such as those produced by Jaymart, can be used on all areas and specialist applications such as stairs, in a complete tread, riser and nosing piece, which is adhered to the floor surface.

Lighting

Internal circulation spaces

Illumination requirements vary according to the time of day, the task for which illumination is required and the relative brightness of the surfaces in the space being lit. General principles for good internal lighting include: light-coloured walls, floor and ceiling; vertical windows rather than roof lights; and light fittings which have a large downward light spread, positioned and designed to avoid glare.

A commonly quoted statistic is the fact that an older eye requires many times the light input to generate the same change on the retina of a younger eye. Unfortunately, this has been interpreted by designers as a need to increase the light level by many times. However, it is almost the reverse of this commonsense decision – the older lens reduces the transmission of light because of the coagulation of the protein, rather like the cooking of the white of the egg. The co-agulated particles scatter light causing glare to the viewer. Increasing the amount of light increases the glare and reduces the amount of information that is transmitted.

A much more effective approach is to improve the modelling of the space using lighting that more clearly indicates the features of the room. Lighting provided by 'shadowless' fluorescent do not provide well-directed lighting, but a combination of uplighters and directed downlight can be used to give clear guidance to the user. Pools of light should not be avoided where they impart information such as regularly spaced downlighters indicating the route of a corridor, but large changes in illumination across areas should be avoided as accommodation takes longer in older people.

Light received on the working plane (i.e. 850 mm AFFL) consists of a combination of direct light and light which has been reflected off walls, floor, ceiling, furnishings, etc. Good lighting is achieved when the direct light in the space is not excessive in comparison to the reflected light in a space. All surfaces in the space will appear adequately lit if the reflected light level in a space is more than half of the direct light level on the horizontal working plane.

Choice of luminaires

Reflected light in a space is influenced by the pattern of downward light spread achieved by an electric light fitting (or the BZ classification, stated in manufacturers' catalogues). A low BZ number (i.e. less than BZ 4) indicates a relatively concentrated beam of light which is useful for highlighting but too harsh for general lighting. A high BZ number indicates a dispersed light distribution with more light falling on walls and floors. Too great a dispersal of light (i.e. greater than BZ 10) will increase the risk of glare.

Choice of finishes

Reflected light in a given space is greatly influenced by the reflectance, or relative brightness, of the surfaces. Dark-coloured surfaces have a low reflectance, absorbing much of the light hitting them, whereas light-coloured surfaces have a high reflectance, reflecting a larger proportion of incident light. For example, a room with dark-coloured walls, floors, etc. will appear gloomy and shadowy, while a space with light-coloured walls, floors, etc. will appear bright and airy. However, shiny surfaces will encourage glare, and should thus be avoided. Therefore the optimum wall surface colours are light matt finishes.

Modelling

Although all surfaces in a space should be adequately lit, uniform, shadowless distribution of light in the space should be avoided. Such lighting would provide insufficient contrast, between highlight and shadow, to give firm modelling of three-dimensional objects. Detailed principles of modelling will not be discussed here. Suffice it to say that good modelling can be achieved when there are horizontal as well as vertical light sources in a space. Light fittings which emit light sideways as well as downwards, or a combination of light fittings and daylight coming through side windows, are effective.

Levels of illumination

Recommended illumination levels vary depending upon the source of information. Different sources have recommended between 54 lux and 150 lux for a lift landing. The light levels in Table 16.1 have been taken from a variety of sources and discussions with people with visual disabilities.

Scalar illuminance has to be calculated, whereas it is easy to measure the planar illuminance with a light meter. The levels referred to here are therefore planar illuminance recommendations.

Electrical outlets

The general principle behind the location of most electrical outlets or control switches is that they should:

- Be within the reach of a wheelchair user, i.e. not located at floor level (bending down) or too high to reach
- Be visible to people with visual disabilities, and should therefore contrast with their surround
- Have large, easy-use switching action

Table 16.1 Light levels

Circulation areas	Approximate light levels
Corridors	75–100 lux
Lifts	75–100 lux (on control panel)
Signage	50 lux above surrounding
Ramps	100 lux + from a combination of sources
Stairways	100 lux (at tread level) normal use 10 lux *minimum* for emergency use
Work surface for general use	300–400 lux + task lighting which is user-controlled
Work surface for detailed use	400–1000 lux which is generated by user-controlled task lighting

The basic layout dimensions of electrical fittings can be seen in Figure 16.1.

Fuse/consumer units

Fuse/consumer units should be located at approximately 1200 mm AFFL, and composed of miniature circuit breakers (trip switches) and have residual current circuit breaker protection (RCCB). The unit should have enough space on the marker flap to provide for a large-print or Braille indication of the circuit using large 'Dymo' marking tape.

Light switches

These should be located no higher than 1200 mm AFFL. The front plate, wall and rocker switch should contrast, i.e. a dark front plate is used with a light wall and light rocker switch, a light front plate with a dark wall and dark rocker switch (rocker switches are preferred). Light fittings which make provision for contrasting front plates include the MK 'Accent' range, the Hamilton English, Accord, Pastel and Imperial Touchlite range and the Tenby Harmony range (Glacier White Moulded range have the same large rockers). Especially recommended is the Clipsall range of light switches 'E31/1/25A', which come in a large range of colourways with the faceplates interchangeable with the switch mechanism. For example, the switchplate could be dark blue and the switch unit sparkle blue, giving an effective contrast from two blue components.

Where light fittings are existing or are not available in the contrasting colours then it is advisable to place the fitting on a square of contrasting background, or paint a square so that it forms a 40 mm border around the fitting. Alternatively, a coloured 'light switch plate' such as those from Manger & Son Ltd could be fitted. (The company should be telephoned for details of a local stockist as they only sell wholesale.)

Pull cords

Pull cords should be hung to drop to approximately 1000 mm AFFL and be white with a white

Figure 16.1
Layout of electrical and control elements in the home and office with a low alarm cord in case of falls

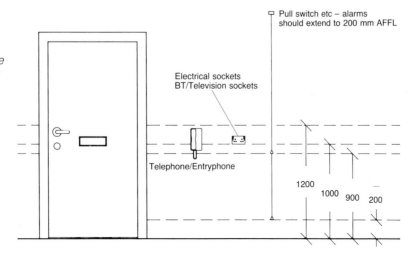

acorn. Because this combination will be almost invisible it is advisable to obtain a large pull handle which is coloured in contrast to the surround, and place a sign on the nearest wall to indicate that the cord is for lights (in lettering no less than 20 mm high, according to the signage specification). The cord should be restrained in a wall guide.

Alarm pull cords should be hung so that they come down to approximately 200 mm AFFL and be red with two red acorns, one at 200 mm AFFL and one at 850 mm AFFL. A pull handle is advisable as above and a sign stating that the cord is an alarm should be added according to the toilet specification.

Sockets and outlets

To obviate the need for excessive bending down, wall-mounted electrical outlets should be located at a convenient height for wheelchair users, and should also clear most commercially available desks. Ideally, they should be located at approximately 850–1000 mm AFFL (no lower than 400 mm AFFL). As with lighting, it is important to have a visually contrasting outlet, which is available from the same manufacturers.

Switched outlets using rocker switches are preferred. The Clipsall sockets are worth noting as they are available with the contrasting rocker switches, which are located at either end of the socket rather than in the centre. This means that it is far easier to identify which switch is controlling which plug. Where the plug is to be wall-mounted and free from obstruction it can be useful to place a plug holder just below the socket to hold plugs off the floor.

Where an outlet must be located at the back of a counter it is recommended that a separate switch is supplied to the front of the counter to avoid having to reach over the counter to access the switch.

Sizes and manoeuvrability

Electrical wheelchair users are regarded to have a turning circle of approximately 1550 mm diameter, as illustrated in Figure 16.2. This then translates into an ability to turn in a corridor 1100 mm wide with a 1200 mm end width (see Figure 16.3). This should be translated into corridor turns with a minimum of 1200 mm.

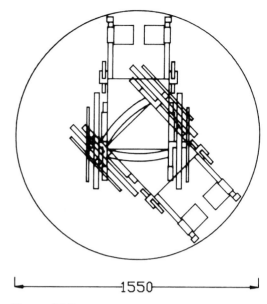

Figure 16.2
Minimum turning circle required by a manual wheelchair user

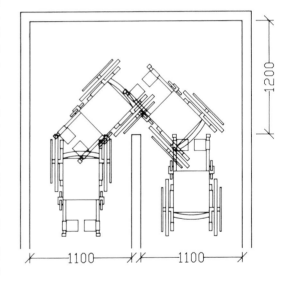

Figure 16.3
Minimum dimensions required for a wheelchair user to negotiate a corridor

The basic reach and dimensions are shown in Figures 16.4 and 16.5. Figure 16.6 shows the reach of a wheelchair user approaching a control console. The clearances required are the same as required in the section on furniture below.

Figure 16.7 shows the dimensions required by a person requiring the use of a cane. Items need to be below 650 mm AFFL to be detected and there should be a clearance of not less than

Figure 16.4
*Typical reach ability
of a wheelchair user
facing the object*

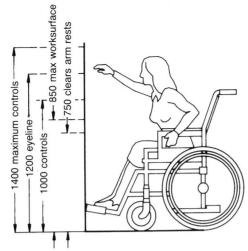

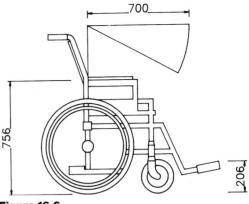

Figure 16.6
*Elevation of a typical wheelchair user with the
forward reach of the user*

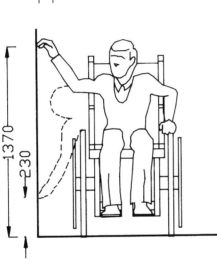

Figure 16.5
*Typical reach ability of a wheelchair user side
on to an object*

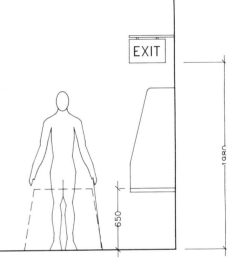

Figure 16.7
*Clear dimensions needed for a stick user to
detect objects and clear space below
suspended signs*

1980 mm to overhanging obstructions. The basic
dimensions of a standard wheelchair are illustrated in Figure 16.8.

Furniture and joinery

Furniture and joinery should be designed bearing
the following in mind.

Approach

The prime concerns for wheelchair users operating in front of and behind counters are the height
of the work surface, the clear height below the
surface, and the clearance below the surface for
the knees, kickplates and toes. These clearances
should be provided on both sides of a counter to
allow for wheelchair access for both staff and
patrons/customers.

Counter-tops

Maximum height of counter-tops should be 850–
900 mm. For instance, a bar or reception desk
which is usually too high for wheelchair users
but acceptable for most ambulant people should
have at least a 1000 mm long section which is at a
height accessible to wheelchairs.

Figure 16.8
Elevation of a typical wheelchair user with the need for toe space of 150 mm

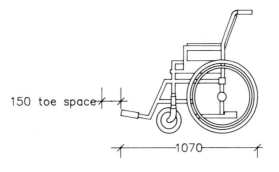

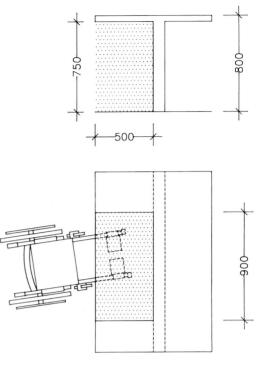

Leg space

There should be at least a 750 mm high space under worktops, desks and counters to provide leg room for wheelchair users and at least a 1200 mm wide space behind desks and counters to allow wheelchair access behind them.

Reach

The vertical reaching ability of a wheelchair user depends upon the orientation of the chair. The reach of 1220 mm AFFL is more restricted when the user is expected to approach head-on – this is due to the size of the chair and limited torso mobility.

There is a higher reaching ability when the chair can be brought alongside, and the reach can extend to approximately 1370 mm AFFL. However, it is important to note in both cases that the wheelchair can be brought flush with the desired target. When a wheelchair user must reach across, say, a counter, the height to which they can reach is much less. Where there is a counter, the reach and vision are further restricted and high shelves or displays may not be visible to a wheelchair user at low level. It is important therefore to design displays and distribution points so that an independent wheelchair user can obtain a representative sample of the literature. These requirements are summarized in Figure 16.9.

Hazards

People with a visual disability, or who are blind and use a cane, can be severely injured by unmarked projections from the wall at a height above 650 mm AFFL. Objects below this height

Figure 16.9
Elevation and plan of the requirements of a wheelchair user for clear leg room and accessible table top

are detected using the sweep of the cane, but are not desirable. It is important to ensure that objects such as telephone hoods and drop boxes (e.g. suggestions) are located either in recesses or in a unit detectable by people with a visual disability.

Reception desk

Reception desks represent the 'shop front' of the organization and should be welcoming to all visitors. Visitors frequently either have to sign in or sign items out, and often need to communicate with the receptionist, so it is important that the counter-top be of the right height for signing and not obscure the receptionist. They should be fitted with induction loops as recommended in Chapter 7.

Height

Counter-tops should be either 800 mm high or have at least a 1000 mm long section at 800 mm high, with a 500 mm deep × 750 mm high leg space below to allow wheelchair users to approach the counter either from the side or head-on for signatures. Leg space should be provided at the front for the visitor and at the rear for the receptionist.

Lighting

Illumination of the counter-top should be sufficient for people with a visual disability to read reasonable print – approximately 300 lux.

Office/studio desks

The prime requirement of desks is that they provide clearance for the arms on a wheelchair. All but the largest power chairs will fit under a 750 mm AFFL table top, with 800 mm AFFL preferred. Care should be taken to select desks that have the maximum clearance from legs – with cantilevered worktops offering the best solution. Fixed drawer units should be avoided and units which are mobile should be provided and designed to fit under the worksurface.

Cafeterias

Canteens and restaurant areas can present the disabled user with a daily difficulty, which is compounded by the fact that he or she will be carrying food. Serving counters should conform to the same specification as the reception desk above, with the tray slide being no more than approximately 300 mm wide and the highest reach-over shelf no more than 1150 mm AFFL.

The tray slide should be continuous to the till, with the leg room available no less than 750 mm AFFL, with 800 mm AFFL preferred, and with tray dispensers arranged so as not to block travel around the tray slide. These are summarized in Figure 16.10.

Where possible, food should be displayed on a tray, so that this can be dragged forward to reach items at the back. A clear corridor of 900 mm must be provided in front of the counter to allow adequate wheelchair manoeuvring space. In small tea bars, it should be remembered that a wheelchair has a turning circle with a diameter of approximately 1550 mm and adequate space should be allowed for this.

Chill cabinets

Where chill cabinets are used that do not have space available for a chair to approach from the front, enough clear space should be provided for the wheelchair user to pull alongside the counter, and food displayed no higher than 1200 mm AFFL and no deeper than a 600 mm reach. Chill cabinets which display foods/drinks in a vertical format should operate so that food is arranged vertically rather than horizontally, i.e. each shelf should contain a selection of all the produce, rather than one shelf holding one product, with the next one up holding another, etc.

Checkout tills

Checkout tills should, wherever possible, be connected to the tray slide to avoid lifting or prolonged holding of a heavy tray while waiting. The till should have a display (approximately 15 mm LED or back-lit LCD display) facing the customer, showing the price of the items being rung up and displaying the sub-total requested.

Prices on shelves

The prices of items on display should be clearly marked on or near the item in numerals no less than 10 mm high, using either black lettering on a white background or white lettering on a black background.

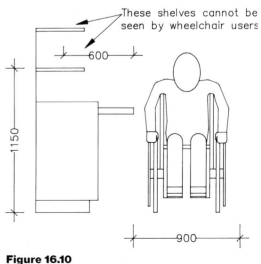

Figure 16.10
Canteen counter layout for wheelchair users

Price lists on walls

Prices for the produce on sale in the tea bar should be displayed on a list with text no less than 20 mm high, using either black lettering on a white background or white lettering on a black background.

Vending machines

Where vending machines are used they should have a clear display panel. Prices should be displayed in lettering no less than 10 mm high, using either black text on a white background or white on a black background. Instructions on use of the machine should be clearly displayed in lettering no less than 15 mm high, with the same colours as above. The coin slot should be no more than 1200 mm AFFL and the machine should be of a type which automatically returns rejected change. Selection buttons should be no more than 1200 mm AFFL. The type of machine which selects by number overcomes the difficulty of having buttons in one location.

A shelf located at 800 mm should be provided close to the vending area to allow produce to be arranged before being carried away. Where hot drinks are being vended, and it is anticipated that they may be carried any distance (even within the tea bar), then a supply of lids should be provided to avoid spillage.

Seating

Seating (e.g. for receptions or waiting rooms) should be firm and easy to rise from, upholstered in an absorbent material and have armrests. The armrests should begin in line with the front of the seat. Seating should be arranged to allow wheelchair users to sit out of the main flow of traffic through the space.

Kitchens

Small college kitchens can now take into account the growing number of wheelchair users attending colleges. Stainless-steel kitchens can be fabricated to provide accessible worktops for wheelchair users. Figures 16.11–16.13 show the typical layout of a university communal kitchen with enclosed cabinets which are seldom used. Figures 16.14–16.16 show a proposed adaptation to allow wheelchair users to participate fully in the kitchen area.

Conclusion

This chapter is a collection of a wide range of pieces of information on the design, layout and decoration of many areas. These discussions seem like common sense, but more than any other chapter of this book, as they are implemented in the building, usage of these guidelines will gradually have the most effect on the greatest number of people and probably cost the least to implement.

Recommended reading

1 Disabled Living Foundation, *Information Service Handbook*, section 11 on Household and Environmental Fittings, Disabled Living Foundation, London.

Figure 16.11
Existing kitchen plan being converted for wheelchair users

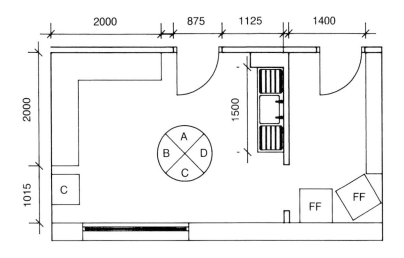

Figure 16.12
Existing kitchen elevation A being converted for wheelchair users

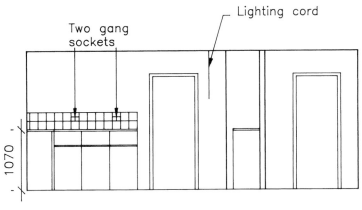

Elevation A

Figure 16.13
Existing kitchen elevations B and D being converted for wheelchair users

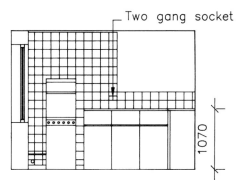
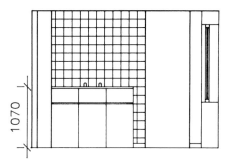

Elevation B   Elevation D

Figure 16.14
Proposed kitchen plan for use by wheelchair users

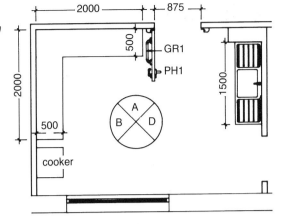

Figure 16.15
Proposed kitchen elevation A for use by wheelchair users

Figure 16.16
Proposed kitchen elevations B and D for use by wheelchair users

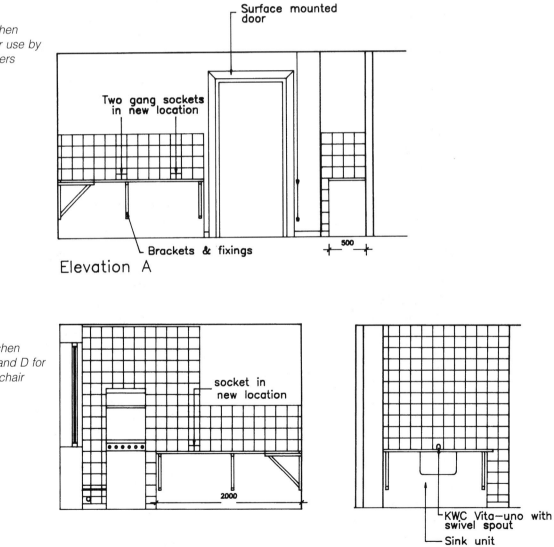

Surface mounted door

Two gang sockets in new location

Brackets & fixings

Elevation A

500

socket in new location

2000

Elevation B

KWC Vita—uno with swivel spout

Sink unit

Elevation D

Appendix: Addresses

3M United Kingdom plc
3M House, PO Box 1
Market Place
Bracknell
Berks RG12 1JU
Tel (01344) 858000
Floor finishes

Abloy Security Ltd
2–3 Hatters Lane
Croxley Centre
Watford
Herts WD1 8TT
Tel (01923) 255066
Security systems

Access Control Services
215 London Road
Stone
Dartford
Kent DA9 9DQ
Tel (01322) 284222
Fax (01322) 284408
Security systems

The Access Officer's Association, contact your
local access officer normally located in Planning/
Building Control or Equal Opportunities
Departments

ACE (Access Committee for England)
12 City Forum
250 City Road
London EC1V 8AF
Tel (0171) 250 0008
Fax (0171) 250 0212

Acrydur, *see* Veitchi (East) Ltd

AIRS
Gateshead Central Library
Prince Consort Road
Gateshead
Tyne & Wear NE8 4LN
Tel (0191) 477 3478
Services for people with visual impairments

Airstream Products Ltd
Airstream House
Brook Street
Cheadle
Cheshire SK8 2BN
Tel (01614) 287544
Warm air driers

Albert Marston & Co Ltd
Planetary Road
Willenhall
West Midlands WV13 3ST
Tel (01902) 305511
Wellington ironmongery range

All Clear Designs Ltd
3rd Floor, Cooper House
2 Michael Road
London SW6 2ER
Tel (0171) 384 2950
Fax (0171) 384 2951
EMail allclear@easynet.co.uk
Architectural access advice

Altro Floors
Altro Ltd
7 Caxton Hill
Hertford
Hertfordshire SG13 7NB
Tel (01992) 584212
Non-slip flooring

Architectural Association School of Architecture
34–36 Bedford Square
London WC1B 3ES
Tel (0171) 636 0974

Armitage Shanks Ltd
Armitage
Rugeley
Staffordshire WS15 4BT
Tel (01543) 490253
Sanitary ware

Arts Council of England
14 Great Peter Street
London SW1P 3NQ
Tel (0171) 333 0100

Artsline
54 Chalton Street
London NW1
Tel (0171) 388 2227
Information on access to arts buildings

Athmer, *see* Strand Hardware Ltd

Audio Communications
Unit 6, Elm Court Industrial Park
Station Road
Wootton Bassett
Wiltshire SN4 7ED
Tel (01793) 851440
Communications

British Telecommunications plc
81 Newgate Street
London EC1A 7AJ
FREEFONE Telecom Sales
Telephone equipment

Cannon Hygiene Ltd
Middlegate
White Lund
Morecambe
Lancashire LA3 3BJ
Tel (01524) 60894
Sanitary dispensers

Carbo Grip Ltd
45 Grove Lane
Camberwell
London SE5 8SR
Tel (0171) 708 1300
Non-slip surfaces

Centre on Accessible Environments
Nutmeg House
60 Gainsford Street
London SE1 2NY
Tel (0171) 357 8182
Fax (0171) 357 8183

Cliffhanger, available from DIY stores

Clipsall (UK) Ltd
24 Dalston Gardens
Stanmore
Middlesex HA7 1DA
Tel (0181) 204 9494
Electrical accessories

Concept Systems
1–7 Mount Street
Stapleford
Nottingham NG8 9AW
Tel (01602) 499455
Equipment for people with visual impairments

Connevans Ltd
54 Albert Road North
Reigate
Surrey RH2 9YR
Tel (01737) 247571
Fax (01737) 223475
Equipment for deaf and hearing-impaired people

Construction Specialities (UK) Ltd
Conspec House
Springfield Road
Chesham
Bucks HP5 1PW
Tel (01494) 784844
Entrance matting

Crabtree Electrical Industries Ltd
Lincoln Works
Walsall
West Midlands WS1 2DN
Tel (01922) 721202
Electrical fittings

CTS Security Ltd
Southgates Corner
Wisbech Road
King's Lynn
Norfolk PE30 5JH
Tel (01553) 765429
Toilet alarms and radio alarms

Deb Ltd
108 Spencer Road
Belper
Derbyshire DE56 1JX
Tel (01773) 822712
Soap dispensers

Delta Design
Primrose Hill
Kings Langley
Herts WD4 8HD
Tel (01932) 269522
Xenon beacons

Dewhurst plc
Inverness Road
Hounslow
Middlesex TW3 3LT
Tel (0181) 572 5986
Lift equipment

Disability Resource Team
Bedford House
125–133 Camden High Street
London NW1
Tel (0171) 482 5062
Disability equality training

Disabled Living Foundation
380/384 Harrow Road
London W9 2HU
Tel (0171) 289 6111
Advice on equipment for disabled people

Dolphin Systems
Unit 96C, Blackpole Trading Estate
Worcester WR3 8TJ
Tel (01905) 754577
Software for people with visual impairments

Dorma Door Controls Ltd
Dorma Trading Park
Staffa Road
London E10 7QX
Tel (0181) 558 8411
Fax (0181) 558 6122
Door fittings

Dragon software, contact your software supplier

Dryad Simplan Ltd
Omega House
Blackbird Road
Leicester LE4 0AJ
Tel (0116) 253 8844
Fax (0116) 251 3623
Ironmongery

Dudley Thomas Ltd
PO Box 28
Birmingham New Road
Dudley
West Midlands DY1 4SN
Tel (0121) 557 5411
Toilet cisterns and levers

Effeff-Fritz Fuss GmbH & Co
Elektrotechnisch Fabrik
D-7470 Albstadt 1
Johannes-Mauthe-Strasse 14
Postfache 490
West Germany
Tel (07431) 123-0
Security locks

The Emergency Bolt Company
Cann Common
Shaftesbury
Dorset SP7 0DF
Tel (01747) 54536
Cooperbolt

Emergi-Lite
Wesley Place
Wellington Road
Dewsbury
West Yorkshire WF13 1HX
Tel (01924) 450880
Emergency lighting

Esco Carpet Tiles Ltd
Hitching Court
Blacklands Way
Abingdon Business Park
Abingdon
Oxon OX14 1RB
Tel (01235) 554848
Fax (01235) 553583
Carpet tiles

Ezi-Line Ltd
East Street
Wareham
Dorset BH20 4NP
Tel (01929) 552005
Fax (01929) 550422
Automatic door openers

Flowcrete Systems Ltd
Radnor Park Industrial Estate
Back Lane
Congleton
Cheshire CW12 4XS
Tel (01260) 270631
Flowcoat systems

Gimson Stairlifts Ltd
62 Boston Road
Beaumont Leys
Leicester LE4 1AZ
Tel (0116) 236 6779
Stairlifts

Gradus Ltd
Georgian Mill
Park Green
Macclesfield
Cheshire SK11 7NE
Tel (01625) 428922
Stair nosings

H & R Johnson Tiles Ltd
Highgate Tile Works
Tunstall
Stoke on Trent
Staffs ST6 4JX
Tel (01782) 575575
Tiles

Hamilton, R & Co Ltd
Quarry Industrial Estate
Mere
Wiltshire BA12 6LA
Tel (01747) 860088
Electrical switches

Harmer Holdings Ltd
Kennelwood House
Hatfield
Hertfordshire AL10 0LG
Tel (01707) 273481
Drains

Hewi (UK) Ltd
Scimitar Close
Gillingham Business Park
Gillingham
Kent ME8 0RN
Tel (01634) 377688
Grabrails, etc.

Hewlett Packard, contact your local computer outlet

IBM, contact your local computer outlet

Impulse Engineering Ltd
Head Office
Unit 76
Woolmer Trading Estate
Bordon
Hants GU35 9QF
Tel (01420) 473130
Toilet alarms

Infratech
2 Dukes Court
Wellington Street
Luton
Bedfordshire LU1 5AF
Tel (01582) 455239
Fax (01582) 488227
Infra-red systems

Institute of Contemporary Arts
12 Carlton House Terrace
London SW1Y 5AH
Tel (0171) 930 0493
Arts venue

Jaymart Rubber and Plastics Ltd
Woodlands Trading Estate
Eden Vale Road
Westbury
Wilts BA13 3QS
Tel (01373) 864926
Rubber flooring

Jebron Ltd
Bright Street
Wednesbury
West Midlands WS10 9HY
Tel (0121) 526 2212
Door closers

Kimberly-Clark Ltd
Service and Industrial Division
Larkfield
Aylesford
Kent ME20 7PS
Tel (01622) 717700
Sanitary dispensers

KRS Electronics Ltd
Dynamic Works
Saltaire Road
Shipley
West Yorkshire BD18 3HN
Tel (01274) 584115
Electric toilet alarms

KWC UK Ltd
Philip House
Ravenswood Road
London SW12 9PJ
Tel (0181) 675 9335
Taps with temperature control

Langley London Ltd
161–167 Borough High Street
London SE1 1HU
Tel (0171) 407 4444
Tiles

Lendrum R. J. Ltd
Stourbridge Road Industrial Estate
Bridgnorth
Shropshire WV15 5BA
Tel (01746) 767272
Automatic door openers

Lorient Polyproducts Ltd
Fairfax Road
Heathfield Industrial Estate
Newton Abbot
Devon TQ12 6UD
Tel (01626) 834252
Door seals

Magrini Child-Care Products Division
Magrini Ltd
Unit 5
Maybrook Industrial Estate
Brownhills
Walsall WS8 7DG
Tel (01543) 375311
Baby-change unit

Manger & Son Ltd, products available direct from outlets

Marley Floors Ltd
Commercial Flooring Division
Lenham
Maidstone
Kent ME17 2DE
Tel (01622) 858877
Slip-resistant flooring

Marlin Lighting Ltd
Hanworth Trading Estate
Hampton Road West
Feltham
Middx TW13 6DR
Tel (0181) 898 6661
Lighting

Menvier-Amberlec Systems Ltd
Astley Lane Industrial Estate
Astley Lane
Swillington
Leeds LE26 8UE
Tel (01532) 870551
Emergency lights

Mercury Communications Ltd
Mercury House
Brickhill Street
Willen Lake
Milton Keynes MK15 0DJ
Tel (01908) 833000
Telephones

MK Electric Ltd
Edmonton
London N9 0PB
Tel (0181) 803 3355
Electrical switches

Modulex Systems Ltd
North Portway Close
Round Spinney
Northampton NN3 8RQ
Tel (01604) 494222
Signage systems

Moflash Company Ltd
Forrest Lane
Walsall
West Midlands WS2 7AX
Tel (01922) 35616/7
High-intensity beacons

Mölnlycke Ltd
Calder House
Central Road
Templefields
Harlow, Essex CM20 2DL
Tel (01279) 439791
Paper towel dispensers

Neaco, *see* Norton Engineering Alloys

Nichols & Clarke Ltd
3/10 Shoreditch High Street
London E1 6PE
Tel (0171) 247 5432
Sanitary ware

Normbau, *see* NT Architectural Hardware Ltd

Norton Engineering Alloys
Norton Grove Industrial Estate
Norton
Malton
North Yorks YO17 9HQ
Tel (01653) 695721
Neaco Neatgrille

Nottingham Rehab
Ludlow Hill Road
West Bridgeford
Nottingham NG2 6HD
Tel (01602) 452345
Equipment and fittings for disabled people

NT Architectural Hardware Ltd
Straight Road
Short Heath
Willenhall
West Midlands WV12 5QY
Tel (01922) 401606
Architectural hardware

Nuffins Ltd
Brunswick Industrial Estate
Newcastle upon Tyne
NE13 7BA
Tel (0191) 236 4126
Non-slip flooring

Nuways Manufacturing Co Ltd
Halesfield 19
Telford
Shropshire TF7 4QT
Tel (01952) 680400
Matting

Panasonic UK Ltd
Panasonic House
Willoughby Road
Bracknell
Berks RG12 4FP
Tel (01344) 862444
Consumer electronics

Paraid Ltd
Paraid House
Weston Lane
Birmingham B11 3RS
Tel (0121) 706 6744
Evac chairs

The Partners
Albion Works
Greenhills Rents
London EC1M 6BN
Tel (0171) 608 0051
Graphic design

Photographer's Gallery
5 Great Newport Street
London WC2H 7JA
Tel (0171) 831 1722
Photographic gallery

Pilkington Glass Products Ltd
Prescot Road
St Helens
Merseyside WA10 3TT
Tel (01744) 692000
Glass

RADAR (Royal Association of Disability and Rehabilitation)
250 City Road
London EC1V 2AS
Tel (0171) 250 3232

Radio Spares Components
PO Box 99
Corby
Northants NN17 9RS
Tel (01536) 201201
Electrical components

Recognita Plus, contact your local software supplier

Recognition Express
PO Box 7
Rugby Road
Hinkley LE10 2NE
Tel (01455) 238133
Tactile signage

Redring Electric Ltd
Celta Road
Peterborough
Cambs PE2 9JJ
Tel (01733) 313213
Hot air driers

Reliance Water Controls Ltd
Worcester Road
Evesham
Worcs WR11 4RA
Tel (01386) 47148
Fax (01386) 47028
Temperature-controlled taps

Reynolds, John & Sons
Church Lane
West Bromwich
West Midlands
Tel (0121) 553 2754
Fixings and fastenings

Rowmark, supplied through Spandex or Recognition Express

Royal National Institute for the Deaf
105 Gower Street
London WC1E 6AH
Tel (0171) 387 8033
Fax (0171) 388 2346

Royal National Institute for the Blind
224 Great Portland Street
London W1N 6AA
Tel (0171) 388 1266

Royal National Theatre
Upper Ground
London SE1 9PX
Tel (0171) 928 2033

RS components, *see* Radio Spares Components

RWC, *see* Reliance Water Controls Ltd

Sapphire Systems
193 Summers Lane
London N12 0QH
Tel (0181) 361 7577
Balustrades

Scotch-Clad, *see* 3M United Kingdom plc

Sealmaster Ltd
Brewery Road
Pampisford
Cambridge CB2 4HG
Tel (01223) 832851
Weatherseals

Sensory Visionaid
Unit 10, Cameron House
12 Castlehaven Road
London NW1 8QU
Tel (0171) 485 4485
Equipment for people with partial vision

Seton Ltd
Canada Close
Banbury
Oxon OX16 7RT
Tel (01295) 269955
Signage

Signs and Labels Ltd
Latham Close
Bredbury Industrial Park
Bredbury
Stockport SK6 2SD
Tel (0161) 4946125
Signs

Sony, contact your local electrical outlet

Sound Advantage
1 Metro Centre
Welbeck Way
Peterborough PE2 7UH
Tel (01733) 238020
Fax (01733) 361161
Equipment from the RNID

Southern Sanitary Specialists Ltd
Cerdic House
West Portway
Andover
Hants SP10 3LF
Tel (01264) 324131
Sanitary equipment

Spandex plc
1600 Park Avenue
Aztec West
Almondsbury
Bristol BS12 4UA
Tel (01454) 616444
Fax (01454) 618012
Signage systems – tactile signs and Rowmark

Stocksigns Ltd
Ormside Way
Redhill
Surrey RH1 2LG
Tel (01737) 764764
Signage

Strand Hardware Ltd
Strand House
Long Street
Walsall WS2 9DY
Tel (01922) 39111
Athmer door seals

Tactyle Ltd
Mallard House
The Old Station
Little Bealings
Woodbridge
Suffolk IP13 6LT
Tel (01473) 620100
Tactile signs

Tenby Industries Ltd
17–21 Warstone Lane
Birmingham B18 6JG
Tel (0121) 200 1999
Electrical products

Terry Lifts Ltd
Longridge Trading Estate
Knutsford
Cheshire WA16 8PR
Tel (01565) 650376
Lifting platforms

Tormax, *see* Langley London Ltd

Travis Perkins
Lodge Way House
Lodge Way
Harlestone Road
Northampton NN5 7UG
Tel (01604) 752424
Building products

Tunstall Telecom
Whitley Lodge
Whitley Bridge
Yorkshire DN14 0HR
Tel (01977) 661234
Radio toilet alarms

Twyfords Bathrooms
Lawton Road
Alsager
Stoke on Trent
Staffs ST7 2DF
Tel (01270) 879777
Sanitary ware

Veitchi (East) Ltd
Olympic Business Centre
Unit 4
Paycocke Road
Basildon
Essex SS14 3DR
Tel (01268) 534132
Flooring systems

Viking Security Systems
Unit 4, Lismirrane Industrial Park
Elstree Road
Elstree
Hertfordshire WD6 3EE
Tel (0181) 207 3838
Ironmongery and security

Wellington's, *see* Albert Marston & Co Ltd

Wessex Medical Equipment Co Ltd
Budds Lane Industrial Estate
Romsey
Hants SO15 0HA
Tel (01794) 830303
Wheelchair stair lifts

WordPerfect, contact your local software supplier

Yannedis
Riverside House
Southend Road
Woodford Green
Essex IG8 8HQ
Tel (0181) 550 8833
Ironmongery supplier

Index